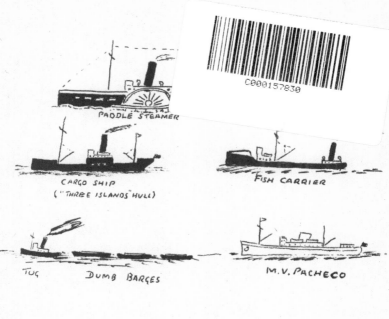

PADDLE STEAMER

CARGO SHIP
("THREE ISLANDS" HULL)

FISH CARRIER

TUG   DUMB BARGES

M.V. PACHECO

ENTERING YARMOUTH HARBOUR.   15·1·43

Little Ship, Big Story

To David

with Best Wishes

Rod Bell

With lots of Love
Stan.
10/8/44

AT REST OFF HOLEHAVEN.

10 AUG. 44.

Drawings by Stanley Dodd Royal Navy Volunteer
Reservist (RNVR) Mechanic on the armed HMY *Sheemaun*.

Little Ship, Big Story

the adventures of HMY *Sheemaun*
and the amazing stories of those
who have sailed in her

RODNEY PELL

Little Ship, Big Story

Published by The Conrad Press in the United Kingdom 2019

Tel: +44(0)1227 472 874
www.theconradpress.com
info@theconradpress.com

ISBN 978-1-911546-46-7

Typesetting and Cover Design by: Charlotte Mouncey, www.bookstyle.co.uk with appreciative acknowledgement to Tim Hunt who took the photograph of *Sheemaun*.

The Conrad Press logo was designed by Maria Priestley.

Printed and bound in Great Britain by Clays Ltd, Elcograf S.p.A

Contents

PART TWO
The War Years

PART THREE
The Post-war Years

PART FOUR
The 21st Century

OWNERS 1935 – 2018 (Current)

1935 -   Mr. Ernest Richards

1935 -   Mr. L. S. Saunders

1936 -   Mr. Harold Bell

1939 -   Lt. R. H. Calvert-Link RNVR

1941 -   His Majesty King George VI
           (The Royal Navy)

1945 -   Naval Department of Sea Transport

1949 -   Mrs J. O. M. Scott

1950 -   Mr. H. E. Chubb M.I. Mech.E. MBE

1950 -   Mr. T. H. V. Haydon

1959 -   Ingram. O. Capper MN. RNVR.

1962 -   SHEEMAUN YACHT CO. Ltd.
           (Captain I. O. Capper)

1965 -   Flt Sgt. T. W. H. Burton Ex-RAF

1967 -   Rear Adml. G. T. S. 'Peter)'Gray CB. DSC.

1981 -   Lt Cmdr. Ian Pearson RN

1987 -   Dr Rodney L. Pell

INTRODUCTION

'An ethereal shuttle clatters back and forth in the Loom of Time endlessly weaving the Tapestry of History'

Anon.

The *Sheemaun*, 25-tons was launched in 1935 from James Noble's Boatyard in Fraserburgh Scotland and is now recognised internationally as a fine surviving example of a G L Watson designed 1930's Gentleman's Motor Yacht. The history of *Sheemaun* is inextricably interwoven with the widely differing stories of a unique group of people who over the past eight decades have put their hands to her wheel. World events and contemporary experiences are revealed as *Sheemaun* shuttling her way back and forth in the 'Loom of Time' has woven a colourful and unique tapestry of adventures and stories which fall naturally into a tetralogy.

1/ The pre-Second World War period

2/ The Second World War Period

3/ The Post-War Period

4/ The 21st Century

Commissioned in 1934 by Banker Ernest Richards, design No 561 by the Leading Yacht Designers, Messrs G L Watson & Co. Ltd was agreed and *Sheemaun* was built and launched in 1935. The stories around her building and naming, and her adventures as she passed through the hands of her four pre-war owners are revealed.

A unique and colourful record of reminiscences and echoes of events, sometimes thousands of miles and many years apart have come to light. I have introduced some imaginary characters who in order of appearance are – 'Jock' Bell, 'Sandy' Stewart, Skipper Buckie (based on real life skipper Buchanan), Andy, Lt Clive Baker RNVR, 'Chalky' White, 'Paddy' Docherty, Jim, Pete and 'Taff' Davies. The stories otherwise are those of real people and all the events happened.

Requisitioned by the Admiralty in 1940, *Sheemaun* served in the Second World War as His Majesty's Yacht *Sheemaun*, a Thames Estuary Patrol Services boat armed with two Hotchkiss heavy machine guns. Her many patrol duties included dealing with the dangerous magnetic mines dropped by German bombers into the Thames. She was damaged by the concussions from some of those mines, she was strafed by German fighter-bombers and was present at the sinking of the ammunition ship the SS *Richard Montgomery* in the Medway approaches.

Amazingly, the memoirs of the late Stanley Dodd RNVR, who served as mechanic on HMY *Sheemaun* in the Second World War, have been discovered and revealed to me by the Dodd family. Stanley's writings provide a vivid personal first-hand account of life in East London during the 'Blitz'; of life and death in London's Docklands and the adventures of a Royal Navy Armed Thames Estuary Patrol Services boat. The extracts from Stanley's writings provide a unique, never-before revealed, primary historic source.

The stories of bravery and of gruesome sea-battles involving the men who would one day come to put their hands to *Sheemaun*'s wheel are recounted. One of those men, Lt. Gordon Gray RN, who preferred to be known as 'Peter', was later to become Rear Admiral 'Peter' Gray CB. DSC.

'Peter' purchased a 'Visitor Book' in March 1942 and kept it with him on every vessel on which he served or sailed. The 'Visitor Book' tells its own stories as it is shaken by broadsides crashing out, by mines exploding and by bombs. One day it would accompany 'Peter' aboard *Sheemaun*. The 'Visitor Book' provides another fascinating and previously undisclosed primary historic source.

Post-War, *Sheemaun* continued with her adventures as did those who would in their turn hold her wheel. She was present in 1953 at the spectacular Coronation Celebrations and Spithead Fleet Review by Her Majesty Queen Elizabeth. She engaged in some clandestine gold smuggling in the 1950s! Later, when owned by former Lancaster Bomber Captain Thomas Burton, *Sheemaun* was taken to the Mediterranean and berthed in Spain for a while before becoming, for fourteen years, the private yacht of Rear Admiral 'Peter' Gray CB. DSC. She would spend her next six years as the Cadet Training Flagship of Pangbourne Nautical College.

Sheemaun in her sailing rig off Dover in 2010,
Photo courtesy Roland Kenward

The 21st Century sees *Sheemaun* certified by Admiral of the Fleet Sir Julian Oswald GCB, as being of National Historic Merit. In 2010 the National Historic Ships Committee, a British Government funded Authority, appointed *Sheemaun* to be the

2010 Flagship of the United Kingdom Historic Fleet. *Sheemaun* was present, by invitation, when a thousand vessels and millions of cheering sight-seers joined in the 2012 Thames Diamond Jubilee Pageant in celebration of the Sixty Years that Her Majesty Queen Elizabeth had been on the Throne of the United Kingdom.

For anyone born after say 1950 and living today in the modern 'here and now', unless a war historian or coming from a family that has retained sentimental war stories and mementos, then it would be very difficult to imagine what life was like during those turbulent years 1939 to 1945.

However, should one recline comfortably in *Sheemaun's* snug saloon, maybe with a glass of decent claret in hand, lulled by the gentle rocking of her hull, the rhythmic creaking of leathered gaff jaws on pine and the chuckling of wavelets against her timber hull; then there come magical moments when the old boat stirring slightly, whispers her adventures and her reminiscences into one's head. Sounds from the past echo from her solid timbers, ghostly figures clamber the companion ways. Voices from the helm call for compass courses and position fixes, give orders or shout warnings to brace as explosions pound her timbers.

After the War, when once again functioning as a private yacht and in happier and less frenetic circumstances, friends and families have laughed and conversed. Sounds of singing, of a guitar, a fiddle, a concertina or whistle have all echoed in her timbers. Lovers have shared with *Sheemaun* their giggling experiences of secret moments and tanned bodies have sunbathed on her decks. Her sails have filled to the wind and her engines have rumbled. *Sheemaun* has taken her part together with other classic and historic vessels as bands have played, and parades have been held at Maritime Festivals in the UK and in France, Belgium and Holland. She has sailed around England, she has cruised the Baltic Sea, she has sailed to the Channel Islands, to Paris and to Minorca in the Mediterranean Sea and back.

ACKNOWLEDGEMENTS

I am especially grateful to Mike and Barrie Dodd, sons of the late Stanley Dodd RNVR who served as mechanic on HMY *Sheemaun* in the Second World War during her role as an armed Royal Navy Auxiliary Patrol Services Boat. Mike and Barrie kindly passed to me the hand-written memoirs of their late father from which the reader will find sections quoted word for word. I am also most grateful for the material, pictures and stories kindly provided by Nicholas Gray whose father the late Rear Admiral Gordon Thomas Seccombe 'Peter' Gray CB. DSC. came in his retirement to own *Sheemaun*. Nicholas Gray told me how his father had described his years of cruising in *Sheemaun* as providing

'Some of the happiest times in my life.'

Nicholas Gray also kindly provided the 'Visitor Book' which his late father had kept with him on every vessel in which he had served or commanded - including *Sheemaun*.

I am very grateful to Lt. Cmdr. Ian Pearson who passed on precious log-books when he parted with *Sheemaun*. I express my sincere appreciation to Bill Macdonald who so vividly recorded the story of Fraserburgh Boat Building; to Helen Richards and Sue Reid, daughter and granddaughter of Ernest Richards who commissioned the building of *Sheemaun*. Thanks, and appreciation also to Shirley Critchley, granddaughter of Judge Haydon KC. Shirley sailed on *Sheemaun* together with her Grandfather and her uncle Vernon Haydon. My appreciations also to Christopher Crouch DFC. grandson of Judge Haydon KC; and to Brian and Andrew Burton son and grandson of Flt. Sergeant Thomas Burton RAF. To Lord Hayter cousin of Emory Chubb, to Captain Richard Forward MN, to Nick Hewitt

Maritime Historian formerly of the Imperial War Museum; to Dan Houston editor of 'Classic Sailor' magazine and to a dear friend, the late Martyn Heighton past Director of National Historic Ships UK and to Denys Tweedell, past Commodore of the Royal Temple Yacht Club, who tutored me for my Yacht-Master examinations.

Very important also is my wife Maura who has been encouraging and supportive and who has applied her IT skills so successfully with the genealogy researches. Without Maura's unfailing support and encouragement, the necessary hard work and sacrifices, the restoration of *Sheemaun* and the researches into her history may not have happened. My appreciation also to shipwright and good friend Steve Parish, whose dedication and traditional skills have served *Sheemaun* so well; and to the late James Rennie Barnett who designed her and to the late James Noble who built her.

Also, my thanks and appreciation go to James Essinger of Conrad Publishing Ltd, who with his boundless energy has been so encouraging and to Charlotte Mouncey of Bookstyle for her inspired cover illustration and skilled type-setting.

PART ONE
The Pre-War Years
1934

The Dream
Matlock Town, Derbyshire 1934

'There is nothing – absolutely nothing half so much
worth doing as simply messing about in boats'

Kenneth Graham – 'The Wind in the Willows'

A Derbyshire drizzle misted down onto the grey Matlock rooftops, insufficient to bring much of a gurgle to the Bank Road gullies but enough to bring reason to the minds of those about to go out and about, that maybe it might be prudent to delay any such venture for a while. Standing at a first-floor window of the imposing stone building that was the Matlock branch of Williams Deacons Bank, manager Ernest Richards looked out at the grey scene, but in his mind's eye he was seeing white wispy clouds in blue skies their reflected images dancing on the wake of a passing yacht. Ernest cut a resplendent figure in his bank-manager's 'uniform' of pin-striped trousers and grey spats, his dark charcoal jacket, grey waist-coat worn over a white shirt and starched collar; but unless tied loosely his neck tie could press the collar stud uncomfortably against his throat. Turning away from the window, Ernest went back to his roll-top desk and settled into his favourite swivelling captain's chair.

But deep inside him there was a very different person. A man who when freed from his formal banker's 'uniform', and away from his office was someone who preferred to be comfortably attired. He favoured a soft open-necked shirt with loose red neckerchief, light slacks and moccasin style canvass deck shoes. Ernest was at heart a sailing man who liked to have a burgee fluttering overhead in the wind, to hear the chuckling sound of wavelets slapping against a hull and to feel the comfort of a soft roll-neck jumper which was also handy for the chilly evenings.

With origins as far back as the year 1771 the Williams Deacons Bank business had been through the governance of numerous executive partners and several name changes, but by means of speculations and clever use of the legal structures within which banking had to be carried out the bank had prospered. The privations and set-back of the disastrous First World War had however been followed by a boom in world business and within five years of the end of that 1914-1918 War the Williams and Deacons bank had opened fifty-two new branches.

Ernest's father had been a missionary working on the Island of Raitaea, one of the 'Iles de la Societe'[1] in French Polynesia, but at the age of only forty-two years he had been struck down by illness and died leaving his wife Margaret and their little son Ernest almost destitute. Ernest's widowed mother had closed the simple home in Raiatea and had taken a passage back to England to live with her widower brother, Alderman and Magistrate Ernest Wragg. From his early years Ernest Richards had been vaguely aware of that far distant existence, he had been told stories of life on Raiatea, he had been shown pictures of those beautiful Polynesian islands with white waves endlessly expending their rolling energies on warm sandy beaches under lazy blue skies. He had seen the pictures of palm trees and pictures of tall sailing ships. It is hardly surprising perhaps, that somewhere deep in his soul lurked a free spirit with a need for freedom and adventure, a penchant for that vibrant energy and exhilaration that prevails when a sailing ship plunges its bow into blue seas.

His kindly uncle Ernest Wragg had no children of his own and

---

1.   As told to me by Sue Reid, granddaughter of the late Ernest Richards.

together with his sister, Ernest's mother, the avuncular Alderman Wragg had seen to it that Ernest received a good education. But Ernest had been a dreamer and showed little interest in a future career, he felt no calling to the ministry as might have been anticipated and neither did a career in law hold any attraction for him. However, he was good at maths, indeed he was quite sharp with mental arithmetic and he was sensible and present-able. He had been grateful to accept, when through his uncle's connections, a position with Williams Deacon's Bank Ltd had come open to him.

The Richards family lived at the rather grand Bank House which held the advantage that Ernest didn't have to travel to and from work but, living where he also worked, made it all the more difficult to set aside time and space for himself and his family. This was a good reason for the family to take occa-sional breaks away from Matlock when able. On most winter's evenings the Richards family would gather in the living room. Ernest liked to sit in his comfortable arm-chair at the fireside reading his travel books and boating journals while Margaret might sit playing the piano or more often sewing, darning and knitting. He was particularly proud of the roll-neck sweaters she produced, they were warm, comfy and snug. When unable to do so himself he might send his clerk out to bring back the latest monthly yachting journal which came out for sale on a Friday. Fridays were always busy days at the bank and it was nice to have some reading to relax with and enjoy over the weekend while sipping a wee drachm of Bruichladdich whisky and savouring that unique, evocative taste of sweet brine with just a hint of peat, pepper and malt.

Ernest Richards' dreams of sailing free across far-off waters were reflected in his reading. He was an avid reader of 'Yachting World and Motor Boat' magazine and a subscriber to 'Yachting Monthly'. His first motor boat - the *Gypsie* had rolled uncomfortably when at sea and was a little cramped for his height. His wife Margaret didn't like it and his sister-in-law Betty was always sick! Ernest felt that time had come for him to invest in a bigger and better boat with some greater headroom.

Seated one evening in his study, Ernest was perusing a sea-chart spread out in front of him. He enjoyed a good whisky and his crystal tumbler rang out like a ship's bell as his pencil gently tapped against the rim. The timbre of the ring deepened a little with each sip, and the mischievous boy that still lurked somewhere deep in his psyche, could barely resist the temptation to sip in semitones... hmmm... no no... a decent Bruichladdich was not for playing tunes!

Ernest focussed again on the chart which showed that Colwyn Bay was the nearest harbour offering good facilities for keeping a boat, but it was seventy-five long miles from Matlock. He was a busy man, and as there was little enough time available to him for sailing he reasoned that he might as well enjoy to the full such time as he could get to be on the water. If only he could find the right boat in these difficult times, a decent seaworthy vessel which might also make a worthwhile investment while providing some enjoyment. Then it occurred to him. Why not commission the design and building of a boat? The right boat of course and waste no more time fingering through advertisements in yachting journals! Come to think of it, he knew of an excellent firm of naval architects in Glasgow.

Seated at his leather topped desk in his office, Ernest gazed wistfully for a few moments through the window, then rubbing his eyes as if to expunge the outside world, he pulled his spectacles down onto his nose and attended to the world inside. The columns of figures came back into focus and he gathered his thoughts. Marking with red ink the over-drawn accounts, considering carefully the requests for loans and the while making mental notes to tactfully pursue enquiries as to an applicants' standing in local society. But these were difficult times nationally and internationally and an informed banker's 'weather-eye' had to balance borrowing requests against future risks. His clerk was excellent, but it was best to check the calculations and as with the captain of a ship, the staff - his crew - required his supervision and their set duties. As ever, there were in-trays of letters for checking and signing, some to be set aside for re-drafting. He always felt as if a weight had lifted from his shoulders when the contents of the piled in-tray had been transferred to the out-tray and he could press the bell to summon his clerk to take it away.

A fine copper-riveted leather waste-bucket of which he was rather proud, stood close by the side of his desk. The bucket was filled with crumpled papers and torn envelopes some of the latter having been franked in Glasgow. Set in the Victorian fire-grate behind him was a coal-gas fire, the blue flames poppling quietly in the glowing clay burners. In front of the warming fire was a little dish of water – put there to 'absorb the fumes' as fashion and the Bank Directors decreed. Against the wall to his right was a mahogany roll-top desk. A closer glance showed that not all those papers vying for his attention were related to the dry world of banking. To the side of the desk was a mahogany book-case, the glass doors of which protected some of Ernest Richard's treasured books and magazines on sailing and cruising, all well-thumbed and annotated. Amongst the books there were nautical charts, almanacs and dividers. On the upper shelf lay his precious leather cased Jules Huet stereoscopic binoculars with twelve times magnification. In a separate drawer Ernest Richards carefully filed his correspondence with James Rennie Barnett, Managing Director and chief Naval Architect of Messrs G. L. Watson & Co. Ltd.

Time-Line –

- That year King George V was on the British Throne
- The Royal Mail Ship Queen Mary was launched at Clydebank
- Unemployment in the USA was 22%. Britain also was facing a depression
- The German President Hindenburgh had just died and Chancellor Adolph Hitler had declared himself Fuhrer and absolute leader of Germany
- A hundred or so of Hitler's critics had mysteriously disappeared – presumed murdered
- In San Francisco the Golden Gate Bridge was being built

1934

Drafting the Dream
Glasgow

'Ships are the nearest things to dreams
that hands have ever made,
For somewhere deep within their wooden
hearts the soul of a song is laid.'

Robert Rose
Toms River NJ

Blytheswood Street in Glasgow is one of the bustling city's main streets and within reasonable walking distance up the hill from the docks and the Rail Station. Halfway up on the left side stood number one hundred and forty-seven, the address of Naval Architects Messrs G. L. Watson & Co Ltd. It was and still is an imposing stone building, its grand windows typical of the style of many similar period buildings to be found in the surrounding streets of the City of Glasgow. On the first floor Managing Director James Rennie Barnett was applying his mind to the design of a sturdy and seaworthy vessel of a size that was becoming popular with the discerning yachtsmen of the time.

James Rennie Barnett
1846 – 1965.
Picture courtesy
Life-Boat Journal Vol
XXXII, issue 343
Sept. 1947

His instructing letter from a banker in Derbyshire required that such a vessel could be easily handled by a crew of two, would provide comfortable accommodation for the owner and his wife, while able to accommodate a further two crew or guests plus a paid hand. The vessel should be capable of safely cruising for some five or six hundred miles at a stretch.

James Barnett was well acquainted with the yachting and cruising fashions and requirements of the period. He was able to draw down not only on his own considerable expertise but on the vast accumulation of records stored at the premises of G. L. Watson & Co Ltd. Furthermore, James Barnett was familiar with the practical skills and experiences built up by Scottish shipwrights over centuries. Such skills and knowledge as had been handed down from father to son being expressed in the sturdy, powerful fishing vessels that had been launched down the slipways over generations. Vessels capable of withstanding heavy seas and gales; vessels that could be relied upon to bring their crews and catches safely back to port.

Back in Matlock, Ernest Richards found James Barnett's drawings very interesting. They detailed a canoe-stern twin-screw motor yacht of some 25 tons with an auxiliary ketch rig and a decent Teak deck-house. A sturdy hull of Oak frames planked in Pitch Pine and Larch. It looked to be every bit as tough and seaworthy as those renowned Scottish Ring-Netters. His wife agreed that such a vessel might be just what he had been looking for. Although no sailor herself she knew her husband well and their daughter Helen, taking after her father, just loved the water and messing about in boats. And so Messrs. G. L. Watson & Co design No 561 was approved and accepted; this boat would now be built. Following further correspondence with his client Ernest Richards, and having made some agreed amendments, James Barnett finally lifted design No. 561 from the drawing board for copying and filing.

All that remained to do now was to select and contract a suitable boat yard for the construction.

As one of the leaders in the world of naval architecture, the company of Messrs G L Watson & Co was well used to instructing and working with shipyards all around Britain. Ship-building yards varied enormously. There were those that built only in steel, there were yards that could handle the largest of vessels, yards that specialised in fast motor boats such as the British Power Boat Company in Southampton and Camper & Nicholson also in Southampton and renowned for their beautiful motor yachts. Messrs Berthon of Lymington had a reputation for building fine sailing yachts. There were reputable boat-builders along the South Coast, on the Welsh Coast and the East Coast. There were many excellent boat-builders, some located relatively inland such as Messrs Bates of Chertsey; the list of possible choices was almost endless. But this was 1934, the United States was still suffering from what would become known as the 'Great Depression' and those financial and economic hardships had seeded across to this Eastern side of the Atlantic. Britain's world trade had fallen off by almost a third, the industrial and mining towns in the North of England and in Scotland had been hard hit with some areas seeing more than fifty percent of workers unemployed.

James Barnett's world was that of yacht designing, while Ernest Richards lived in the world of banking. James Barnett had found his conversations with Ernest Richards very interesting in this respect. Quite properly the two men had a professional need to discuss the anticipated costs of the project and in so doing it was inevitable that their conversations came to embrace the global financial circumstances and issues of the time. It was clear that if Design No 516 was to be built, then it would have to be at the most economic costs yet without sacrificing the required quality and strength.

James Barnett gave this a good deal of thought. He was aware that despite the exhaustive effect of the First World War on raw materials and the not so distant economic crash of the late 1920s, good quality Oak and other ship-building timbers such as Larch, Pine and Elm were still available at very reasonable cost in Scotland. Furthermore, he had heard that there was a boat-builder in Fraserburgh who could build to just the standard that was required and very economically. Discrete enquiries confirmed this to be so. The only drawback being the not inconsiderable distance that separated Glasgow and for that matter also Matlock, from the boatyard in far-away Fraserburgh. These findings were put to Ernest Richards, who when appraised at what were very reasonable build costs, considered the project to be an attractive investment. There would be the issue of travelling to and from Fraserburgh and Ernest Richards did not drive or for that matter did not own a car, but there were good rail connections. He was happy to sign his agreement.

1934

Fraserburgh[2]
'Broch' to the Locals

'Alsua for thay that mony thinges passes out of the realm
withoutten Custome, it is ordained and decreeted, etc., that
there be paid to the King for custome of like thousand of
freche herringe sauld, of the sellar, one penny, and of like last
of herringe barrelled foure shillings, and of like thousand red
herringe made in the realm, foure pennies'

James 1st declaration by Act of Parliament[3] in May 1240

And so, it was recorded that even in the early thirteenth
century, that the efforts of the Fraserburgh fishermen and
their kinsmen underwrote an industry that was more than locally
significant, it was an industry also dear to the heart of the Royal
Coffers in London!

Abundant herring fish stocks matched with the availability
of sturdy home-built fishing boats and their brave crews, had
been the foundation of a major and valuable fish-export market
between Scotland and Germany, the Baltic States and western
Russia, but the First World War had largely put an end to that.
Furthermore, the inshore Scottish fishing industry had been hit
by the Great Depression of the late nineteen twenties and early
thirty's, and herring was no longer the fashionable and staple
food it had been. As a result, many Scottish fishermen were
left with little choice than to look elsewhere in the world for a
living. It was not just the international situation that was causing
hardship. The sail-powered Scottish drifters and the Fifie and

---

2. Fraserburgh Town is closer to Stavanger in Norway than it is to London.

3. Fraserburgh Past and Present by John Cranna. Rosemont Press 1914.

Zulu fishing boats that had once reigned supreme in these waters were now being displaced by foreign engine-powered vessels. Powerful boats that could easily outrun the traditional Scottish sailing fishing boats whether there was wind or no.

The Scottish boat-builders in the decades before the First World War had enjoyed what might be termed the 'Golden Days' of Scottish boatbuilding, and the Fraserburgh boatyards had enjoyed their share. In 1899 cabinet maker and shipwright Alex Noble had set up as a boat-builder, his skills soon became so well respected by local fishermen that he moved to bigger premises and was soon employing numbers of tradesmen but Alex finding he had no head for administration handed the business to his elder son Wilson who was also a skilled shipwright.

The First World War had brought a mixture of good and bad for the men of Fraserburgh. At that time the Lords of the Admiralty had an urgent need for sturdy small to medium vessels to serve as harbour launches, anti-submarine net-tenders and mine-sweepers etc. Their Lordships recognised that Fraserburgh was one of the ports that could provide such vessels and the men to serve in them. Accordingly, the Admiralty had requisitioned for War Service some fifty Fraserburgh steam-drifters along with their crews and had ordered the building of ten more. At the same time the Admiralty facilitated the acquisition of best timbers for the construction of these vessels.

With order books full despite the deep general recession, the Fraserburgh boatyards found themselves busy building anew and adapting such other vessels as might be required. Conversely the local fishing industry suffered badly through loss of boats and the loss of the men who went with them as crew. This loss of manpower became endemic, for hundreds of the brave men who had volunteered for service in the First World War had never returned. That terrible 1914-1918 war had thankfully passed into history but in the late 1920s with no orders from the

Admiralty, the yard of Wilson Noble with empty order books, was having to lay-off fit and skilled men. Paradoxically the now idle Fraserburgh boatyards found themselves with surplus stocks of first class timbers.

Four hundred and fifty miles north east of Matlock, the view from Fraserburgh, looking out across the Broch Harbour in the early spring of 1934 was a depressing sight. Blustering grey skies and lashing rain brought visibility to just a half mile, the light at the end of the South Breakwater was barely visible. Fifty or so wooden fishing boats lay tugging and chafing at their moorings, but even when the weather abated not many would be putting to sea.

For Wilson's younger brother James, there was no choice other than to leave his employment at the Wilson Yard and to set off in the hope of finding work elsewhere. But James' only skills were in boat-building. So, taking a chance James set himself up as an independent boat-builder and repairer on the Broch Breakwater not far from his brother's yard. Young James Noble doubted that the traditional Scottish fishing boat industry would ever recover, but he did believe that the economy would improve and anticipated that his future probably lay with building private yachts. His younger brother Charles, who worked with him, supported this view as did James' wife. Although no orders to build private yachts were forthcoming, his new yard did find some repair work and re-fitting to do, so there was a modest income and he was able to pay the bills. When he did eventually have an order to build a fishing boat, he looked very carefully at cutting the costs, in which respect he was greatly helped by a readily available supply of cheap but good quality timber. James' hard work paid off and was followed by further requests for him to build similar boats. James then began to enjoy a reputation for building quality vessels at very reasonable cost. A type of vessel that was becoming popular with the Scottish fishermen was the motor-powered Ring-Netter. This was a sturdy vessel the hull crafted of Oak frames on an Elm or Oak keel, the sides planked in Pitch-Pine, decks laid of stout Canadian Pine and with a Teak deckhouse.[4] All of these being strong weather and rot-resistant timbers. These fishermen began to favour James Noble's yard with orders for their vessels.

> 'James Noble could produce a completed boat,
> exclusive of gear for £1,100[5]'

James remained ever hopeful that orders for private yachts would one day materialise. But now the day was ending and his brother and the few shipwrights he could still employ had put their tools away and left to go home. As he left, he picked up an unopened letter and stuffed it into his pocket, then turning off the light he stepped out into the windy street, locked the yard door behind him and set off for home.

It was getting dark and it was cold, James shivered. Looking briefly across at the Harbour Commissioner's office he turned his back on the grey and dismal harbour, pulled his donkey jacket tighter, strode away from the breakwater in the dimming northern light and made toward his nearby cottage from where a cosy glow at the windows beckoned with its offer of warmth and respite from the biting wind. As he entered the cottage the wind almost tore the door from his grip and a small gale briefly whirled in scattering some skeins of wool[6] and papers. He heaved

---

4. Per 'Boats & Builders - *The History of Boatbuilding Around Fraserburgh*' by Bill Macdonald ISBN 0 9521551 0 9 p28

5. Per Bill MacDonald *'Boats & Builders – The History of Boatbuilding Around Fraserburgh'*. The sum of £1,100 in 1934 would in 2017 be equivalent to around £72,250. A very modest sum for a quality-built 25 tons displacement,45 feet in length motor yacht!

6. Unlike a ball of wool, the wool in a skein is loosely wound on itself so that it unfurls easily as the knitting progresses.

his back against the door and as suddenly it had been let in the gale was shut out and quietness descended once more.

Settled in front of the fire with a steaming bowl of neeps[7] and barley broth he looked at the window, watching the rain drops like hesitant tadpoles wriggling their way down the glass until gathering in clumps they fell sploshing on the window-sill. Glancing seawards out over Main Street and down across Broad Sea shore, his eyes were drawn to the merciless grey surf pounding out there on the Craig rocks. At least the vessels lying sheltered behind the Balaclava Quay would be safe, but no fishing boats would be venturing forth in that sea and heaven help those who might be still out there weather-bound somewhere in the grim North Sea.

James watched the almost hypnotic, rotating beam of the Kinnaird Head lighthouse as it strove to penetrate through the pouring rain yet, seeming to suddenly leap as it flashed intensely on the cottage window making the tadpoles sparkle. It was the oldest lighthouse in the Kingdom. Powered by a paraffin vapour-lamp, as it had been since seventeen hundred and eighty-seven, its glass lens so powerful, that during daylight it had to be kept rotating or be covered least it might accidentally focus the sun's rays which could melt the vapour lamp!

His wife standing behind his chair, her hands on his shoulders, said nothing, she knew him well and shared his concerns about the yard business. She also understood how a tired man, coming in from the wet and cold after a hard and physical day at the yard, needed warmth and good plain food. Every other day she baked a batch of sodabread and this one loaf was still warm. James broke open the crusty loaf savouring the aroma that wafted into his nostrils - the perfect accompaniment to go with a bowl of broth. Wiping the bowl clean while enjoying

---

7. Neep – A Scottish turnip like root vegetable with a purple skin and orange flesh. Known in Sweden as Rotobagga and the USA as Rutabagga.

the last morsel, he glanced across to the hearth where the kettle sang quietly and then at the shelves next in the alcove. As his wife placed a mug of sweet tea at his side... a glint caught his eye... the whisky bottle that had been a gift from an appreciative West Coast fisherman. There it was on the shelf reflecting the twinkling logs. The thought of a wee tot of Bunnahabhain was tempting indeed, but... well... maybe not this evening. As he eased his chair back from the table, his foot brushed on something soft.

Reaching down to rescue the skein of wool he noticed an envelope. It was a bit damp 'Ah yes...' as he left the yard he had stuffed a letter into his pocket to read later at home, it must have blown out as he came in the door. Noting the Glasgow franking mark as he slit it open his pulse quickened. The letter was from James Barnett the Director of G. L. Watson & Co Ltd., Yacht Designers & Naval Architects. James Noble's little shipyard had been approached by one of the leading firms of naval architects with a proposition to build a motor yacht! The mug of tea lost out to the Bunnahahbian. Next morning a telephone call was put through to James Rennie Barnett of G. L. Watson & Co. It was agreed that drawings and proposals would be forwarded.

1934

The Building of Design No 561
At James Noble's Yard

'A skilled shipwright takes good wood that's dead
And gently breathes into it a new life instead.'

Anon

There was no time to waste. Mr Barnett had been specific as to the timbers from which this new motor yacht would be built. The first and all-important timber lay waiting under cover in the yard. Fortunately, among the yard's selection of carefully stacked Elm trunks, there was one which would provide a keel in one piece and was just right for this new boat. It was duly marked with a cross of white paint. The Scottish Elm can grow to close on a hundred feet (about 30m) high and this one with a trunk of about four feet diameter (1.2m) would have been at least a hundred years old when felled a decade earlier. The fine-grained timber is very strong and resistant to splitting. Although susceptible to rot if left exposed to rainwater and air, if kept away from air by being submerged in saltwater or mud it can last indefinitely. It is an ideal timber from which to make a boat's keel. This trunk was soon hauled onto the yard saw bench, carefully checked for shakes, aligned and quarter sawn to produce a long straight keel piece of some forty-five feet by ten by twenty inches (13.7 x 0.25 x 0.51 m).

This, the first piece of the vast jig-saw of timbers that would become the *Sheemaun* was carefully aligned on the slipway cradle that would one day carry it with a whoosh out from the shed and down the slip-rails into the waters of the Broch. James Noble together with a couple of carpenters then 'lofted' or transferred the drawings prepared by Barnett onto seasoned Oak timbers from which the frames or ribs would be created. There would be thirty-six stout Oak frames on the starboard side and thirty-six on the port side. Each frame four inches (10.16 cm) thick but differing from the next in length, depth and curvature. The frames were to be spaced fore and aft with their centres fifteen inches apart in compliance with the Lloyds Insurance A1 requirements. The eight frames on each side of the engine room would be doubled to provide a massively strong support for the heavy engines and fuel tanks.

For the next six weeks saws buzzed and rasped, while adzes swung and thunked. Sweet smelling Oak saw-dust hung in the air blending with the mildly pungent yet sweet odour of Stockholm tar together with wafts of hemp, of hot pitch, of coke braziers and of a hundred-other heady olfactions so familiar to a shipwright's senses. Wood shavings and saw-dust gathered on the cement floor. At the end of each day the floor was cleared and swept for there was the ever-present hazard of fire. Filled fire buckets were always to hand. Timber off-cuts of no use for ship-building were bundled and allocated, James Noble and his team seldom wanted for good dry timber to burn at home in their stoves and grates!

As the work progressed a heavy Oak keelson was overlaid and bolted to the frames where they met the Elm keel. The Oak keelson would effectively double up on the strength and stiffness of the Elm keel and provide the backbone of a boat that would be able to power safely through heavy seas. With completion of the framing and assembly of the bow stem, apron, beam shelves, stern horns and rudder trunking and deck beams, the three-dimensional outline of a sturdy forty-five feet (13.7 m) motor yacht was now declaring itself. Naval Architect James Rennie visited to make his inspection and give his approval for the next stage of the building. For the business of planking the hull, best knot-free Pitch Pine was selected for the underwater area and Larch for the topsides. For optimal hull strength and stiffness, the planks had to be at least a half of the hull length. Each plank was individually crafted so that it could be fitted precisely and take on the hull curvature and twist without too much strain. The contiguous longitudinal edges had to almost touch at the frames while leaving a sufficient gap outwardly to allow for caulking with oakum and red lead below the waterline where flexibility was needed, and white lead above which being harder would take a coat of paint.

Where necessary the planks would be steam heated until they became pliant enough to be bent onto the frames and iron spiked in place. This was hot work and protective leather gloves had to be worn. As a necessary finger-saving exercise, the iron spikes were held with tongs while being hammered in! The matter of fastening the planks to the frames had been detailed by James Barnett. Hand forged five-inch (12.7 cms) iron spikes were to be used, alternating with iron bolts. Unlike steel, forged iron while tough, retains a degree of malleability and would stand up to the wringing forces suffered by a hull in heavy seas. Furthermore, forged iron has good resistance to corrosion whereas steel will easily rust. Strong hand-forged iron spikes[8] produced by local blacksmiths and still used in trades other than boat-building were readily available. This boat would need several thousand!

An 85-year-old 5 ½ inch (12 cm) iron spike found in mint condition when removed from *Sheemaun* during a re-fit

---

8. Unlike steel which rusts easily, iron is relatively resistant. *Sheemaun's* iron spikes are virtually as new.

The decking of a wooden ship is much more than a cover to keep water out, it is an integral part of the hull structure. Thirty-two oak beams six inches (15.24 cms) by four inches (10.16 cms) and gently curved would need to be laid across the hull. Each deck beam had to be precisely carved with at its ends a locking dove-tail into its supporting Oak beam shelf. The Beam Shelves each some four inches (10.16 cms) by eleven inches (27cms) in section and running the whole length of both sides of the hull were bolted securely to the upper ends of the frames. Securing all thirty-two of the deck beams to the beam shelves now 'locked' the hull into a very strong three-dimensional frame. Where the main and mizzen masts would be mounted on the deck, those deck beams were further secured by strong Oak hanging knees and lodging knees and mast partners; six inches by four inches longitudinal Oak beams dove-tailed and locked into the transverse deck beams. A similar method of construction would provide for the hatches and coach-house carlings. Before any of the foredeck beams were in place a sixty gallon (272 litres) galvanised water tank was installed well forward and low down in the bow. With the deck beams, hatches and coach-house base frames established the carpenters could now lay the inch and a half thick (4 cms) pine decking which was 'secret nailed' with screw nails into the deck beams. As senior carpenter Jock Bell explained to a confused apprentice -

'Weeell laddie... af we hae tae build ah commerdation hoose on ti er deck o' a ship ye kid call it a 'Cooch-Hoose' but ait 'comes a 'Fwheel-Hoose' if ait hais ter ship's fwheel init... d'ye noo see?'

Two sixty-gallon (272 litre) paraffin fuel tanks and five-gallon (22 litre) petrol tanks were secured into the engine room wings and then the two 27 horsepower Parsons petrol-paraffin engines with their gear boxes were lifted in and bolted securely onto the sturdy Oak engine bearers. Beneath each engine bed there had been previously placed a large copper 'drip tray'. Work proceeded with installing the propeller shafts. These were in two sections flange bolted and supported on thrust bearing blocks. The after shafts ran through the bronze stern glands and bearings secured into the Oak propeller shaft logs that passed through the hull. The propeller shaft tubes were run through the cavity of the shaft logs and the cavities injected with a thick mixture of paint and white-lead that would make a perfect water-tight seal. On each side of the aft 'deadwood' bronze A brackets were carefully lined up on the shafts and bolted securely to the hull. A pair of twenty-one-inch diameter (53.4 cms), three bladed bronze propellers were then secured on the splined and tapered aft end of the propeller shafts. The propellers were mirror images of each other, one left-handed and the other right-handed. Mounting them so that in forward gear the outer tips of each would rotate upwards thus ensuring the optimal forward drive and manoeuvrability for the vessel. Careful final alignment by adjusting the engine mounts achieved such free-running of the shafts that each propeller could easily be turned by finger pressure! Lead and iron pigs[9] of ballast as prescribed by James Barnett were close packed into the bilge on strong wooden stringers and the Pitch-Pine flooring screwed securely down over them. While the engineers and electricians sorted out the fuel systems, the batteries and the electrical systems, the yards specialist joiners set to work.

The skill-set of joiners differs from that of ship's carpenters in that the joiners are not working with massive structural timbers, their task is to build the internal structures, the bulkheads and cabins. It is the joiners who create the fixed furniture such as the cot-bunks, dressing tables and wardrobes, the storage drawers and lockers, the seating and the galley and heads arrangements.

---

9.   A cast lump of unrefined iron or lead weighing half a hundred-weight.

They install the wheel-house fittings, and in conjunction with the engineers, the engine and electrical control panels and any wheel-house seating.

James Barnett's design, called for a fine Teak wheel- house built on an Oak frame. The wheel-house would have drop-sash sliding windows each of which could be lowered down into a vertical copper tray hidden in the cavity of the double 'skin' of the coach-house. The purpose of the tray being to keep the coach-house or wheel-house dry by collecting the rain water and sea spray that would inevitably be driven into the sash housing and discharging it out onto the deck. Once the deck planking had been laid and caulked with hot pitch, the deck fittings could then be attended to. Setting up the cast iron mooring bollards was a matter of accurately positioning and bolting them in place. The mast tabernacles were secured and under-pinned by Oak deck beam knees and partners.

The rail stanchions had been a true test of skill. The amidships stanchions could be mounted vertically but there was a graceful upward fore and aft sweep of the deck and so to keep the forward and aft stanchions perpendicular to the waterline, each had to be cast with a slightly increased tilt on its base. Furthermore, the forward six stanchions and the aft four, as well as standing perpendicular to the waterline also had to tilt inwards and they had to be cast as port and starboard mirrored pairs. James Barnett had prescribed for all this and the stanchions cast by the specialist firm Messrs Ballatynes had been delivered with each one marked appropriate as to its location.

In the final months while the internal details and fixtures were being completed, a team of men working from trestles and ladders secured all the hull seams with oakum, red lead and putty under the water line and white lead and putty above. Likewise, the thousands of recessed fastening spike-heads and through bolt-heads were sealed over. When the white-lead and putty had 'set off' the whole hull was sanded smooth in preparation for three layers of best undercoat. Paints were made up on site as needed. The following traditional recipe[10] producing a good undercoat –

'Red lead powder .... ¾ oz
Litharge .... ¾ oz
Manganese powder .... ¾ oz
Raw linseed oil .... 1 pint'

For a quality top coat that would provide a glistening white finish with good weather and wear resistance another recipe was favoured. To ten pounds of paint base were added –

'8lb best white lead in oil
4lb best zinc white in oil
1 lb manganese dryers or marine dryers
1 pint best turpentine
¼ pint copal varnish
¼ oz ultramarine or Egyptian blue powder.'

Best results would be achieved if the paints were mixed fresh and used within a few days of preparation and that these paints gave good protection against mildew and rot. The underwater profile of the hull was treated with what was termed 'anti-fouling' in order to discourage attachment of barnacles, weeds and wood-boring creatures such as the gribble. This would have to be applied within a few days of the launch. Also prepared on-site to a well-tested traditional recipe [11]–

---

10. *Motor Cruising* – The Lonsdale Library Vol 6 1935. Pp 242-243 Published by Seely Service & Co Ltd.

11. *Motor Cruising* – The Lonsdale Library Vol 6 1935. Pp 242-243 Published by Seely Service & Co Ltd.

'If to a hundred parts of a good readymade ant-fouling paint 6 parts of mercuric oxide, 3 parts of copper oxide and I part of arsenical oxide are added and well stirred in, the result will generally be found to be entirely satisfactory. When applying the anti-fouling paint two persons are required – one to do the painting and the other to keep the paint well stirred and mixed, for mercuric oxide is very heavy and inclined to sink to the bottom of the can...'

Local fishermen reckoned this mix could keep a boat free of weed and barnacles for up to two years while Sandy Stewart reckoned it the best unguent for treating ringworm in horses!

1935

Sheemaun's Mahogany Wheel

Since its invention early in the seventeenth century when it replaced the awkward whip-staff and the heavy tiller, the traditional ship's wheel has become an intricate and beautiful construction, usually built of Teak or Mahogany. The natural properties of both these fine-grained woods are ideally suited to the shape and function of a ship's wheel. Both lend themselves to precise and accurate carving, both are resistant to salt water and the challenging exposure many years of marine weathers. Both timbers have a pleasing colour, and both will offer a smooth hand-kindly texture. Teak however being an oily wood does not take well to varnish and so Mahogany is generally the more favoured, which when varnished gives such a pleasing and sparkling deep colour. James Barnett had not seen any need to prescribe drawings for the wheel; he knew that the experienced joiners would enjoy constructing just the right sized wheel for this boat. So, one might well ask as to just what goes into the construction of a ship's wheel.

Like its predecessor the cart wheel, a ships wheel while looking simple enough is a beautifully crafted and precise 'jig saw' of some thirty-seven parts! There is the wooden hub into which are lodged eight spokes, each turned on a lathe to give a pleasing appearance like a stair banister. The radiating spokes are held equidistant apart at their outer ends and secured by wooden pieces called 'fellowes' of which there are three layers or circles, each circle consisting of eight fellowes. The fellowes are secured and bound at the fore and aft sides of the wheel by inset brass bands. A brass axle spindle is centred into the hub and a brass cap is fitted to the spoke that will be uppermost when the rudder is central. This brass-capped 'King Spoke' allows the helmsman to discern when the wheel is centred by either looking at it or in the dark by feeling it. Finally, a polished dome of brass is screwed onto the face of the hub to both decorate the hub and to protect the nut which secures the wheel to the steering gear shaft. An apprentice shipwright, so as to impress his employer and hoping to become in his turn a journeyman shipwright, might carefully craft and assemble a miniature ship's wheel as a demonstration of his joinery skills and attention to fine detail.

For most people who step on board a traditional vessel, the ship's wheel is perhaps the immediately eye-catching object and invokes in the observer an almost irresistible urge to touch it, to hold the spokes and to just turn it a little!

Sheemaun's historic Mahogany Wheel
which so many adventuring hands have held

A unique wheel that together with the little ship of which it is a vital part, begs to tell the amazing stories and exploits of those who have stood to it in past years.

1935

How a Little Ship came by her Name

'I a light canoe will build me,
Build a swift Cheemaun for sailing,
That shall float upon the river like a yellow leaf in Autumn,
Like a yellow water lily.'

Henry Wadsworth Longfellow – The Song of Hiawatha

At Bank House Ernest Richards settled back in his armchair by the warming coal fire, was deep in thought. His last boat had been called *Gypsie*. The new boat could hardly be called '561' it must have a name, but what name? Perhaps *Gypsie 2* or *Sea Dawn* or may be *Sea Spray*? Across the room his wife Margaret relaxed on the sofa and their daughter fourteen year old Helen lay on the shag-pile rug chin cupped in her hands reading Henry Longfellow's moving poem the - 'Song of Hiawatha' –

'…Straightway then my Hiawatha
Armed himself with all his war-gear,
Launched his birch-canoe for sailing;
With his palm its sides he patted,
O my Birch-canoe! Leap forward,
Where you see the fiery serpents,
Where you see the black pitch-water!
Forward leaped Cheemaun exulting
And the noble Hiawatha
Sang his war-song wild and woeful
Dead lay all the fiery serpents,
And among them Hiawatha
Harmless sailed, and cried exulting:
Onward, O Cheemaun, my darling!
Onward to the black pitch-water!'

Ernest showed his list of possible names to his wife but somehow none of the names that came to mind bore that... 'je ne sais quoi'... that indefinable sense of appeal...

The Richards Family at Bank House in the mid-1930s. Helen Richards sitting on the rug, Ernest Richards in his comfortable armchair and Margaret Richards sitting on the sofa.
Photo courtesy of Helen's daughter Sue Reid.

Helen held up her book –

'Oh Father... look... do look... Cheemaun is such a lovely name, do let's name our boat Cheemaun.'

The family then assembled around the table to take another look at the various papers about the new boat and the drawings and discussed the names. For those who are fascinated by the sea and the elements and who love boats and boating, there is always deep down in the psyche a romantic attachment. Ernest Richards immediately felt drawn to his daughter's proposal. He rather liked the sound, a name lifted from such evocative writing, an unusual name but clear and easy, quite catchy in fact. Simple and short, with just two syllables... but... something was not quite right. They repeated the name trying different inflections. Ernest rubbed his chin…

'Why don't we soften it, let's change the C for an S?'

Helen agreed, her mother nodded, and so it was to be –

Sheemaun

Helen Reid nee Richards at 92 yrs. Photo courtesy Sue Reid

In recounting as to how the naming of *Sheemaun* came about, on 5th July 2012 I received an email from 92-year-old Helen Reid -

'Hi Rodney,

Sometimes I wondered what became of Sheemaun so many years go. Finding her through Sue and Doug's research[12]

---

12. Helen's daughter Sue and son-in-law Doug had seen the article about *Sheemaun* in 'Classic Boat' magazine of March 2011.

was astonishing, and wonderful. It stirred a memory of my family sitting round the dining room table discussing what to name the new boat.

At that time, I was reading Longfellow's poem 'Songs of Hiawatha' in which a mythical character built a birch-bark canoe from what the forest and the water had to offer. The canoe became Hiawatha's treasure, and had the power to help him through difficult times and those of his people. He called his canoe Cheemaun.

My father liked the name and I was very pleased to have chosen the one that seemed to fit. He changed the first letter from a "C" to an "S" because Sheemaun had a softer sound.

I do hope to hear more of Sheemaun's history and perhaps something of how you made the changes. The sails enhance her.

Bye now,

Helen B. Reid'

1935

The Launching
Four hundred miles north Of Matlock

In the warming early spring weather at James Noble's Yard in Fraserburgh, Launch Day at last had arrived. A handsome new boat with colourful bunting flying at her masts, lay on the greased slipway, only a half dozen or so timber props and some strong ropes preventing her from sliding down into the waiting Scottish waters. John Cranna[13] relates how by tradition, the local schoolmaster might let it be known that a launch was to take place. The school would be closed for an hour and the boys would gather at the Broch. Inevitably there would be some mischievous lads who would attempt to hide on the boat for the sheer thrill of the bucking ride down the slip and huge splash as the boat hit the water!

A crowd of around a hundred had gathered including the boat yard crew and the Noble family. James Noble with a dozen men stationed on the boat, made a quick check for schoolboy stowaways. Ernest Richards, Margaret and Helen gathered on the little railed platform that had been raised just in front of the vessel's Oak stem. At a signal from James, Ernest Richards nodded to Helen who clasping a bottle of white wine[14] that was

---

13. *Fraserburgh Past and Present* by John Cranna Harbour Treasurer. Rosemount Press. 1914.

14. A ceremony described by John Cranna – 'The crowds... anxious to see the chosen lady discharge the graceful duty of baptising the new craft, by breaking a bottle of wine upon the stem.' The early Vikings launched their Long ships over the bodies of prisoners to appease the blood-thirsty 'Sea Gods'. Later, sacrificial goats replaced the human offerings. It was not until the 15th Century that a libation of wine became a more civilised ritual' Red wine would have stained the white paint.

strung from the head of the sturdy Oak bow stem, then leaned forward splashed the contents over the little ship's bow –

'I baptise this boat *Sheemaun* and may she safely carry all who sail in her'

Helen's words were almost drowned out as the carpenters cast off the retaining ropes and with heavy mallets knocked away the timber shoring. For an anxious moment nothing happened, then with a creaking grunt the cradle moved and slowly the bow stem receded from the raised platform as *Sheemaun* gathering speed began to thunder down the slip. Amidst fountains of white spray, her twenty-five tons sent a substantial wash surging out into the Broch waters. As soon as she had settled on an even keel the men on her decks ran from one side to the other until she was almost dipping her gunnels. Having passed this traditional test of stability, the warps were hurled ashore.

While *Sheemaun* was being made fast, another traditional ceremony was being enacted as journeymen shipwrights grabbed the nearest apprentice carpenter and to the horror of those lads' mothers they were dunked fully clothed into the sea. A speedily rowed boat being already present to haul out from the water any apprentice who appeared to be floundering!

When *Sheemaun* had finally settled on an even keel Ernest Richards climbed proudly aboard this now alive and floating vessel. He put his hands to the wheel. It felt solid and secure, it felt good. The wheelhouse was clearly going to be weather-proof and snug. He then went below and re-explored the accommodation which now *Sheemaun* was afloat felt so alive and different, so removed from the two-dimensional drawings and different even from what he had seen while the vessel was being constructed. Ernest Richards noted that she was floating nicely to her painted waterline and reflected on the skill of her designer James Barnett and of James Noble's team of shipwrights. James Noble joined him and together they checked the bilges. There were some trickles as might be expected when a newly built boat took the water for the first time. This would cease as the timbers swelled as they absorbed the sea-water and came to squeeze tightly on the oakum and cotton caulking that had been payed into the seams. A few gallons of salt bilge water could quickly enough be bailed out and the bilges sponged dry.

Shipwrights at James Noble's Yard celebrate a Launching in the 1950s – some of those men would have taken part in the building of *Sheemaun*. From *'Boats & Builders – The History of Boatbuilding Around Fraserburgh'* by Bill Macdonald ISBN 0 9521551 0 9[15]

Following the launching ceremony, the Richards family the Noble families, the carpenters, shipwrights and joiners gathered at trestle tables quickly set in the now empty boatshed for a traditional meal of boiled beef, tatties[16] and swedes followed

15. Ian Smith kindly donated his copy to me. The Macdonald family were involved in the running of James Noble's boatyard, however. I have been unable to contact the Macdonald family.

16. Potatoes

by rice-pudding with currants and sprinkled with cinnamon. There was also sherry trifle. Beers and spirits helped to lubricate the vocal cords. Afterwards the younger generation went off to continue the merriment. The only complaint came, from James Noble's ten-year-old son who didn't like sherry trifle![17]

Ian Smith, nephew of the late James Noble, was a little boy at the time of *Sheemaun*'s launching. Sixty-seven years later, in the year 2002 Ian Smith told me –

'All I can remember of those times is seeing boats launched amid a flurry of excitement, followed by a big splash, and later being given a sweet biscuit and a cup of lemonade if my relations were involved. The stronger stuff was given to the tradesmen.'

Time-Line 1935 –

- In the USA unemployment was at 21%.
- Allen Lane established Penguin Books.
- The huge German airship the Graff Zeppelin was making regular trans- Atlantic passenger flights between Germany, Brazil and Argentina.
- Richter described a way of measuring earthquakes.
- Britain celebrated the Silver Jubilee of King George V.
- The German peoples generously presented Adolph Hitler with a gift of sixty warplanes for his 46th birthday.
- Jack Meyer established Millfield School at Street in Somerset UK
- The Golden Gate Bridge of San Francisco was being built.

---

17. As told to me by Ian Smith, nephew of the late James Noble.

1935

The Keel of HMS *Stork* is Laid

'Ho, Mates! Go lay the keel-blocks down,
And bring along the keel,
For we must build an iron ship,
And that right off the reel,
And that right off the reel, my boys!'

Iron Shipbuilding on the Clyde (1888) by Bass Kennedy

Some two hundred miles south west from Fraserburgh, where the river Leven joins the Clyde, a white flag with a blue elephant emblem fluttering proudly marked the ship-building yard of William Denny & Brothers. Over the decades many distinguished vessels had slipped from the Denny Yard to receive their baptism in the salty Clyde waters. The list includes the famous Tea-Clipper the *Cutty Sark* and many others ranging from tugs to ocean liners and ferries. One most remarkable steamer was the *SS Coya* of 546 tons. The *Coya* was not launched into the Clyde, instead she was de-constructed, packaged and shipped across to Peru in thousands of parts to be tractor and mule transported up into the Peruvian Andes to Lake Titicaca, at an altitude of twelve thousand five hundred feet (3.812m), where in 1893 she was re-assembled. The SS Coya is still there today, now functioning as a floating restaurant!

As the *Sheemaun* was being launched in Fraserburgh and the war clouds were gathering over Europe, at the yard of William Denny & Brothers the cranes and heavy lifting gear were laying the solid and strong steel keel of what was to become the HMS *Stork*. Officially the ship was destined for 'survey work' in the Far East but her design allowed for easy conversion to a warship. At

266 feet (81 metres) in length and 1,190 tons, HMS *Stork*, as a Bittern Class heavily armed sloop, would come to fight ferocious battles variously in the North and Arctic seas, the Mediterranean, the Far East and the North Atlantic. Her strong keel and especially her bow would one day be tested when rammed against one of Hitler's U-Boats.

The badge of HMS Stork depicting –

On a field of blue, a Stork Proper.

The passage of time and fate, hard-fought sea-battles together with their attendant brave actions and tragic deaths, would bring a personal link between the wheel on HMS *Stork* and the wheel on *Sheemaun*.

1935

James Barnett's Clever Design

'It is not generally realised that size is no criterion of the seaworthiness of a vessel. A corked bottle is quite a fragile thing, but it will survive the worst hurricane that ever blew'

Humphrey Barton – 'Atlantic Adventures in Small Craft'

Tiny by comparison with HMS *Stork,* the *Sheemaun* was forty-five feet in length, twelve and a half feet at her beam and drew four feet ten inches[18]. But with a displacement weight of twenty-five tons[19] she was a substantial little ship. A special feature was her 'flush' deck which ran from stem to stern and save for the deckhouse without interruption. She had fore and mizzen masts, both mounted on tabernacles that would allow them to be lowered. The rigging as fitted had been kept simple at Mr Richard's request. 'Steadying Canvass' as it was termed could be set in the way of a forward triangular staysail, a simple triangular mainsail and a triangular mizzen or after sail. This rig, although it could provide only a modest forward drive, would significantly steady the vessel in lumpy seas. There was scope to increase the area of canvass if required. The mizzen mast mounted a stout boom, almost a sprit, for hoisting the dinghy aboard. Substantial mooring bollards and fairleads allowed for secure mooring and iron stanchions and railings provided security.

The accommodation had been planned largely in accordance with Ernest Richard's requirements. Forward was a foc's'l [20]cabin which could be accessed below deck via a door from the galley

18. 13.7 m in length, 3.8 m in beam and 1.5 m draught.

19. 25,400 kg.

20. Ancient term – Forecastle, the front of the boat with accommodation and a raised fighting platform – fo'c'sl.

or from above deck via a deck hatch and ladder. To port there were two cot berths, one above the other. To starboard there was a hanging locker, a seat and toilet. Forward of this foc's'l accommodation was the anchor chain locker. Below the floor a sixty-gallon[21] galvanised water-tank serviced the galley sink and the washroom or heads. Next aft was the galley with on the portside a dresser, work surface and sink with shelving and a locker. On the starboard side was a Rippingille® Patent paraffin stove providing two hot-plates and an oven. There was further shelving and storage. Above, was a lantern-hatch which cleverly positioned astride the bulkhead and door way between the galley and saloon gave ventilation and light to both the galley and the saloon. The saloon provided a roomy, comfortable area with on the port side an L shaped settee and berth. A table and two chairs arranged in conjunction gave seating for up to six. On the starboards side there was another settee and berth. Just to starboard of the midline a companion way led up the wheel-house or deck-house and to port of that was a convenient side-board and drawers. There were bulkhead mounted oil lamps and twelve-volt electric lighting. Additional ventilation and light was provided by two glazed opening ports on each side.

Amidships, good comfort and protection from the elements was provided by the wheelhouse which was teak clad, and pine-wood lined. The floor being set some twenty inches (51cms) lower than the deck, there was ample headroom for even a tall person. To port there was a full-length berth which could double as a seat. Three windows, two of which were 'Drop-Lights' gave plenty of light and vision and could be opened for ventilation. The sash drop-light window was a simple and practical design dating from stage-coaching days whereby for ventilation, the glazed window suspended on a leather strap, could be dropped down into the door cavity. The window could then be pulled

---

21. 272.7 Litres.

closed again by simply pulling up on the strap which in turn was fastened onto a retaining hook. Such windows were made by the thousands in Victorian times and mostly used in railway carriages. On the starboard side there were two further 'drop-light' windows and the deck-house door opening, via three steps up, onto the deck.

Transversely mounted in the fore part of the deckhouse was a dash-board with the engine instruments, steering compass and throttle controls. To each side of the windscreen were 'drop-light' windows. The traditional spoked mahogany ship's wheel was mounted centrally on the bulkhead just aft of the dash-board. Two gear levers protruded up through slots in the floor from the engines below and it would be between these that the helmsman stood at the wheel. A wet hanging-locker aft on the starboard side within easy reach of the deckhouse door would be convenient for anyone coming into the deckhouse with wet sea-gear.

From the deckhouse a hatch led down five steps into a capacious engine-room in the wings of which a man could stand. A pair of Parsons petrol/paraffin four-cylinder engines each of twenty-seven horse-power gave an easy hull speed of 8 knots (9.2 mph). Each engine drew from its own sixty-gallon fuel tank, one on the starboard side and the other likewise on the port side. There were two small petrol tanks for engine starting. The dynamos linked to a twelve-volt battery charging system with split supply to each engine battery and a third 'domestic' battery. There was adequate provision for tool storage, spare oil etc.

A companion-way led aft down six steps to a lobby leading through to the owner's 'State Room'. To port was a store-room/workshop which opened into the lobby. To the starboard a door led from the lobby into the washroom and sea-toilet facility or 'Heads'. The owner's 'State Room', as ever, thoughtfully laid out by Barnett provided a double depth, full length hanging wardrobe starboard-side. On each side there were comfortable cot-berths of six feet three inches in length and fitted with folding tables. Beneath each, two generous drawers provided further storage below and two lockers which doubled as comfortable cushioned bench seats. Ventilation and lighting was provided by a lantern hatch above and there were oil lamps and twelve-volt electric lights. Between the berths aft, against the aft bulkhead was a dressing table with drawers and mirror above. Behind the aft bulkhead there was further storage space accessible via a deck hatch and containing the steering quadrant and storage.

1935

Ernest Richards has Second Thoughts

'If at first you don't succeed, try, try again. Then quit.
There's no point in being a damn fool about it!'

W C Fields

Following satisfactory sea-trials, arrangements were made for a delivery crew of local Fraserburgh fishermen to sail the *Sheemaun* south via the Caledonian Canal to Conwy Bay in North Wales. Although located at the closest proximity of the sea with Matlock, Conwy was still a good seventy-five miles away from Bank House. A journey that from Bank House to Colwyn Bay and then by dinghy out to the *Sheemaun* took some three or more hours. After making several journeys between Matlock and Conwy the family found it increasingly inconvenient, for without a car and with Sunday train services the travelling time ate deeply into the weekend. Furthermore, without a car it was awkward and cumbersome to transport luggage and essential belongings between *Sheemaun* and Bank House. The demands of maintaining a substantial sea-going vessel from a distance began to weigh heavily on Ernest and his family.

Meanwhile Major Heckstall-Smith, editor of the 'Yachting World and Motor Boating' journal had written an article on *Sheemaun* and this was published on Friday September 7th, 1935. Another article was due to be published shortly in 'The Motor Boat' journal. With such publicity Ernest Richards considered this would be an opportune time to put *Sheemaun* up for sale and make the best of things.

The article by Editor Heckstall-Smith and published on September 20th, 1935 - *Sheemaun* in "Yachting World & Motor Boating Journal" No 2162 Vol 83., was indeed propitious for *Sheemaun* was a vessel of some significance at the time on account of her being one of the first small flush-decked motor cruisers designed to undertake serious off-shore cruising in most weathers. Major Heckstall-Smith described *Sheemaun* as -

'...something which even Messrs G. L. Watson may be reasonably proud of...'

In describing the construction Heckstall-Smith noted that aside from the excellent accommodation –

'The construction generally is extremely strong, as one would expect from builders with long experience of fishing craft. Those who believe that the sea-going qualities of a fishing boat far exceed those of the average motor cruiser need have no doubt of a vessel such as this, for, by virtue of her carefully proportioned under-water body, she should be unquestionably superior to any fishing boat of similar dimensions.'

Ernest Richards anticipated that he would in another ten years or so be able to retire to his favoured Cornwall, where he would be free to enjoy his love of things nautical. He firmed up on his decision to part with *Sheemaun*. Accordingly, Issue number 2162 for Friday, 20th September 1935 of 'Yachting World and Motor Boating Journal' duly carried an advertisement –

'25 tons Twin Screw Motor Yacht. Built this year to our design and under our supervision. Dimensions: - Length O.A. 45 ft; breadth 12.5 ft: draft 4.8 ft. 2 Parsons 4-cylinder paraffin motors 20/25 h.p. each. A strongly constructed and able sea boat. Fully fitted out, and immediate delivery could be given.'

Shortly afterwards the 'The MotorBoat' journal carried a short article on *Sheemaun*.

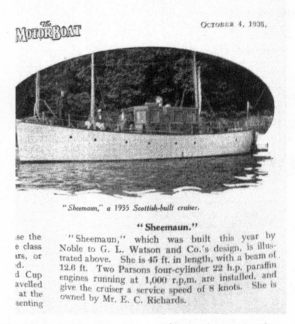

OCTOBER 4, 1935.

"*Sheemaun*," a 1935 Scottish-built cruiser.

"Sheemaun."

"Sheemaun," which was built this year by Noble to G. L. Watson and Co.'s design, is illustrated above. She is 45 ft. in length, with a beam of 12.6 ft. Two Parsons four-cylinder 22 h.p. paraffin engines running at 1,000 r.p.m. are installed, and give the cruiser a service speed of 8 knots. She is owned by Mr. E. C. Richards.

'The MotorBoat' magazine on 4th October 1935 featured
Sheemaun berthed at Colwyn Bay in summer 1935

Referring to the above picture, Helen Richards told me -

'That's my father standing on the foredeck and my mother sitting on the hatch; she always wore that white hat ...'

The Richards family and Helen were sad to say goodbye to *Sheemaun,* but given the restraints of a demanding profession, the little time available and the responsibilities that came with such a boat Ernest Richards felt it was the right decision. The advertisement attracted immediate attention and in November

Sheemaun was sold to Mr L.S.L. Saunders for £1,100.00. For Ernest Richards that was a very satisfactory outcome. He had realised a modest profit on the sum he had paid for her construction, and on the plus side he had enjoyed a Summer cruising season and he had learned a lot.

Sheemaun salutes Ernest Richards, James Barnett, James Noble and Helen Reid

Mr Saunders was well pleased with his new possession. This was a proper little ship. From the moment he put his hands on the wheel it felt secure and safe, it felt good and she was clearly seaworthy. In the spring of 1936 he sailed her down through the Irish Sea calling in at Dublin, the Isle of Man, Rosslaire, then across to Falmouth and on to Southampton Hamble. However, a handsome little ship like that would not go unnoticed very long at The Hamble!

Time-Line-

- 20th January King George V died and Edward VIII ascended to the British throne amidst the scandal of his relationship with Mrs Wallis Simpson.
- In Newport Gwent, in March, Joyce Pell bore a son – to be named after the battleship HMS Rodney.
- In East London Winston Churchill observed as the Battle of Cable Street took place.
- 200 'Hunger Protesters' marched from Jarrow to London.
- King Edward VII abdicated and was succeeded by his brother 'Bertie' who became King George VI, King of the United Kingdom, Emperor of India and First Head of the Commonwealth.

1936

A Change of Plan and a New Owner

'The lovely thing about cruising is that planning
turns out to be of little use!'

Tom Degnon

Harold Bell[22] wiped the salt spray from his eyes as he helmed his yacht up Southampton Water. A Force four gusting force five wind from just West of North made it necessary to tack and tack across as the plunging bow sent stinging salt-sprays flying back onto the helmsman. Shipping traffic in Southampton water was busy as usual and despite the rule that '*Power gives way to Sail*' the reality was that skippers tacking back and across in their sailing yachts had to bear in mind that the huge leviathans steaming by had very limited manoeuvrability. 'Might is Right' some would say.

There were not a lot of sailing craft on the water that day but quite noticeable was a rather fine white hulled motor-yacht with steadying sail set, tramping up from aft at a good pace heading straight into the wind and seas. As she over-hauled Bell's yacht with her high stem cleaving the waves she not only remained dry on deck, but the helmsman at the wheel was in the comfort of a snug and dry wheel-house. Harold Bell made a mental note of her name.

Sheemaun

---

22. Per letter 25/9/02 Ian Smith of Noble Bros (Fraserburgh) Ltd., then in his mid-seventies, wrote that the Bell family were well-known farmers, owning many large farms in the Fraserburgh area. They bred fine cattle and competed in the Highland Games. Later, Harold Bell sold the farms and 'moved to warmer climes' in the South.

After only a few weeks, Harold Bell's enquiries at his local Yacht Club led him to a fruitful meeting with Mr. Saunders. Fruitful, in the sense that Mr. Saunders was willing to part with *Sheemaun*. He had after all enjoyed a season of cruising and was quite happy to look for a change of vessel. Hands were duly shaken and the sum of £1,050.00 agreed and Harold put his hands to the mahogany wheel. It felt sound, it felt good.

The *Sheemaun* handled every bit as well as Harold Bell had expected, she was indeed very sturdy and had a useful turn of speed while keeping her decks dry from spray. As with any craft of her size and hull form she tended to roll in a side-sea, but that could be managed well enough by paying attention to the swell and setting the steadying sails. Her saloon however could perhaps be improved to better reflect his style; he would think about that and take the best advice.

Warming himself in front of his lounge fire and peering into the mirror on the mantle-shelf, Harold stroked his white goatee beard and straightened his neat little bow-tie. Above the mirror was a painting, one of his favourites, although for some tastes perhaps a little heavy. It was the 'Funeral at Sea' painted by an acquaintance, Sir Frank Brangwyn. Frank Brangwyn, who enjoyed an international reputation as an artist and was also a skilled lithographer, illustrator and a designer of furniture, glass and ceramics. He had produced many posters during the First World War but his poster 'Put Strength in the Final Blow – Buy War Bonds' depicted a British Tommy bayonetting a German soldier, this had upset a lot of people. The German Kaiser himself it was rumoured had put a price on Brangwyn's head!

Aside from his creative nature, Brangwyn had also been a keen voyager, sailor and explorer and it was this part of his friend's character that Bell so much admired. Harold arranged to meet Brangwyn at the Bull Hotel at Ditchling in East Sussex. This was convenient for Brangwyn who had semi-retired and it was near to his house 'Jointure'. Over a roast beef lunch chased down with a little Claret the two men discussed travel, art and explored the pleasures of sea-faring. Bell took the opportunity to introduce his desire to improve the layout and style of the saloon in his motor yacht *Sheemaun*. Brangwyn was fascinated by the sketches and photographs produced by Harold and made some suggestions but at sixty-nine years of age and suffering increasingly from depression, he had no wish to be 'hands-on'. Instead, Brangwyn proposed that Bell approached his friend and neighbour Albert Rowley.

Albert Rowley lived close by at 'Hillway House' indeed, so close by that it had been built on a part of the plot of land in which stood Brangwyn's home - 'Jointure'. Rowley was the founder and director of the Rowley Gallery of Decorative and Fine Art located at 140 Church Street, Kensington. An establishment that still enjoys a reputation as one of London's leading galleries in fine art. Albert's son Laurence having an interest in carved wood panels and furniture. Discussions and sketches were produced, hands were shaken and the new design for the *Sheemaun's* saloon would go ahead. The settee berths port and starboard, the sideboard amidships of the companion-way and the saloon table would all go, there was to be a complete make-over.

Berthed nearby at Littlehampton, *Sheemaun* was easily accessed for the necessary surveying and joinery work. Harold also instructed the shipwrights to install a bridge-deck and a second steering wheel at the after end of the wheelhouse, and a second set of engine controls. This would allow *Sheemaun* to helmed from outside in fair weather, be generally beneficial to navigation and add to the pleasure of sailing the boat.

In the saloon; the port and starboard settee berths, sideboard and table were removed to optimise on the available space. On the port side two specially designed armchairs were installed with between them a sideboard and cupboard. There was an arrangement whereby the chairs could be converted to two single beds or one double. Useful stowage was available behind the chairs. On the starboard side a drop-leaf writing desk was provided forward. Aft was placed a cocktail cabinet fitted with a hinged lid that secured down over the decanters while under the decanters was a fitted cutlery drawer. A comfortable arm-chair seating arrangement between these allowed the owner to work at the desk or just sit easily as might suit the social occasion.

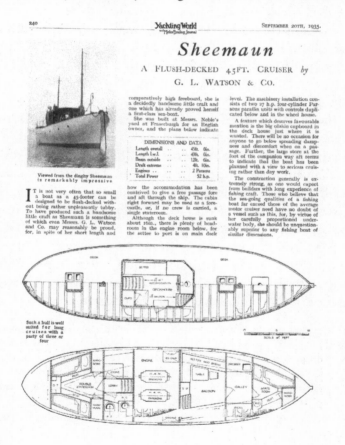

240   Yachting World   SEPTEMBER 20TH, 1935.
Motor Boating Journal

Sheemaun

A FLUSH-DECKED 45FT. CRUISER *by* G. L. WATSON & CO.

Viewed from the dinghy Sheemaun is remarkably impressive

comparatively high freeboard, she is a decidedly handsome little craft and one which has already proved herself a first-class sea-boat.

She was built at Messrs. Noble's yard at Fraserburgh for an English owner, and the plans below indicate

DIMENSIONS AND DATA		
Length overall	..	45ft. 0in.
Length l.w.l.	..	43ft. 6in.
Beam outside	..	12ft. 6in.
Draft extreme	..	4ft. 10in.
Engines ..	..	2 Parsons
Total Power	..	52 h.p.

IT is not very often that so small a boat as a 45-footer can be designed to be flush-decked without being rather unpleasantly tubby. To have produced such a handsome little craft as Sheemaun is something of which even Messrs. G. L. Watson and Co. may reasonably be proud, for, in spite of her short length and

how the accommodation has been contrived to give a free passage fore and aft through the ship. The cabin right forward may be used as a forecastle, or, if no crew is carried, a single stateroom.

Although the deck house is sunk about 16in., there is plenty of headroom in the engine room below, for the settee to port is on main deck

level. The machinery installation consists of two 27 h.p. four-cylinder Parsons paraffin units with controls duplicated below and in the wheel house.

A feature which deserves favourable mention is the big oilskin cupboard in the deck house just where it is wanted. There will be no occasion for anyone to go below spreading dampness and discomfort when on a passage. Further, the large store at the foot of the companion way aft seems to indicate that the boat has been planned with a view to serious cruising rather than day work.

The construction generally is extremely strong, as one would expect from builders with long experience of fishing craft. Those who believe that the sea-going qualities of a fishing boat far exceed those of the average motor cruiser need have no doubt of a vessel such as this, for, by virtue of her carefully proportioned underwater body, she should be unquestionably superior to any fishing boat of similar dimensions.

Such a hull is well suited for long cruises with a party of three or four

To the aft bulkhead just amidships of the companionway was placed a sliding rail on which the saloon table which could be hinged up and out of the way or hinged down onto a supporting leg to provide a table that would seat five. The slide-rail allowed the table to be moved a little to port or starboard of amidships as might be convenient. Two further alterations that Harold required related to the ship's 'Heads'[23]. The for'ard heads to the starboard side of the fo'c'sle accommodation was removed and replaced by a hanging locker. In the after heads, which could be accessed without disturbance to the after cabins, the sea toilet and wash basin were re-arranged to make way for inclusion of a cast-iron 'Hip Bath'. The port-side store-room/workshop was converted to a snug little cabin with a single full-length cot berth extending forwards into a 'trotter box'[24], and a seat and stowage drawers.

The engine controls were not so straightforward. Bowden cables and 'off the shelf' lever controls could be linked to the existing levers in the wheelhouse. The forward and reverse mechanism however posed a problem. The installed Parsons paraffin engines fed into what were known as epicyclic gearboxes, a clever system that required long hand-levers to pull the braking bands into 'Astern' and to push for the system engage 'Ahead', somewhere in between these positions the epicyclic mechanism whirled around but with no rotation of the propeller shaft although still mechanically connected! As for the control linkage his engineer came up with a clever

---

23. Centuries ago when ships generally sailed with a wind blowing from astern, the very basic toilet facilities consisted of wooden planks with convenient holes in them, protruding out on each side of the bows or head of the ship and sometimes with a primitive shelter. The following wind would blow the smell away from the ship. Those toilet facilities became known as 'The Heads' - a term still used today when referring to a ship's toilet!

24. An enclosed box-like extension to a short berth to accommodate the feet of a tall person.

solution. Instead of putting in a complicated system of jointed levers leading to and from the wheelhouse to the bridge-deck aft of the wheelhouse, two concentric hand wheels would be mounted on the aft starboard side of the wheelhouse and connected to the gear levers below in the engine room by chains and cables. In all this became a significant undertaking. To provide for the additional control systems, the starboard wet-locker in the coach-house had to be removed but as *Sheemaun* had proved to be a remarkably 'dry boat' a wet locker was unnecessary. It was replaced by a cushioned seat, which in turn made possible the installation of an aft facing window and in all it created a very convenient position for the navigator. The wheelhouse port berth/settee was shortened, and a new port doorway installed. Of course, the coach-house decking had to be taken up to allow full access to the engines and gear-boxes and for the cables and chains to be installed. Meanwhile the Rowley joiners removed the existing built-in saloon furniture and piece-by-piece the new layout and furnishings were crafted in place. Finally, there was the painting and varnishing to Harold Bell's satisfaction.

Two months later and *Sheemaun* now had not only a new saloon layout but also an external control station with throttle levers and wheel gear controls mounted at the aft of the coach-house. For the convenience and safety of the helmsman a raised aft bridge-deck was added with safety rails. From this vantage the helmsman had excellent all-round vision which greatly improved the convenience and precision of close-quarter manoeuvring and berthing – a feature that in years yet to come, subsequent skippers and helmsmen would greatly appreciate. Indeed, it was a feature that may have contributed to *Sheemaun's* very survival.

An article published in 'The MotorBoat' 17th September 1937 featured this work -

IN his first season, Mr. H. C. Bell has already completed 1,500 miles' cruising with his motor yacht "Sheemaun," and hopes to top the 2,000 mark before the end of the year. A sturdy, sea-going type of vessel, "Sheemaun" is 45 ft. in length and is equipped with two 25 h.p. Parsons paraffin motors.

During last winter Mr. Bell arranged with the Rowley Gallery of Decorative Art the redesigning and refurnishing of the saloon, which gave him increased dresser and cupboard space and, at the same time, increased the available floor area.

Comfortable armchairs take the place of settees and are ingeniously devised so that at night they may be used either as two single beds or one double bed.

The saloon table is fixed to a slide rail attached to the bulkhead, which allows it to be turned back against the bulkhead when not in use, and also permits of a limited amount of athwartships movement. A very neat writing desk of the drop-leaf type has been provided;

"Sheemaun."

an attractive cornerwise cocktail cabinet and fitted sideboards on the port and starboard sides of the saloon give a large amount of stowage space.

The work has been attractively carried out and provides an interesting and an unusual alternative to standard practice. Plans and a description of this cruiser were published in *The Motor Boat* of February 22, 1935.

Sheemaun's distinctive silhouette, as she sailed around the Isle of Wight, anchored sometimes in Studland Bay or put into one or other of the popular harbours, was to be become a familiar sight along the South Coast while she was being cruised by Harold Bell together with Mrs Bell, a paid hand and maybe one or two guests. Harold put his mind to studying charts, journals and tides as he made plans for future cruising.

Time-Line -

- The Short Brothers of Rochester delivered their twenty seventh Short Empire Flying Boat to Imperial Airways.

- Imperial Airways commence regular flights of 2,300 miles (3,700 km) between Southampton and Alexandria via Marseilles – Rome – Brindisi - Athens and Alexandria. A journey that could take three days.

- The Duke of Windsor married Mrs Wallis Simpson.

- Sulphonamides were used to treat infections.

1937

Meanwhile on the Other Side of the World
Shanghai

'The two most beautiful things are a ship under sail and a
woman in love. But you must be their master. Be strong and
they will serve you to the end – be weak and they will drive
you to Hell – and if to Hell I must go, give me a ship.'

Lt. G.T.S. 'Peter' Gray RN II.XI. 38[25]

Japan had been effectively at 'war' with China since the
Japanese had seized control of the South Manchuria Railroad
Company following the Russo-Japanese war 1904 - 1905. There
had been various nasty skirmishes with the Japanese claiming
need to protect the railroad against 'Chinese saboteurs'. These
'skirmishes' resulted in the Japanese gaining each time a little
more of Chinese territory. In 1931 the Japanese Kwangtun Army
by the subterfuge of claiming a need to protect the railroad,
had seized the entire Manchurian Province. Given the hugely
superior strength of the Japanese in the air, on the sea, and their
great military strength, there was little that the Chinese could do
about it. Officially the British and the United States were neutral
regarding both China and Japan in this tense international situation. However, both Britain and the USA enjoyed profitable and
important trade with China. To protect the British and international trading establishments and British citizens, the Royal
Navy had stationed two gunboats, the HMS *Ladybird* and the
HMS *Bee* in the Huangpu River and for similar reasons the USA
had put on station the USS *Panay* and the USS *Tuckwo*. These
shallow-draught but heavily armed vessels had been specially

---

25. Written in the same year that Lt Gray was married!

built for river and estuary duties. They were fully crewed and armed and were intended to present an inhibitory but to all intents and purposes a 'Peace-Keeping' presence in the time honoured traditional spirit of Imperial 'Gunboat Diplomacy'!

It was August the Second 1937. In the British Military Hospital, bored, sweating and occasionally swatting at the irritating flies, Lieutenant Gordon Thomas Seccombe Gray R.N. lay on the damp, thin sheets. He was looking through the ward window down across to where in Suzhuo Creek four warships lay at anchor, wisps of smoke curling up from their funnels. Lieutenant Gordon Gray RN was a serving lieutenant on the gun-boat HMS *Ladybird*. 'Peter', as he was known to his family and friends, had been hospitalised ashore for a few days with an ankle injury but with the help of a stick he was now regaining a somewhat painful mobility.

As he lay there, he became aware of a discordant throbbing, felt more in the chest than heard with the ears. Increasing in intensity the throbbing became a disturbing sound that could mean only one thing. After a few more minutes, high overhead, the unmistakeable throb of Mitsubishi Kinsei radial aero-engines was now distinct and clear above the general hub-bub of noise from the city – there must be a dozen or more aircraft up there. High up but distinctive with their twin engines and twin tails; they were the renowned Mitsubishi G3M long range heavy bombers. Clearly this was not just another reconnaissance sortie. As 'Peter'Gray watched, the air was rent by screaming howls as scores of bombs rained down onto the docks area. They seemed to fall indiscriminately onto the Shanghai South Station, onto the docks and wharves, into the river and onto the densely packed houses and warehouses. Thunderous explosions shook the town and the air misted to the supersonic shock waves. The hospital windows rattled, and the white enamelled gallipots and glass medicine bottles jingled on the ward trolleys. A scattering of fires had quickly broken out in the town and great plumes of black smoke were billowing up into the air. Ships sounded their sirens and bells and a rapid crackle of pom-pom and the thump of defensive ack-ack fire came from the warships. But having taken the town quite by surprise and having brought death and mayhem within minutes, the bombers flying at 233 mph (375 km/h) were already fading from sight and out of range. The sweet almost oily smell of spent cordite wafted up through the air interspersed with the rancid nostril searing odour of burning wood, fats and timbers. Momentarily stunned by this sudden and vicious attack, a dramatic intrusion that was proof as to why the American President and the British Government had agreed to maintain a deterrent presence in China, but as today's events had shown, clearly not a sufficient deterrent!

Matron Ruddock and Dr Patrick with their attendant nurses and orderlies scurried through the wards and corridors reassuring the patients and checking for damage. Dr Patrick glanced across at Lieutenant Gray –

'You'd best be back on your ship. Take care with the ankle, no weight-bearing on it for a couple of weeks then you can change the strapping for a crepe bandage… I'll see if can get someone to help you down to the creek.'

This was no time to be in hospital, he had to re-join ship and fast. An orderly heaved him onto a wheel chair and rattled him across the gardens that sloped gently for a couple of hundred yards down to the jetty, where already there were numbers of sailors scrambling to board a picket boat. By the time the picket boat had returned Lieutenant 'Peter' Gray to HMS *Ladybird* and he had been helped aboard, the bombers had long gone. There was mayhem in the town of course. There were fires to be put out, the dead collected; there were injured to be attended to and much clearing up to be done.

The Royal Navy presence however, and likewise that of the

United States Navy, was solely to guard and protect their respective countries' citizens and their commercial properties and interests. Otherwise they were strictly neutral, and any firing of weapons could be done only in defence of ship or British interests. After that unpleasant and worrying event shipboard routine had to sharpen up. There were still the occasional formal duties to be attended to; the routine shore leaves and re-supplying duties as needed. But what had been a monotonous life for the crews and their commanders had changed. Now there was an increased sense of unease and vigilance. The guns and weapons systems were overhauled, and the anti-aircraft weapons kept either loaded or with ammunition immediately to hand.

December 5th 1937 - six Japanese bombers attacked again. This time the little 'Deterrent Fleet' of British Imperial and United States vessels was the target and two of the vessels were quickly damaged. On HMS *Ladybird* 'Action Stations' had been sounded and crew scrambled to their battle stations. 'Peter' Gray raced up to the bridge as bombs screeched down all around. Only the pom-poms and the Lewis guns could elevate sufficiently to get a sight on the raiders but the fast Mitsubishi G3Ms were well above the range of the Lewis guns. The pom-pom gunners made a good show, but no raiders were shot down and as quickly as they had appeared the planes were fading into the distance. All around there was chaos. The USS *Tuckwo* had been badly damaged and was on fire. Her surviving lifeboats were being lowered and crew were abandoning the ship. HMS *Ladybird* also put out her boats and assisted with the rescue. It was not long before the USS *Tuckwo*, now a burning hulk, settled on the river bed with just her upper-works above the water. Attention turned to the USS Tatung which was also on fire and taking in water. The Commanding Officer ordered HMS *Ladybird* to be positioned so that a tow could be passed to the USS *Tatung* with the intention of beaching the USS Tatung on the opposite shore, where hopefully repairs would enable the vessel to be kept afloat. This was not an easy manoeuvre as there was a real risk that HMS *Ladybird* could also run aground.

The USS *Tatung* was towed as close to shore as was judged reasonable, then by using the flow of the river, the USS *Tatung* was 'Ferry Glided' and securely beached. A tug skipper would have been proud! The displaced crews now had to be accommodated as best possible and some were temporarily taken aboard by HMS *Ladybird* while arrangements were made for their future. The more seriously injured were taken to the British Military Hospital where Matron Ruddock and Dr Patrick would look after them. At 620 tons, with two 6-inch (15.24 cms) guns, one 3-inch (7.6 cms) gun, two quadruple 'Pom-Pom' guns, several Lewis guns and small arms, HMS *Ladybird* was now the main deterrent warship at Shanghai. Having seen what considerable damage the Japanese bombers could inflict, her commander and crew were uneasy at the prospect of being a sitting target and uncomfortable at not being able to take a take a pro-active stance. This was frustrating indeed, but they were under Admiralty orders.

In an un-authorised action, Colonel Hashimoto Kingoro on December 12th, 1937 ordered the newly positioned Japanese shore batteries to shell both HMS *Ladybird* and HMS *Bee* resulting in significant damage to both vessels. Fortunately, there were no serious injuries, but much work had to be done to make repairs and to return the ships to a fighting capacity. HMS *Ladybird* was shortly afterwards withdrawn from her Yangtse River duties and ordered to the Mediterranean. It was perhaps of some consolation for 'Peter' Gray to learn later that Colonel Hashimoto had been severely disciplined by his Commanding Officer General Matsui and for atonement he had been made to resign his commission and enter a Buddhist monastery!

Time-Line –

- 13th December 1937 The Japanese Army invaded China, capturing Nanking and murdering and raping hundreds of thousands of Chinese – The Nanking Massacre.
- President Roosevelt commenced his second four years inoffice.
- Sir Frank Whittle successfully tested the first British prototype jet engine.
- The German Zeppelin *Hindenburg* exploded into flames while mooring in New Jersey.
- A fierce and bloody Civil war had erupted in Spain between the Nationalists and Republicans. Hitler supported the Nationalists and his Condor bombers had attacked the Spanish city of Jain.
- The coronation of King George VI took place at Westminster Abbey.
- Fourteen thousand sea-miles West of Shanghai a little wooden ship *Sheemaun* was being re-fitted at Littlehampton in England.
  She would one day feature closely in 'Peter' Gray's life.

1938

A Shady Guest At the Branksome Tower Hotel
Dorset in England

'He has a charming manner and disarming smile,
But behind this façade he logs a sinister file.'

Anon

Discretely situated in twelve acres of beautiful gardens and woodland above the south coast cliffs of Branksome Chine, the grand and resplendent Branksome Tower Hotel offered un-interrupted southerly views out to the English Channel, south across Poole Harbour and Studland Bay and Eastward across to the Solent and the Isle of Wight. Dating from the early 19th Century the Branksome Tower had been for more than seventy years home to the Bury family. In 1892 the estate was acquired by the far-sighted property developer and hotelier, Mr D H Dore. Mr Dore was to develop the Branksome Tower into one of the finest hotels on the South Coast, which with its beautifully laid out gardens and woodlands was rightfully claimed to rival anything on the French Riviera. In subsequent years many well-known personages stayed as guests, dined there or just met to socialise. It was a place to be seen at. The Prince of Wales dined there, Lord Braybrooks and Hugh Lupus, Duke of Westminster stayed there. Ambassadors from around the world were often accommodated at the Branksome Tower Hotel as guests of the British Government. Among the many of the distinguished guests we find the names of Signor Marconi, whose steam-yacht 'Elettra' was moored in Pool Harbour at the time. Among many signatures in the guest books were those of

Prime Minister Lloyd George, of the Rajah of Sarawak and the Sultans of Muscat and Johore. The hotel was of also popular with authors, film stars and entertainers such as Edgar Wallace, Gertrude Lawrence, Al Johnson, George Formby and the dance band impresario Vic Oliver.

One of the guests staying there – ostensibly to absorb and enjoy the Hotel's luxurious ambience and fine cuisine, was Baron Werner Blomberg, a strikingly tall German gentleman with a slight limp and a haughty aristocratic demeanour. Baron Blomberg, who spoke perfect English had insisted that he was booked into one of the splendid suites of balconied rooms on the third storey overlooking Studland Bay and Pool Harbour. Such accommodation would have been perfect for the real purpose of his visit. A clandestine role that required he blend into the background discretely anonymous amongst his fellow guests while he made his covert observations. But Baron Blomberg had not expected to be so exasperated and unsettled by the antics of two tiresome children, the niece and nephew of the manager, who were also staying at the hotel.

Only two days after his arrival, as he was assembling his camera and tripod the Baron had become aware of a rustling noise. Somehow the corridor door had not latched and the door to his apartment suite was ajar so Werner on proceeding to shut it had been startled when two children jumped out from a laundry basket that was just outside the door and ran away down the corridor giggling. Baron Blomberg could not avoid the very uncomfortable feeling that they had been spying on him. Was that such a ridiculous notion? After all these were just little children, but what if an adult had put them up to it? What had they seen and what stories might they be passing on to whoever might be there to listen? Further-more die kleinen tuefel[26] had been mixing up the pairs of shoes that the guests

---

26. The little Devils

would put outside their room doors each night to be cleaned and polished. As a result, Werner had a rather un-welcome visitor in the large shape of the retired Colonel from two suites away who, on coming to retrieve his shoes had glanced rather too penetratingly into the Baron's suite. The Baron had been on the point of complaining to the Manager Mr Vernon Haydon, but to do so would have made him conspicuous. Fortunately, those wretched children[27] would soon be returning to their boarding schools - gute riddance!

Settling back comfortably in the Lusty Lloyd Loom high-back wicker chair and feeling more relaxed, Werner Blomberg contemplated the silver salver which had just been set down before him, the black coffee still steaming in its bone china cup. He glanced into the suite behind him. Yes, the steward had shut the door as he left the room and the latch had closed. Werner lit an Eckstein zigarette, inhaling deeply and expiring slowly as he gazed out across Studland Bay. At least here in the privacy of his suite at the Branksome Towers Hotel, he could freely indulge in a habit which his supreme boss back in Germany, Adolph Hitler, vehemently detested.

The bright sunshine at four o'clock was almost perfect for his photographic needs as it was now beginning to cast just enough shadow to make buildings stand out with almost a three-dimensional effect. He stubbed out the Eckstein and spread out on the wicker table an Ordnance Survey map of the area alongside a marine chart of the sea area off the Dorset Coast. The Imray Norie and Wilson charts gave much better detail of the near-shore and shallow beach areas than the British Admiralty charts which were prepared by oceanographers with primarily the needs of big ships in mind. He then set to work with his Carl Ziez

---

27. Shirley Crouch and her older brother Christopher – niece and nephew of the hotel manager Vernon Haydon.

Jena binoculars and his Ernst Leitz Wetzlar camera on its tripod, taking many photographs and making copious notes.

Although a keen Bridge player, Werner avoided the hotel card-tables and kept to himself. When not engaged in watching from his balcony, his attentions were focussed on exploring and examining the Dorset countryside, the conurbations, army barracks, road and rail facilities and the coast-line and beaches; always with his camera and note-book to hand. He admired the English in many ways. He considered the English to be civilised and cultured like the Germans. The British Nation was hugely rich and successful and Britain controlled a global Empire; but now the British stood in the way of his Fuhrer's ambitions to build a German Third Reich that would last a thousand years. Hopefully, the Fuhrer with his now mighty forces and global ambitions would bring these arrogant Britishers to their senses and to the negotiating table. But just now Baron Werner Blomberg[28] was feeling lonely and looked forward to his return to the Fatherland and his new and frisky young wife Ema. Following the death of his first wife Charlotte in 1932, he had re-married. His second wife Ema Gruhn had formerly been his secretary and was his junior by thirty-five years. The Fuhrer Adolph Hitler himself had been present at their wedding. Ema who most men found fascinating, had a hidden raunchy side to her and she had at one time covertly appeared in erotic films. Werner found her exciting and daring but the revelation of her role in certain films had caused something of a scandal[29] and his Fuhrer had not been best pleased!

He looked down from his balcony at the confident and rather

---

28. Blomberg survived the War, was imprisoned, and testified at the Nuremberg Trials. He died on 14th March 1946 and was buried in the Nuremberg Prison grounds.

29. Morphine addict Herman Goering, who had been a witness at the Blomberg marriage, later used this information to force Baron Blomberg to resign from his position as Field Marshall.

hocknasig Britishers with their steife ober lippees as they strolled imperiously through the lovely grounds or reclined sunbathing near the beach, he smiled inwardly at the thought of how Ema might stir this lot up!

With his covert observations and fact-findings completed he was looking forward to his return to the Vaterland, to the embraces of Ema and to make his report to the Fuhrer. Diese Englischen leute would soon enough find themselves being stirred up and discomfited by German discipline and hard work! Werner's last duty in England, as protocol and formality required, had entailed a formal visit to the Bovington Army Camp; where as he finished his inspection of the paraded troops he had given Hitler's Nazi salute to the troops and their Commanding Officer! That had not gone down too well with his hosts, but so what! The Fuhrer would be well pleased and there was one of the hotel's Rolls Royce cars waiting to take him to the German Embassy in London and then on to Harmondsworth airport.[30]

Time-Line –

* Werner Eduard Fritz Blomberg was Hitler's Generalfieldmarshall, the Minister of War and Commander-in-Chief of the German Armed Forces. During his stay at Branksome Towers he was spying for his Fuhrer and the Fatherland. Hitler's plans for a Second World War were already in an advanced stage. The plan called 'Operation Sealion' was for a massive sea-borne invasion of Great Britain that would be launched after the defeat of the Royal Air Force and coastal defences. Following the defeat of Hitler's Axis powers in 1945 it was revealed how that very area of Dorset

30. Harmondsworth Airport in 1946 was greatly expanded and re-named London Air Port, soon afterwards to become known as London Heathrow Airport.

had been marked as a suitable location for the German invasion plan.

- Werner Blomberg probably watched *Sheemaun* as Harold Bell cruised her in the Studland Bay area.

In the early post-war years *Sheemaun* would come to be owned by Vernon Haydon and she would feature at the Branksome Tower Hotel. *Sheemaun* would take wealthy guests for day-trips. Vernon's father Judge Haydon KC and Vernon's niece and nephew Shirley and Christopher, then grown up, would embark on some exciting cruises. And in Vernon's hands *Sheemaun* would engage in some very covert and clandestine activities!

1938

A Summer Cruise to the Continent

'My soul is full of longing
For the secret of the sea,
And the heart of the great ocean
Sends a thrilling pulse through me.'

Henry Wadsworth Longfellow

The distinctive outline of the *Sheemaun* had already become a familiar sight on the Solent waters and off the Isle-of-Wight as Harold Bell cruised in his comfortable little ship, but Harold had his eyes set further afield. He had plans to take *Sheemaun* to the prestigious Pavillon d'Or (Golden Standard) rally competition for motor yachts. The event had been initiated by the Union Internationale Motonautique based in Paris where in 1937 the first Pavillon d'Or rally had taken place. The 1938 rally and competition had been scheduled for July, it was to be held in Holland at Vlissingen and would be hosted by the Royal Netherlands Motor Boat Club. Fifty-two motor yachts including *Sheemaun* were to participate. The month was convenient and all going well *Sheemaun* would be back in the Solent in time for the internationally famous Cowes Week Regatta.

Together with his 'First Mate' Mrs. Bell and with a paid hand aboard, they departed from the Hamble taking the tide to Littlehampton where *Sheemaun* moored up until the next east-going tide which would take them on to Eastbourne. They continued to tide-hop eastwards to the picturesque Ramsgate Royal Harbour where they were made welcome at the prestigious Royal Temple Yacht Club. A few days were spent enjoying

Ramsgate and replenishing the stores[31], with special attention to putting aboard some decent British marmalade before heading East across to Oostende where they berthed overnight, and the following day took the tide North-East up to Vlissingen in Holland. At Ramsgate they had meanwhile been joined by several other vessels issuing variously from the East Coast, from the Medway and the Thames Estuary - all similarly bound. This little fleet included Captain Charles Lightoller's *Sundowner*[32]. On their arrival the *Sundowner* preceded *Sheemaun* into Vlissingen to moor up by convenient quayside steps on the starboard side, and *Sheemaun* tied up starboard-to-port, alongside Sundowner.

July 1938 – Vlissingen (photographer unknown)

31. There was no refrigeration on small vessels, nor indeed in most homes. Meat and fish was purchased fresh, salted, dry-smoked or canned. Fresh meat and fish had to be consumed quickly. Butter would last a few weeks wrapped in grease-proof paper. It could be bought in sealed tins which lasted indefinitely. Fresh milk could be made to last several days by adding two drops of formaldehyde to a pint (0.57 L) but powdered milk or canned condensed milk was easily available.

32. In May 1940 Captain Lightoller would take *Sundowner* to the Dunkirk Evacuations in Operation Dynamo and bring back to Ramsgate 130 exhausted soldiers. He died in 1952 aged 78yrs.

Sheemaun seen on the left of this contemporary photograph is moored starboard-side-to against *Sundowner*. Mrs Sylvia Lightoller in the white jumper is seen adjusting a coir fender assisted by Harold Bell while 'First Mate' Mrs Bell is seen emerging from the wheelhouse door of *Sheemaun*'s deckhouse.

The Bells and the Lightollers lost no time in socialising and there was much to talk about. First of course as to the immediacy of the Pavillon d'Or Rally, then to discussing details and experiences of the southern North Sea passage just completed. They shared their mutual passions for cruising abroad in their little ships and the Bells learned at first hand from Charles Lightoller, of his experiences in that awful and terrible sea disaster of the Fifteenth of April 1912; for Captain Charles Lightoller had been Second Captain on the allegedly 'unsinkable' R.M.S.[33] *Titanic* and had been one of the few to survive that historic and terrible maritime tragedy.

Charles Lightoller showed Harold Bell around *Sundowner*. At fifty-two feet in length she was slightly longer than *Sheemaun* but at twenty-six tons was about the same displacement weight. She had a single screw powered by a seventy-two horse-power Glennifer diesel engine of which Captain Lightoller was particularly proud. He had never been quite satisfied with the original sixty horse-power petrol-paraffin Parsons engine. Changing it for the bigger six-cylinder Glennifer diesel engine had given *Sundowner* an additional two knots in speed. In his turn, Skipper Harold Bell showed Captain Lightoller around *Sheemaun*. Captain Lightoller approved the wheelhouse layout, the mahogany wheel felt sound, secure and good. The accommodation was much admired, the skippers noting with a grin that the washroom facilities of both vessels included almost identical cast-iron hip-baths, they had a chuckle as they joked about cold bottoms!

---

33.   Royal Mail Ship

Settled in *Sheemaun*'s saloon, the conversation turned inevitably to the deteriorating European political situation, about which there was such unease back home. England still seemingly safe and secure on the other side of the Channel! But here in Vlissingen they were so much closer to Germany where the European tensions were almost palpable. Back home 'The man on the Clapham Omnibus'[34] was not much bothered that Hitler having abolished the Office of President was now in effect the German Dictator. Of course, the strict and repressive German anti-Jewish legislation was worrying and distasteful from the perspective of those back home in Britain, but here in Holland it was too close to ignore. An absence of German motor yachts at the Rally had been evident and much concern was expressed that only four months earlier Hitler's had marched his troops into Austria, and so German speaking Austria now found itself part of Germany. Harold expressed his concerns that the pleasure of being able to cruise private yachts off the European coasts and on the European canals might soon become a distant memory. The conclusion being that they should continue this cruise and enjoy the experience while they could.

Accordingly, after the four-day Vlissingen rally, *Sheemaun* set course to cruise through the Northern German waters before returning in time for the Cowes Week Regatta. Little did those skippers and their crews realise how in just over a year they would find their country entangled in a terrible European war, yet let alone dream, that their two little ships would come to take part in that war.

---

34. A British legal term used to refer to an imaginary, ordinary reasonably educated, respectable but non-descript man sitting on a bus/coach in Clapham, London and against whose views a Claimant's or Defendant's evidence might be judged. The ancient Romans used a similar precedent in the sense of the 'Bonus Paterfamilias'.

Forty-eight of the expected fifty-two motor yachts made it to Vlissingen and the event was reported in the local paper -

VRLJDAG 1 JUL 1938 DE LRIDSCHER COURANT
VIERDE BLAD – PAG 13

ereed, 5

3 eerste
rs over

vee ren-
m, over
ij J. v.
d van 1

lasse de
K.M. of
erreden.
Renaud-
lwillend

club zal van 18—25 Juli a.s. een inter nalen stertocht voor motorbooten o seeren om den Pavillon d'or. Hie hebben 48 deelnemers ingeschreven, uit Vlissingen, Delfzijl en Nijmegen Amsterdam zullen varen.

Uit Vlissingen vertrekken de volgende booten: Zenith van H. W. Nijman (War mond), Cormoran van C. F. Antheunissen (Warmond), Pantouflard van M. de Clercq (Gent) Ma Joie 2 van Ph. G. Back (Lo westoft, Pinguin 2 van M. Cock, Sheemaun van H. C. Bell (Oostende), Aring van A. F. Linse (Veere), Nora 3 van R. de Bock (Antwerpen), Jone 2 van S. Wilson (Ports-

‹ Vorige   Volgende ›

Harold Bell, set on experiencing the North German waters, then helmed *Sheemaun* East to continue with his planned cruise through the delightful German rivers and canals. Then he laid a course South East via the river Elbe to Hamburg, where they stayed for a few days before returning via the River Elbe. Then they sailed to Cuxhaven via the Kurstenkanal, aiming to arrive at the North coast and thence to re-trace their course West from Oostende to Dover, and on to the Solent in time for Cowes Week[35]. *Sheemaun's* cosy and dry wheelhouse came into its own when they met with some heavy Solent weather, but which fortunately cleared for the weekend.

---

35. Cowes is a small town on the Isle-of-Wight. The Cowes' Week Yachting Regatta is the oldest Regatta in the World. It is held in the first week of August and dates from 1820 when the Prince Regent offered the prize of a gold cup to the winner.

COWES NOTES

ANNUAL YACHTSMEN'S SERVICE

The annual Yachtsmen's Service arranged by the East Cowes Sailing Club took place at Northwood Church, Isle of Wight, on Sunday, and was conducted by the Rev. W. E. Longney.

During the week-end there was an improvement in the weather, and an increased number of yachts out. Mr. C. R. Fairey's motor yacht Evadne made its first appearance on the station this season, and as he is the Commodore of the Royal London Yacht Club his flag received the Commodore's salute of 11 guns.

Royal Yacht Squadron vessels seen out were :—

Lieutenant-Colonel J. A. Cole's ketch Harebell, Mr. J. R. Parsons's motor yacht Esmeralda, Viscount Gort's yawl Thanet, Sir Spencer J. Portal's schooner Xarifa Lance, and Mr. W. H. Askew-Robertson's ketch Mary Askew.

Other yachts in the Roadstead included :—

Mr. T. C. Ratsey's sloop Evendale, Mr. G. F. Carlisonian's sloop Zelita, Mr. Alexander L. Howard's motor yacht Papakura, Sir Connon Guthrie's motor yacht Creole, Mr. K. Macomber's motor yacht Crusader, Mr. H. M. C. Girling's motor yacht Marita, Mr. M. D. N. Wyatt's sloop Freedom, Mr. S. S. Taylor's sloop Rosemary IV, Mr. C. E. Donne's sloop Content, Messrs. H. S. and P. S. Whitmore's motor yacht Oceana, Mr. C. G. Blaxter's sloop Gairney, Mr. C. G. Vickers's cutter Allegro, Mr. A. L. Howard's ketch Wasfarer, Mr. W. J. Cutcliffe's sloop Nanette, Mr. C. C. Sander's ketch Dorbet II, Lady Acland's sloop Alpha, Mr. A. C. Barley's yawl Maid, Mr. M. Sharp's cutter Roselle, Captain R. T. Dixon's sloop Sea Crest, Mr. A. W. Wilson's ketch Lady Constance, Mr. E. Williams's cutter Mazurka, Mr. H. C. Bell's ketch Sheemaun, Mr. C. C. Reanan's ketch Cleome, Mr. G. W. Powell's cutter Charmian, and Mr. A. H. Rose's cutter Natanis.

Harold wrote a diplomatically worded account of this adventure shortly after arriving back at Southampton in late August 1938 and submitted it to "The Motor Boat and Yachting" magazine. It was published the following year in the issue of March 10th, 1939 pages 224 to 226. Only six months prior to Britain's Declaration of War with Germany.

Courtesy – Archivist at the National Maritime Museum of Cornwall

224   THE MOTOR BOAT AND YACHTING   MARCH 10, 1939.

On the Continent With "Sheemaun"

A Cruise Along German Rivers and Canals

By H. C. Bell

WE left England on the Pavilion d'Or cruise to Holland with the vague idea that, as Germany was only next door, we need certainly go there after the international event was over. Neither the mate nor I had previously visited that country. Accordingly, we had procured visas, triptyque, tourist marks and a few charts. In Amsterdam, however, we made more definite plans and bought more charts. We set forth from Sixhaven (the splendid yacht harbour of Amsterdam) at the end of July, and passed out through the Orange locks into the Zuider Zee or Yisl Meer.

Our 28-ton yacht "Sheemaun" is a bulky 45-footer with plenty of beam and draught. Watson-designed and Scotch built. She is propelled by two 28 h.p. Parsons kerosene engines, and has a useful auxiliary ketch rig. The Germans whom we met in the course of our cruise agreed that we had "too gútte Sée-Schiff."

In addition to my wife and I, we had one paid hand, and all had plenty to do.

Our first port of call after leaving Amsterdam was Hoorn. It had been suggested that the Island of Marken was worth visiting en route, but as the Zuider Zee was not entirely flat that morning, and our draught so nearly approximated the charted datum of the entrance channel (10 decimetres), I decided to take no risk.

The approach and entrance to Hoorn present no difficulties, and a considerable berth (apart from congestion) was found in the inner harbour, opposite the steamer quay. The mate was loth to leave this pleasant place, but as we had decided to make Hamburg our main objective, a start was made the following morning for Friesland.

Navigation on the Zuider Zee for vessels of 6-ft. draught or less is quite simple, but the Dutch chart No. 212 is a necessity. In thick weather it is advisable to keep the lead going. Stavoren was our next port of entry into Friesland. It took the rest of that day and all the next to reach Groningen. There are plenty of buoys and beacons to mark the channels through the shallow meres and, with a large-scale inland

(1) "Sheemaun" in a Continental port. (2) Herr Pappe, the genial custodian of the Bremen Yacht Club. (3) To reach Groningen much had to be lowered. (4) At Hamburg. (5) The yacht station at Emmerich.

A full transcript of Harold Bell's article follows -

On the Continent with "Sheemaun"
A Cruise along German Rivers and Canals
(The Motor Boat and Yachting March 10th, 1939)
By H.C. Bell

We left England on the Pavillon d'Or cruise to Holland with the vague idea that, as Germany was only next door, we must certainly go there after the international event was over. Neither the mate nor I had previously visited that country. Accordingly we had procured visas, tryptique, tourist marks and a few charts. In Amsterdam, however we made more definite plans and bought more charts. We set forth from Sixhaven (the splendid yacht harbour of Amsterdam) at the end of July and passed out through the Orange locks into the Zuider Zee or Ysel Meer.

Our 25-ton yacht "Sheemaun" is a hefty 45-footer with plenty of beam and draught. Watson-designed and Scotch built. She is propelled by two 25 h.p. Parsons kerosene engines, and has a useful auxiliary ketch rig. The Germans who we met in the course of our cruise agreed that we had "ein guttes See-Schiff".

In addition to my wife and I, we had one paid hand, and all had plenty to do. Our first port of call after leaving Amsterdam was Hoorn. It had been suggested that the island of Marken was worth visiting en route, but as the Zuider Zee was not entirely flat that morning, and our draught so nearly approximated the chart datum of the entrance channel (16 decimetres). I decided to take no risks. The approach and entrance to Hoorn present no difficulties, and a comfortable berth (apart from mosquitos) was found in the inner harbour, opposite the steamer quay. The mate was loth to leave this pleasant place, but as we had decided to make Hamburg our main objective a start was made the following morning for Friesland.

Navigation on the Zuider Zee for vessels of 6-ft. draught or less is quite simple, but the Dutch chart No. 212 is a necessity. In thick weather it is advisable to keep the lead going. Stavoren was our port of entry into Friesland. It took the rest of that day and all the next to reach Groningen. There are plenty of buoys and beacons to mark the channels through the shallow meers and with large-scale inland waterways map, it is impossible to go wrong.

The first lock after leaving Stavoren was Gaarkenken. Here the lock master advised me to follow the new Noordhornega – Eemskanaal, as otherwise there would be considerable delay in waiting for the railway bridges to open.

To reach Groningen by this route however, the masts had to be lowered, as there were two fixed railway bridges with 7 meters headroom and four road bridges with 4 meters headroom, which can be increased to 7 meters by raising the bridges horizontally. This costs 50 cents at each bridge, so we decided to unstep our masts and keep our guilders; as they are very precious in Holland.

This new canal (only opened last year) is one of the finest in Holland. I was informed that it is to be continued to Lenmer, on the Zuider Zee, thus forming an excellent inland route for moderately large craft wishing to proceed from Amsterdam to the Ems River. We passed through another lock on the outskirts of Groningen, took a turn to starboard, which led us into the southern section of the waterway surrounding the capital of this Dutch province, and made fast near the railway station.

The fifteen miles of canal to Delfzijl is crossed by fifteen bridges but they swung open at our approach and there was no delay. We berthed temporarily in the dock, but later passed through the lock and made fast in the harbour alongside a Dutch training schooner, preparatory to coasting along the German North Sea border.

I had been advised to take a pilot for this part of our passage, as he would be able to take us by some short cuts inside the East Frisian Islands. I came to terms with an elderly Dutchman who spoke good English, certainly looked the part and was highly recommended by the lock master. But, alas, we were to be woefully deceived. The old man came aboard at 2.30 the following morning, as, according to him the tide would then be right for us. In the darkness our pilot took us down the estuary at Ems. As daylight came we passed from the buoyed channel to the narrow channel marked only by perches between, the island of Juist and the mainland. By this time, however, the ebb had started and the shallowness of the water soon became apparent. The pilot was getting anxious, and well he might, for at 6.30 a.m we slowed down to a full stop, stuck fast on the highest part of the Norderny sand. Not only were we in German waters; we had landed on German soil!

Fortunately there was no sea running, and as the tide was falling rapidly we should soon be high and dry. It became evident, almost at once, that the yacht would list to port, so the dinghy was lowered and the kedge laid out to starboard. Even so, and with fenders wedged under the port bilges, we took a list of 30 degrees. It turned out to be a hot day, so most of the idle hours (seven of them) were spent below, sheltering from the heat, but we had little sympathy with our pilot, and in the forecastle he was even less popular. "I could have done this for you sir", was the dry comment from that quarter.

As the morning wore on, the flood began to make. By 2 p.m. we were afloat again, without apparently having suffered anything beyond discomfort. Norderney Harbour was entered two hours later, and, so soon as we were made fast, I interviewed the pilot. This was the first time I had taken a pilot and the first time I had run aground. I was feeling very sore about the incident and told this Dutchman exactly what I thought about him. "Now you must go." I said. "We have our charts – that is better."

The next morning there was "a fine breeze" from the eastward, so a day was spent on the island, which is a popular holiday resort of the German people and not without reason. It was still blowing on the following day, but not so hard, and an early start was made in order to cross the bar of the well buoyed Norderneyer Seegat at high water. We made Dove Tief, the outer channel buoy, at 3.30 a.m. and here, clear of all shoals and dangers (no more inside passages for me), I set course for the North Scharnhorn buoy over 40 miles away.

The North Sea was in a kindly mood that day; the wind abated, the sun shone and the Weser Light Vessel came abeam within four hours to confirm our position. We had no need to alter course, however. So accurate did it prove that the North Scharrnhorn buoy, which guards the north-west corner of the Scharnhorn rift, came up fine on the starboard bow, exactly where it should have done. We left it close to starboard, followed the line of buoys at the mouth of the Elbe, and entered Cuxhaven. A German yachtsman who we had met at Norderney, having recommended the Amerika Hafen, we went there, but in the act of making up we were charged from the other side by a Customs launch, boarded, and directed to proceed to the yacht harbour within the entrance of the Alter Hafen. This is a good place to lie, but the southern end (i.e., on the starboard hand when entering) dries at low water, care is necessary. A day was spent in this busy port visiting the town and going through Customs formalities. On August 6 we took our tide up the mighty Elbe. With the aid of the large-scale Admiralty charts, we had no difficulty in covering the 56 miles to Hamburg.

We entered the lovely yacht harbour on the island of Finkenwerde, the harbour —master came out to meet us in his launch, assigned us a berth, and we found ourselves stable companions with "Dirk III," about which a fine yachting book has been published. This yacht harbour is the finest I have seen, and an excellent example of what is consistently being advocated in the "Motor Boat" for the benefit of yachtsmen in this country. The rise and fall is comparable with that in the Solent, yet each yacht can moor either alongside or stern on to a floating stage, with headropes made fast to piles or small mooring buoys. Each yacht has her own "stall," so that she can come and go without causing inconvenience to others.

Homeward Bound

After a few days in this delightful modern city we began our homeward trip. It is impossible in the space of a short article to go into much detail, so only a brief description of the route can here be given. Another night was spent in Cuxhaven. From here the ebb took charge of us out of the mouth of the Elbe, and the flood rushed us up to the Weser to Bremerhaven. At Bremen the following day we had a cordial welcome from Herr Poppe, the genial commodore of the Bremen Yacht Club, who, together with other members of the club, made our stay enjoyable. We had intended to follow the Wesser to Minden but there was not enough water, so down we went to Elsfleth and took the river Hunte to Oldenberg.

During the next six days progress was slow by way of the Kusten Canal, the river Ems, the Dortmund-Emms canal and the Rhine-Herne canal to Duisberg. There were 23 locks and the barge traffic was heavy, even on a Sunday. All bridges on this route are fixed, but allow about 5 meters headroom. Parts of this great inland waterway are very fine, and the work of improvement is proceeding apace. Duisberg is purely a commercial port and not recommended to yachtsmen. We left it as soon as possible for Emmerich with a pilot aboard, as this is compulsory on the Rhine, but this time we had no tiresome mishaps. Emmerich is a delightful little harbour where we were made very welcome at the yacht club. It was with reluctance that we eventually said "Auf Wiedersehn" to Germany, crossed the German-Dutch frontier, and followed the Waal down to Dordrecht. With the aid of Dutch charts Nos. 204 and 209 (a necessity for this passage), we reached Veere, and so to Middleberg and Flushing. My wife was quite partial to Ostend, so after leaving Holland we lingered awhile in this cheerful Belgian port before returning to our native shores and seeking once more the sheltered waters of the Solent. We crossed to Dover 38 days after leaving Amsterdam. During that time we had covered 865 miles of sea, river and canal, and had run the engines for 173 hrs. Main items of expenditure for this period, apart from wages, were –

	£	s.	d.
Fuel and oil	23	3	0
Wines and provisions (excluding meals ashore)	14	2	6
Pilotage, harbour dues And lock fees	4	5	6
Tips etc.	2	0	0
	£65	11	6[36]

This Continental ditch-crawling along fine inland waterways, amid pleasant scenery, visiting towns of great
historical and romantic interest, and being among such a
clean, kindly and hospitable people was, for us, a happy
experience which we hope one day to have again.

Prosit!

---

36. Equivalent in 2017 to £4,113 or $ 5,496!

1939

International Turmoil and Change - *Sheemaun* is for Sale
Europe is politically falling apart, and War is imminent

'Walls have ears and the sky has spies
Soon falling bombs will take our lives.'

Anon

Harold Bell was becoming increasingly uneasy. Germany had re-armed and had introduced military conscription. Italy wielding an aggressive foreign policy had invaded Abyssinia only four years earlier. In Spain General Franco was embroiled in a brutal Civil War aided by Hitler, while Britain and France were finding themselves increasingly concerned about Germany on the one hand and Italy on the other. Czechoslovakia was about to erupt into civil war and it looked as if Hitler might invade Poland. This was no time to be planning yacht cruises and anyway Harold Bell still had business interests to attend to and safeguard. The 'writing was on the wall' and he would have to part with *Sheemaun*. There was naturally much sadness and nostalgia in the Bell family, but the looming European situation had to be faced. With a heavy heart Harold Bell advertised *Sheemaun* for sale, but at this insecure and critical time whoever would even consider buying a private motor yacht?

Sheemaun salutes Harold Bell

As fate would decree, an experienced yachtsman Acting Lieutenant Roy Calvert-Link RNVR, happened to be on leave, he happened to live in Bournemouth and he happened to notice that a pretty and seaworthy looking motor yacht was for sale. Not surprisingly and given the worrying international situation the asking sum was very reasonable, but could the vessel be as good as was made out? It was little trouble to view a vessel only an hour's drive away and a pleasant one at that for the journey would take him through the beautiful New Forest.

A viewing was arranged. Roy Calvert-Link looked carefully all over *Sheemaun.* He tested the rigging and deck gear. He very much liked the enclosed wheelhouse. He ran up the engines which started well and ran smoothly.

He put his hands to the mahogany wheel which felt secure, the boat responded well. It felt good.

Roy Calvert-Link was impressed with what he saw and Harold Bell in his turn was happy to know that *Sheemaun* would be passing into the hands of someone who knew boats, was a keen yachtsman and would do his best to look after her. After all, anyone who has come to care about and love a boat is very reluctant to see it pass into strange possibly even uncaring hands. If Harold Bell did wonder quite why a thirty-four-year-old Royal Naval Reservist Officer should wish to acquire a boat at such a perilous time, then he kept such thoughts to himself.

It was July 1939. Within weeks, on 3rd September, Britain and France would Declare War on Germany.

Time-Line –

- In the UK Ramsgate Town and The Royal Harbour had been bombed by Kaiser Wilhelm's Zeppelins in WW1. Fearing the worst for Ramsgate in any further conflict with Germany, Alderman Kempe and his Councillors pleaded for some years that Whitehall should agree that Air Raid Shelter tunnels be dug down into the chalk under Ramsgate.

- The Home Office having finally agreed, tunnelling started in June 1939. Some three miles of deep tunnels and chambers would be hewn into the chalk within a year. Many surface entrances dug down from the streets of Ramsgate Town ensured that most of the population would be able to get safely underground within ten minutes or so. The massive tunnels could accommodate over a thousand people. Their facilities included electric lighting, ventilation, sleeping areas, canteens, toilets, shops, a small hospital and even a barber.

- The Royal Harbour and Port of Ramsgate, during what would very soon become the Second World War, would suffer yet further onslaughts and terrible damage at the hands of Hitler's bombers. Those tunnels would prove their worth by saving hundreds of lives when in just one raid some five-hundred bombs were dropped on the town.

- In an evil and cynical move, Hitler's henchman finalised the establishment of the 'Reich Association of Jews in Germany' into which all Jews in Germany had to be registered. At the same time Hitler was planning the invasion of Poland.

1939

The Thames Estuary - August

'The wealth of the World is wafted to London by the Thames, swelled by the tide; and navigable to merchant ships through safe and deep channels. For sixty miles; from its mouth to the City, its banks are everywhere beautiful with fine country seats, woods and farms.'

Paul Hentzner 1598 - 'A Journey into England'

There were very worried men in the British Government and at the Ministry of Defence. The River Thames with its slowly pulsing tides was the main artery supplying the life-blood of essentials and commodities to London and it was essential for the exporting of goods around the world. Much of the foods, goods and raw materials imported into London's huge Docks would be re-distributed around the British Isles. The River Thames and the London Docks provided the pumping heart that powered the trade and commonwealth business on which much of the United Kingdom's wealth was based. Those worried men also knew that Herr Adolf Hitler and his advisors must surely at some stage attempt to deal a crushing blow to Britain by blocking or in some way paralysing this vital water-way. The Thames and its Estuary must urgently be protected. Accordingly, the mile-long Pier at the town of Southend was requisitioned by the Ministry of Defence and duly renamed HMS *Leigh* by their Lordships of the Admiralty. The Grand Pier Hotel and several sea-front properties were also requisitioned and staffed by Royal Navy personnel. HMS *Leigh* then became the headquarters of the Royal Navy Harbourmaster responsible for controlling the movement and mooring of the many vessels big and small that were daily bound inward or outward. A Defence Boom of almost seven miles in length would be created from north to south across the Thames Estuary between the Kent and Essex shores. Large timber, iron and concrete piles would be driven vertically into the sea-bed at approximately eight feet intervals in the less deep sections. Between these and spanning right across the deeper parts of the estuary and the shipping channels a floating barrier would be laid. The floating barrier to consist of massive blocks of wood bound together with iron straps. Hundreds of such blocks, joined together by short lengths of chain would be drawn across the estuary. Hanging down from these floating blocks would be a curtain of steel link-chain. Such a defence boom was deemed to be virtually impenetrable by submarine and surface raiders. Solid wooden blocks had been chosen instead of hollow floats because the latter could easily be punctured by gun fire.

The finished boom would be more than six miles long and span between Shoeburyness on the north bank to Sheerness on the south bank. In the middle of the boom there would be three 200 ton 'Gate Barges' armed with searchlights and anti-aircraft guns. Suspended under those barges would be more steel nets. The barges could be moved to permit passage in or out for the hundreds of war vessels and merchant vessels that had to enter or leave the Thames. The whole structure 'covered' by shore gun-batteries and there would be armed tugs and small but heavily armed warships on twenty-four-hour duty. Electric cables laid on the river bed across the seaward side of the Boom would detect any magnetic disturbance such as might be caused by a steel or iron hull of a warship or submarine. In the event of an enemy submarine being detected a destroyer stood by ready to depth-charge the area. There would also be also several mine fields strategically placed, the mines electrically wired so that detonation could be carried out by observers on the shore.

The Defence Boom was intended to present a major obstacle to any hostile water-born vessel, but it would also present a great inconvenience to the traditional inbound and outbound passages of the hundreds of small coasters, trading barges and fishing boats. Outward bound vessels could be 'waved through' but inward bound vessels would have to be examined. To optimise gate-time such vessels as might be allowed a quick admission would then be examined by awaiting armed Auxiliary Patrol Service vessels.

Time-Line –

- The British Women's Land Army was reformed.
- For the first time ever, a transatlantic air passenger service using 'Heavier than Air' aircraft was established by Pan American Airways.

1939

War is Declared
Meanwhile back in Blighty[37]

'Prepare, prepare the iron helm of war,
Bring forth the lots, cast in the spacious orb,
Th'Angel of Fate turns them with mighty hands,
And casts them out upon the darken'd earth!
Prepare, prepare!'

William Blake 1757- 1872

Twenty-three-year-old Stanley Dodd lived by the Thames at Wapping in East London. His parents ran a small shop and Stanley was employed at the East London Sorting Centre of the General Post Office located close-by at Whitechapel, and convenient to the electric rail service via Whitechapel station. The sorting office serviced a huge population area of some fifty square miles between the districts of Poplar and Chingford. Together with his young wife Ellen - who he always referred to as 'Girl', Stanley had dreamed of getting away from East London in late August and to drive north up to Scotland for a few weeks holiday walking and touring. All the doom and gloom war-talk which was now dominating life in the Capital was unsettling and depressing; they felt a need to get away from it all, to explore open spaces and to enjoy vistas and clear skies and some solitude. However,

---

37. 'Blighty' was a slang word used by British Colonial Servicemen when fondly referring to their British Homeland. It may have had origin from the Urdu vilaayati or bilati meaning Englishman or European foreigner. Homesick British troops in WW1 and WW2 talked of 'Dear Old Blighty'. The War Office published a magazine called 'Blighty'. It was a light-hearted publication with short stories, cartoons, pictures and pretty girls – free to the troops and on public sale for a shilling - £3 in 2017

it really did now seem that a war with Germany was likely and because there was such uncertainty about the European situation they were having last-minute second thoughts. If the worst were to happen, they would need to get back to London quickly. So, instead they headed West to Somerset from where it would be easier and quicker to drive back to London.

Hereafter are extracts copied from the hand-written memoirs of the late Stanley Dodd, which reveal all the resourcefulness and humour of the London Cockney in those difficult and threatening times. Stanley's writings dramatically record unique, personal and atmospheric historic details from those days, his page numbers have been included.

'But... long before reaching Weston[38] we passed little groups of people in the villages and so on, each bearing a grave look of concern on their faces and some of the women were crying. By the time, we reached Weston we knew... (p 201)... that war had been declared, naturally there was a lot of discussion and conjecture and at the finish we stayed the night intending to make an early start in the morning for home. This we did and on the journey[39] passed a continuous stream of traffic all heading West away from London – so much that we thought that London must have been evacuated. There were cars, vans, lorries all loaded to capacity with people, children and household goods, streaming West and away, in fact we seemed to be the only vehicle going East. When we got to the outskirts of London, we found that people were digging trenches and erecting barricades and that the air was electric with tension. Anyway we dropped Dad and Ethel at New Southgate and then tore on

---

38. A town on the north Somerset Coast on the River Severn Estuary in western England
39. They then drove back to London, a distance of 140 miles (225 kilometres).

to Wapping[40], to Nellie and the shop. It appeared that as soon as war had been declared on the previous day, an air raid warning had been given, but it appeared to be a false alarm. Then the excitement had subsided into apprehension and then, as nothing further developed, into wait and see. This wait and see continued, and for a few days all sorts of theories and rumours arose but eventually it became apparent that life was to continue in the same manner. The declaration of war and the fictitious air raid warnings were the only two episodes which were out of step – that is – as far as Wapping and myself were concerned. In the papers and on the BBC there were reports of defensive activity, and, of... (p 202)... course, dominant news of German domination in Poland and in the consolidation of Sudatenland (Alsace and Loraine) which they had annexed previously. But although things were on the move, reservists being called up, ships commissioned, and so on basically everything remained more or less the same. At least, that was as far as Wapping was concerned, although "outside" in the City and Westminster sandbags had been erected around the entrances of important buildings and at strategic green spaces, trenches had been dug. Of course we now know through recorded history that far more than this was going on behind the scenes, for example the use of a tube railway station – the Aldwych – as a headquarters, the fortification of the coast in important places, the establishment of anti-tank traps and pillboxes and so on, but I'm writing this as it affected me. After a few days of this "normality" we resumed our holiday and went out daily with Dad and Ethel and at weekends with Nellie and so the first fortnight passed by and I resumed work at the office. Then things began to happen in a minor way. All the bridges over the

---

40. Wapping – an East London District lying on the north bank of the London Thames

docks leading into Wapping were manned by the army and you had to prove who you were to pass over them. As I was on nights, I used to be stopped regularly by two armed sentries and a corporal with the words "Halt – who goes there?"… (p 203)… Then I would foolishly reply "Friend", show my driving licence (S Dodd, 4 Jackson House, Watts St, Wapping) and then be waved on with "Pass Friend". Within a few weeks of this, the blackout came into being. No lights were to be displayed which were not screened and petrol was to be rationed. In connection with petrol rationing I had an amusing experience which is worth relating – with the Morris 10[41] – because we got out so much I had a specially large carrier made to accommodate our camping equipment. Now it so happened that I managed to "acquire" a large 60 gallon tank used for storing paraffin and at the interval prior to rationing, I conceived the idea of filling up this tank as a reserve. So I had it filled with petrol – petrol 1/6[42] a gallon – through devious means 30/-[43] and keep your mouth shut – I let in the clutch and with the strain at the rear plus the weight of the petrol, the front of the car tipped up, the weight of the petrol and the rear holding it some three ft off the ground. Now I supposed the tank had shifted slightly for when I climbed onto the bonnet my weight brought the front down but when I got off up it went again in see-saw fashion. Well the outcome of this was that the bloke who sold me the £4.10[44] of petrol for 30/- and since killed by a rocket, had to lay on the bonnet so that I could drive the car into the lockup garage and we… (p 204)… had to cross a bridge

---

41. A small 4 seat family car.

42. £3.43 at 2017 value.

43. £92.65 at 2018 value

44. £62.98 at 2018 value

with this "Pass Friend" rigmarole. We didn't know what to expect – be shot, be frisked by the Police, but we passed it OK, for strangely enough the army never questioned us and just waived us through as if a man lying on the bonnet and a car in which the front rose 6 inches in the air was a perfectly normal everyday occurrence. I might add that it wasn't worth the effort whether you have 60 gallons plus, or just 6 gallons, it soon comes to the end and the huge tank remained disconsolately on the floor at the bottom of the garage…' S.D.

Stanley Dodd would come to serve as a Royal Navy Volunteer Reservist (RNVR) Mechanic on the armed HMY *Sheemaun*.

Emotions of fear, disbelief and patriotic fervour were sweeping though the Shires, the Counties, Towns and Cities of England.

RP was aged 3years 8 months when war was declared – named after Admiral Lord Rodney and the Battle-ship HMS *Rodney*. Dressed by his mother Joyce in a patriotic sailor suit!

PART TWO
The War Years

1939

The Dawning of the Thames
Auxiliary Patrol Service

'As they took to their boats those brave few,
That London would need them soon, full well they knew.'

Anon

In the nineteen twenties a group of yachtsmen who, while their boating and sailing lives were separate and diverse, found they had in common that they all lived or worked in London and could easily meet up. They agreed to establish a club, and so the year 1926 saw the founding of The Little Ship Club. Meetings were arranged at which yachtsmen could socialise and share their mutual practical and theoretical knowledge. This progressed to more organised instruction classes covering everything nautical from boat construction and maintenance to coastal and off-shore navigation, meteorology, rope-work, sail-trimming, engine and electrical technicalities etc. Membership blossomed from initially several score to in 1932 some four thousand. The Club leased rooms at Beaver Hall, the headquarters of the Hudson Bay Company. The very high standard of this seamanship training and education came to the notice of the Lords of the Admiralty. So impressed were their Lordships that in 1936 the Admiralty commenced sending to the Little Ship Club, men of the Royal Naval Supplementary Volunteer Reservists for formal instruction. Then in 1937 Alfred Duff Cooper GCMG[45], 1ˢᵗ

---

45. GCMG – Grand Cross of St Michael & St George. Although lower ranks might cheekily interpret the initials as – God Calls Me God!

Viscount Norwich and First Sea Lord, in an unprecedented gesture, invited the Club to apply for the privilege of flying a Blue Ensign[46] defaced appropriately by the Club motif, namely a light blue sky over a dark blue sea with on it a white triangle representing a white sail.

As it become increasingly obvious that war was probably inevitable, a select number of boat owners gathered together along with such motor yachts as they could muster on the London tidal Thames and these prescient men created a unique 'Club' - The River Emergency Service. The members of this River Emergency Service freely volunteered their time and their boats for such duties as might become necessary. Most were members of the respected Little Ship Club. Contingency plans were also made for the supply of fuel and essential equipment for these little vessels.

There had already been some German bombing raids over the Thames but on the night of 7th September 1940 in an unprecedented attack on London, three hundred and seventy-five of Hitler's bombers rained down thousands of high explosive and incendiary bombs causing almost unimaginable widespread devastation, a devastation which was to be repeated for fifty-seven successive nights and would become known as 'The Blitz'.

Under control of the Port of London Authority, the River Emergency Service went into full operation. Those remarkable men with their boats played a significant role in 'search and rescue'. They plotted the positions of mines dropped into the river and they searched for those mines. They also took on a significant role in conveying essential personnel and even taking the injured to hospital, for many of London's Streets and bridges were rendered un-passable due to the devastating

---

46. A prestigious British Ensign based on a dark blue background and only permitted to be used under a granted Admiralty Warrant by certain Naval Officers and Clubs.

bomb damage and consequent raging fires, while London's River Thames remained relatively free from obstruction.

The Royal Navy which pre-war had shown little interest in the River Thames then took offices adjacent to the Tower of London and next to the Port of London Authority Offices. The Admiralty, now recognising the immense contribution and value of these volunteers, in June 1940 took over from the Port of London Authority the task of organising the River Emergency Service from which was created the Royal Naval Auxiliary Patrol Service – the RNAPS or RNXPS. The little boats of the RNAPS were then armed and crewed by trained Royal Naval Volunteer Reservists and some Supplementary Reservists, they were painted regulation naval grey and flew the White Ensign[47]. Some were relatively small fast launches at about thirty-five feet, others could measure up to eighty feet over-all. They were well-built little vessels, seaworthy and sound.

One of the founding 'fathers' of the River Emergency Service was the keen yachtsman, lawyer, historian and Member of Parliament Alan P. Herbert.[48] Herbert lived at Hammersmith where he moored his motor boat *Water Gypsy* and he also sometimes anchored *Water Gypsy* off the Houses of Parliament. Alan Herbert had enlisted in 1914 as an Ordinary Seaman, he progressed to Leading Seaman and in 1915 was commissioned as a Sub-Lieutenant. In 1917 he was wounded by shrapnel. Herbert was a man who knew about war and seamanship.

Per - *Motor Boating*, 572 Madison SA. New York February 1941 -

'Sir Alan Herbert, then A. P. Herbert MP[49] for Oxford University Constituency kept his boat *Water Gypsy* on the

---

47. The Ensign flown by British Royal Navy Ships and Royal Naval Shore Bases
48. Sir Alan Patrick Herbert 1980 - 1971
49. MP – Member of Parliament

Thames at Hammersmith. *Water Gypsy* was one of the early volunteered Auxiliary Patrol Boats, through contacts and devious means APH managed to arm her with machine guns.'

The RNAPS was much more than a 'Dad's Navy', for in addition to the patrolling vessels, the Service provided and maintained some sixty fixed-station observation barges moored along the tidal Thames and far down into the Estuary at strategic locations. These Observation Barges provided a very essential service, their purpose being to observe and record enemy aircraft movements including the fall of bombs and mines and parachutes. Special attention was paid to the fall of the magnetic and acoustic mines that the German bombers parachuted into the Thames on clear moonlit nights. The precise landing locations of these parachute mines were logged by cross-referenced coordinates on large scale area charts.

Those Royal Navy Auxiliary Patrol Service boats served multi-functional duties. They assisted with tending the ant-aircraft Barrage Balloons and their crews and they rescued downed airmen allied and enemy alike. They collected and delivered mail and small goods, and transported personnel to and from various naval and merchant vessels. They carried out highly dangerous anti-mine activities. They examined and searched in-coming vessels and some delivered the Rum Ration to Royal Naval Vessels. They were daily exposed to significant dangers, many were machine gunned by German aircraft, some were bombed, some were damaged by mines and at least one - the steel-hulled Armed Auxiliary Patrol Boat HMS *Aisha* was destroyed by a magnetic mine. The patrol boats stopped and examined all merchant and non-naval vessels coming into the London River, their authority being made clear by the Royal Navy white ensign they flew, and by the presence on their foredecks of one or more substantial machine guns – weapons that their crews had been trained to use and were expected to use if necessary. Whenever the opportunity arose the Royal Navy Auxiliary Patrol Service Vessels used their weapons to fire in anger at enemy aircraft, and in the later war years at the fast flying V1 self-propelled bombs.

In 1945 Sir Alan Herbert MP, whose own boat the *Water Gypsy* had served as a Thames Auxiliary Patrol Boat, was highly critical that the British Government had not thought to award the 1939-1945 Star Medal to those men who had served with the Thames Auxiliary Patrol Service. In what many considered to be a shameful decision, the Lords of the Admiralty had advised Parliament that a medal was not merited because the boats had operated only in 'Sheltered Waters'.

Standing up in Parliament Sir Alan faced the assembled Politicians and demanded that they explain –

'From whom were these vessels sheltered?... They were not sheltered against bombs above or mines below and during the material times, these vessels were patrolling night and day, ready to repel invasion. So that what they were sheltered against we do not know.'

Sadly, Sir Alan's fellow Members of Parliament had other matters on their minds, perhaps understandably, and so the quite clear wrong to which Sir Alan referred was never corrected. An oversight which I hope that Parliament and the Lords of the Admiralty may yet see fit to put to rights, perhaps at a suitable anniversary, such as will fall in June in the year 2039 at the centenary of the founding of the Royal Navy Thames Auxiliary Patrol Service.

1939

Thames Nore Division of the Western Front Defences Command

Nore[50] Command, which came under the direction of Admiral Sir H. J. Studholme-Browning, was defined as the heavily defended section of the North Sea lying between Bridlington in the north and Ramsgate in the south and extending seaward for about eighty miles. Nore Command was itself a subdivision of The Western Approaches Command. A very important part of the The Nore Command was the southern area covering the outer Thames Estuary, the Medway Estuary north Kent and south Essex coasts and the tidal Thames known as the Thames Nore Division.

Way back in those war years 1939 – 1945 the scenario in the Thames Estuary was so very different from what we now see and know that without a description of what it was like in those times, the reader might not appreciate that such a fast-moving and vicious war-time scenario could have existed. Even now, if one knows where to look, there are sombre relics to be found. One very obvious such relic being the sinister wreck of the American Liberty Ship the SS *Richard Montgomery*, which lies in the shallow sand-banks at the junction of the Medway River with the Thames. The rusting masts of the SS Richard Montgomery rise above the surface. Beneath them lying in the rusting holds are some five thousand three hundred and forty-eight tons of very live high explosive munitions!

---

50. Named after the Nore Sandbank in the outer Thames Estuary. The Nore Sandbank used to mark the outer limit of jurisdiction of the Port of London Authority.

The wreck of the SS *Richard Montgomery*
photo by RP from *Sheemaun* in 2010

A massive defence boom had been built stretching right across the Thames estuary from Shoeburyness to the Isle of Sheppey. Built of steel, concrete and wooden piles driven only eight feet apart into the sea-bed and shores and with steel nets dangling down under solid wooden floats[51], it was effectively impenetrable to surface craft and even to miniature submarines.

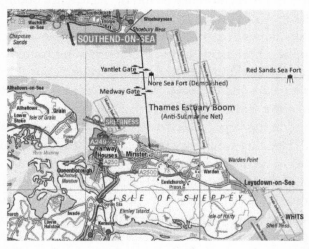

The Thames Estuary Defence Boom 1940 extended from East Beach at Shoeburyness, South for 5.6 miles (9 km) to Royal Oak Point on the Isle-of-Sheppey - Courtesy of John Jones of www.wildfire3.com/richard-montgomery.html

51. A solid wood float could not be sunk by gunfire!

Three electrical sea-bed cable units had been laid across the eastern aspect of the boom. Cables that could detect the magnetic field of any passing steel hull such as a submarine, likewise a fourth cable was laid across the eastern mouth of the Swale and where there was also a mine-field. The Defence Boom was serviced by a dozen or so armed vessels and was covered by shore batteries. The only way into or out through the Boom was via two central 'gateways' of steel nets suspended beneath barges which could be moved by armed tugs to allow the passage of vessels. The entire area was rigidly controlled by the Admiralty. No vessel, little or large could move in the Thames Estuary area unless by order or with permission. Any un-authorised ship movement after dark was forbidden under the penalty of being fired on by armed vessels or the powerful shore batteries. The large area of protected water inland of the defence boom acted as a relatively 'safe' haven for shipping.

Britain depended on importing food and many essential supplies. Merchant shipping convoys were routed across the North Atlantic to keep them as far away as possible from Hitler's warships and U-Boats. These hundreds of ships had to be escorted down Britain's East Coast through the mine-fields, to be assembled in this large protected area inside the Thames Defence Boom. There they would be registered, checked and issued with orders as to further procedure, many would voyage upstream to the London Docks. Scores of destroyers, corvettes, armed tugs, mine-sweepers, motor-torpedo boats, gun-boats and fast Air-Sea-Rescue launches would every day dash in and out of the Defence Boom gates. Many warships including mine-sweepers, armed tugs and escort vessels also needed to berth at Chatham, Sheerness and Queenborough for refuelling, re-arming, repairs and 'wiping' or neutralising of their hull magnetism by use of de-guassing coils. As the war progressed the boomed area became increasingly important for the assembly of craft that would take part in Operation D Day. In addition to this massive naval and merchant shipping operation, there were many dozens of small coasters and hundreds of Thames trading barges and fishing boats all attempting to go about their essential businesses. They were entirely governed by and dependent on the tides and local weather, many relying solely on sail power and they were all without any radio facility.

Virtually every day and every night as the weather allowed the Thames Estuary was over-flown by German spy planes and almost daily during the first three years of the War some sort of aggressive activity took place in the skies. Allied vessels were frequently bombed, strafed, mined and torpedoed.

In the skies above the Thames there were almost daily 'Dogfights' with British Hurricanes and Spitfires whirling and diving around the attacking formations of German bombers and the slower but deadly Stuka Dive-Bombers. The staccato chatter of machine guns and the deeper bark of cannons daily echoed across the waters together with the concussive boom of exploding bombs. Entire aircraft and pieces of aircraft spiralled and pattered down onto the ships and their crews below. Over one hundred and fifty aircraft were shot down into the Thames Estuary and hundreds of airmen parachuted down some of them dead or dying, and many injured and burned. While the majority were from Hitler's Luftwaffe planes there were also British aircraft that had been shot up. Fast German Schnellboots or E-Boats as the British referred them would zoom in at 43.8 knots (50.5 mph) towards the outer Thames Estuary usually at night and shoot up or torpedo any Allied vessels they might find, they also laid mines.

1939 – 1944

The Thames & Medway Estuaries Wartime Scene

For the first four years of the Second World War the waters of the Thames and Medway Estuaries were literally teeming with vessels of all sorts and coming and going, discharging cargoes and servicemen, refuelling, re-loading. There were scores of warships, scores of merchant ships, scores of smaller armed vessels and hundreds of unarmed harbour service vessels and of course the local fishing and trading boats. Of the small armed vessels there were at least a hundred or so, of which some are listed here as at January 1942[52]. The list is not complete –

Royal Navy Armed Auxiliary Patrol Vessels at Cliffe Fort – *Aberdonia, Bill Adams, Blue Peter, Crescent, Dorebet II, Rep Eternal Wave, Eusett, Kinsman rep., Kintail, Maragretta, Narwale, Pride of Sheppey, Samaki,* **Sheemaun***, Valterry, Westcliffe Bell, Windelf, Winona, Zelea.* (20)

Armed Tugs – *Dido & Maud* (2)

Armed Motor Fishing Vessels – *Renaissance, Zee Mew, Clara Simone,* (3)

Royal Navy Armed Auxilliary Patrol Vessels at Chatham - *Fedalma II, Jong, Lazy Days, Reigate II, Snow Bunting, Wairakei, Usanco, Vedette, Wima, West Breeze.* (10)

Mine Watchers at Chatham –

---

52. From British and Other Navies in World War 2 Day-by-Day. Don Kindell. Home Waters, Part Two

Cachalot, Curlew, Ellaline, Grey Dawn, Lavinia, Ona, Usanco. (8) and supplemented by *Wima* and *West Breeze.*

At Sheerness - Naval Armed Auxiliary Patrol Boats - *Freida, Oscar Angel, Andre Marcel, Fezzaea, Marcelle Pierre, President Herriott.* (6)

Minesweeping Depot Ship -
St Tudno (1)

Minesweepers – 24

Various
Medway Motorboat Patrol - 8
Motor Launch Flotilla - 8
Armed Boom Gate Vessels – 3
Armed Boom Defence Tugs – 2
Barrage Balloon Vessels – 23
Target Towing Vessel – 1
Echo Sounding Yacht – 1

Every day substantial numbers of vessels would be entering and leaving the huge protected area of Estuary via the Defence Boom gates, included Royal Navy frigates, destroyers, corvettes, anti-aircraft ships and armed tugs. Scores of large merchant cargo ships, fast motor torpedo and motor gun boats, mine-layers and minesweepers, small trading barges and fishing boats etc. By day and by night, depending on the weather, the area would be overflown by Hitler's bombers with their Messerschmitt fighter escorts. Bombs and mines would rain down and vessels and shore establishments would be machine gunned. The batteries of heavy anti-aircraft guns ashore on the Essex coast and the Isle of Sheppey unleashed thousands of rounds aimed at the invading enemy aircraft, and after they had been established from the Summer of 1942, so did the gun batteries on the Maunsell

Forts in the outer Thames Estuary. These defences together with the British Hurricane and Spitfire fighters made constituted an effective defence against Hitler's attacking squadrons and their escorting Messerschmitt fighters.

This would have been a common and very welcome sight in those skies over the Thames way back in 1942 although then the Spitfire would have been in camouflage colours. Photo – RP

There were aircraft crashing in flames, parachutes descending and all the time the slow pulse of London's River tides, ebbed and flowed through dangerous shallows and sandbanks. Lives by the score were being lost almost daily. Such were the conditions in which little vessels such as HMY *Sheemaun* and her fellow armed patrol boats and their brave and dedicated crews had to operate.

1939

Mine Warfare in the Thames

'Where happy waters sing in solitudes,
The gift of being near ships, of seeing each day
A city of ships with great ships under weigh,
The great street paved with water, filled with shipping,
And all the world's flags flying and seagulls dipping'

John Edward Masefield 1878 – 1967

B ritain was very dependent on trade with the Commonwealth, the United States and the World at large. London had a dockland area of some ninety acres (3,624,217 sq metres) 35 acres (141,640 sq metres) of water, eleven miles (17,703 km) of wharves and one and a half thousand cranes unloading sixty million tons of goods a year of which fifty million tons was food, and comparable immense volumes of goods were exported. London was the biggest and busiest port in the world. Hitler was determined to starve Island Britain into submission by the simple ploy of destroying her major ports and denying merchant shipping traffic from being able, to use the Thames, the Humber and the Severn estuaries. It would be another five long years before the hitherto happy waters of the Thames would again see

'All the world's flags flying...'

Both nations had used sea-mines in the First World War. Sea mines were relatively cheap, easy to produce and were very effective destroyers of ships. There were various types of mine but the commonly deployed mine floated just under the sea surface at the top end of a cable the other end of the cable being attached to a weight on the sea-bed. There were various other types of

119

mine and most were designed to explode on contact with a ship. Counter-measures generally involved 'trawling' or 'sweeping' by shallow draught mine sweepers towing cable-cutting gear. This was not without risk of course but it was reasonably effective. The freed mines that bobbed to the surface could then be destroyed with gunfire. Fearing a German invasion on the East Coast, Britain had laid more than twenty-five thousand coastal mines in a mine-field stretching from the Thames Estuary to as far north as the top of Scotland and virtually blocking German access to the North Atlantic. Britain had also laid over three and a half thousand mines in the Dover Straits and so effectively closing that seaway to the German U-boats and other warships which then had to risk sailing up the North Sea and around the top of Scotland to access the Atlantic and be able to attack the merchant convoys. Further the British and Americans laid some seventy thousand mines between the Orkney Isles and Norway and so, unless carrying accurate charts of the mine-fields, for any U-Boat or other vessel attempting to gain the Atlantic by sailing up the North Sea or vice-versa coming in from the Atlantic, it was a risky and dangerous voyage. This formidable but static deterrent was to be largely neutralised when in June 1940 France capitulated to Germany and gave Hitler unhindered access to the French Atlantic and Mediterranean coasts.

Sea mines or some form of floating explosive device had been known of since the Chinese devised them in the 16th Century. Mines were used in the American Civil War and in the First World War, at which time the possibility of both magnetically and acoustically activated mines had been envisaged. While the British war-lords had initially regarded sea-mines as an ungentlemanly and rather obscene form of warfare, Hitler's technical experts had been re-designing mine-warfare with ever increasing sophistication and deadliness and with attention to Proximity Mines which did not require a direct contact or impact with a passing vessel to trigger the detonation. These deviously clever and highly effective weapons were designed to be laid in shallow waters such as the Thames and Humber estuaries and the Bristol Channel. Lying on a shallow sea bed these mines would explode under the hull of a passing ship usually with devastating effect[53]. The Magnetic Mine was detonated by the slight directional change in the earth's magnetic field caused by a steel ship passing over it. The Acoustic Mine was set to explode when triggered by the noise of the machinery and propeller of any ship passing close. Within only the first three months after the Declaration of War more than a hundred ships, totalling more than one hundred and twenty-one thousand tons, were sunk by Hitler's magnetic mines dropped by his bombers into the Thames and its Estuary! A shipping-loss rate that greatly exceeded the rate of shipping loss in the Atlantic Ocean. Inevitably, hundreds of seamen were injured, and many were killed.

At the commencement of World War II in 1939 the British Admiralty had available less than fifty mine-sweeping vessels and most of those were old coal burning 'Smokey Joes' left over from the First World War. There was a desperate need for more mine sweepers and crews to man them. New minesweepers were specifically built, some imported from America and many small vessels such as trawlers and tugs were converted. The fishing industry had shrunk as Hitler's aircraft and Schnellboots were under orders to destroy any fishing boats. The Admiralty recognised that fishermen, who would have the special experience and skills necessary when it came to be handling heavy trawl equipment, could play a vital role in mine-sweeping. Fishermen were encouraged to volunteer for service with the Royal Naval

53. The heavy cruiser HMS *Belfast*- launched 17th March 1938, was the Royal Navy's most powerful cruiser. On 21st November 1939 she was so badly damaged by a German magnetic mine in the Firth of Forth that it took almost three years to repair her. She is now moored permanently on the River Thames in London as a museum ship.

Patrol Service. Lowestoft was regarded by the Royal Navy as the most suitable location for a training base. With the mobilisation in 1939 of the Royal Naval Volunteer Reservists a land-based reception and training centre HMS Europa was established at Lowestoft and quickly came to be known as 'The Sparrow's Nest'. By the end of the war there would be some 6,000 Royal Naval Patrol Service mine-sweeping vessels and more than 60,000 men active across the world's oceans and seas. So many of these RNPS men were Reservists that the service came to be known as 'Churchill's Pirates' and 'Harry Tate's Navy'[54]. The work was highly dangerous. The vessels were mostly slow and lightly armed and were easy targets for the fast and heavily armed German Schnellboots (E-Boats). The mine-sweepers were vulnerable to enemy aircraft and any faster more heavily armed enemy vessel. Many scores of mine-sweepers were blown up by mines. Hundreds were strafed, bombed and sunk or badly damaged and hundreds of their crewmen were killed or wounded. Despite this the little ships and their brave crews just got on with the clearing of and disposing of mines, a task that was of enormous importance to Britain and her Allies. One of the early volunteers was Londoner Stanley Dodd –

'...I was still keen on the sea and I saw an advert in the paper about Joining Patrol Services – for duty on fast motor boats. So I applied, had an interview and test at the Admiralty and in due course was called up some 6 months before my time, like a fool, ...(p 225)... I put on my best suit and saying farewell to everyone made my way to Liverpool St Station en route for Lowestoft where the base was. H.M.S. Europa. This turned out to be a holiday

54. Ronald Hutchison 1872 -1940. Stage name 'Harry Tate' – was a comedian who played being a fool whose life was shambles. In his stage-act his car fell to pieces around him.

gardens – "Sparrows Nest" – It was inhabited by a sadistic Scotsman, who had never seen the sea and although I was only there a week getting kitted out, inoculated, etc, it was one of the worst memorable incidents in my life. They were all, without exception a shower of Barstards. You couldn't understand their broad Scots accent and they couldn't understand your Cockney accent. The uniform situation patchy, so much so, that I was issued with a Sailors Cap, arm band saying R.N. and a pair of boots two sizes too large for me. Mind you it wasn't entirely the fault of the man, for we spent at least 6 hours of daylight hiding behind sand bags in shelters whilst the German air force nipped over for a quickie and shot or bombed anything in sight. This did not worry me too much as I, at any rate was used to it, but you couldn't move without permission and many a pint of beer lost a good home because they wouldn't let me out sort of thing. After all I'd much rather be sitting in a pub in a raid than hiding under some bushes in a greasy gutter. Besides - apart from my hat and arm band I still had my best suit on until I got... (p 226)... the boots. Talking of the boots – I got them after I had been there some 3 days and on putting them on, we had to march and run out to Oulton Broad – to disperse because of the "hit and run" raids I hadn't worn these boots long before my feet were a mass of broken blisters and the boots filled with blood. On our return to base, I was marched to the M.O. to have my feet hardened with permanganate of potash and then march again to have my photograph taken for my pay book and identity card. When the photographer said to each of us as the photo was being taken – don't laugh – I don't know whether he was a humourist or meant it. Don't laugh! There's the actual photo somewhere around showing Stan Dodd head and shoulders and bearing a blackboard stating

LT/KX128268 which is the complete 100% antithesis of laughter. Fortunately after a week I was away from there – so now for active service. By this time I had been kitted out and so, resplendent in a ill fitting new uniform a small draft of 5 of us set off for H.M.S. Tormentor, Warsash near Southampton…' S.D.

Time-Line –

- Fuehrer Adolph Hitler authorised the German 'Euthanasia Policy' by which policy any persons deemed to have mental or physical disabilities or any persons who were considered by authorised physicians as 'incurable' and thus 'Unworthy of Life' would be put to death. The advising physicians would be legally protected from prosecution.

- It would come to pass that seventy thousand and two hundred and seventy-three innocent German citizens would be put to death. The German State would not have to bear the cost of looking after those people and their hitherto carers would be freed to do productive work.

1939

Chatham Kent - October

Roy Hansen Calvert-Link Acting Lieutenant RNVR had been assigned to shore-based duties at Chatham and another of the so called naval 'Stone Frigates'[55] HMS *Wildfire* the Royal Navy shore-based headquarters at Sheerness on the Isle of Sheppey. The buildings and offices of HMS *Wildfire* placed high up on the cliffs of Garrison Point commanded a wide over-view of the conjunction of the Thames and Medway estuaries. Roy reckoned that this tidal area would provide a splendid cruising ground for a vessel like *Sheemaun*. It would be no great problem to have her moved to the Medway where he had plenty of reliable contacts in the 'yachting world,' and he could berth her possibly at nearby Queenborough Harbour. But Roy had discounted the massive naval build-up that the outbreak of war had brought, for with so many naval vessels, mine-sweepers, destroyers, tugs and harbour duty launches based at Sheerness Garrison Fort, Queenborough Harbour and Chatham, there would be no room for any private yachts, quite aside from possible security issues. So instead, *Sheemaun* crewed by amateur volunteers, was sailed across the Thames Estuary to a berth at Hole Haven[56] on the West bank of Canvey Island.

Meanwhile news of the formation in the London docklands zone of an Emergency River Service had spread throughout the yachting fraternity. Roy recognised that *Sheemaun* would be very suitable for such a role. Using his yachting contacts, he was able to arrange for shifts of volunteer crews and managed

---

55. Slang term for any of the Royal Navy shore-based units.

56. Originally known as Holy Haven - John Purdy 1838 '*The Brazilian Navigator*' p 18.

to get her armed with a couple of Lee Enfield .303 rifles and some shotguns. Together with half a dozen or so similar craft, it seems that *Sheemaun* was virtually a 'Privateer' for although a privately-owned motor yacht, like Sir Alan Herbert's *Water Gypsy* and several others, she carried arms, was crewed by volunteer yachtsmen and had been incorporated into the war-time patrol duties then being organised by the Royal Naval Thames Auxiliary Patrol Service.

As a matter of interest, in the 1930s to own a shotgun needed no licence although the 1920 Firearms Act outlawed the owning of a short-barrelled shotgun or of a machine gun. In 1936 a fire-arms licence could be obtained from the Police and all that was necessary was for the applicant to show "good reason" for having one!

As and when his duties allowed Roy Calvert-Link would join for a short spell with old yachting friends on his little ship. Patrolling that local area of water was exciting as well as exacting and they quickly acquired a sound knowledge of the local tides, the weather and the many sandbanks and shallows. It was however not without dangers.

German bomber formations nightly over-flew the Thames Estuary on their way to drop their bombs over London and the Royal Air Force airfields at RAF Gravesend, RAF Tilbury, RAF Biggin Hill and RAF Croydon. Furthermore, whenever weather conditions were suitable, hundreds of mines were being dropped by the Germans into the Thames and Medway estuaries using specialised bombers, float planes and motor gliders, despite the barrage put up by the many anti-aircraft gun positions and the anti-air craft rocket launchers. At times the night skies were lit up almost across the horizon. Spent shells, bombs, rockets, whole planes and fragments of aircraft rained down. Above their heads Spitfire and Hurricane fighter planes intercepted the German bomber formations, dog-fighting with the escorting

Messerschmitt 109s and targeting the Heinkels, the Junkers 88 and Dornier bombers.

Vapour trials tangled like drifting white spaghetti around the skies, the staccato rattle of machine guns and the bark of 20 mm cannon reverberating and echoing from the cliffs of Sheppey and the Medway hills. Occasional bursts of flame and billowing black smoke marked where some plane with its unfortunate crew had been hit. Parachutes would puff out and billow, then slowly descend with an airman swinging below like a ponderous pendulum, there would be a splash and the silk parachute would settle gently down over the airman's head often as a covering final white shroud. The crews of the Patrol Vessels, *Sheemaun* among, them kept a careful log, timing these events and noting the coordinates of mine and bomb splashes. Whatever patrol vessel or launch might be near a downed and often wounded airman, then that vessel would make signal and proceed to the rescue regardless as to whether it was 'Friend or Foe'.

Stanley Dodd wrote -

'...whilst if there was a dog fight taking place in our vicinity we had to stand by and pick up anyone shot down into the drink. We had our moments and were shot at several times, but by zig zagging and good luck we suffered no real damage. We rescued about a dozen or so. Most of the Jerries[57] who had bailed out, their equipment was extremely good and for the most part they were glad to be rescued apart from the odd fanatic who, when picked up, drew out a revolver and taking aim at one of us shouted Heil Hitler, lost his balance and promptly fell overboard. We let him cool down for a spell and then yanked him in, much subdued. On the whole it was all good clean fun, and although we lived rough – one fortnight I remember,

---

57. A British slang term for anything German or 'Jerry'

we lived on tea, bread butter and corned beef and nothing else, we never suffered in any way and despite being wet and cold, never even developed a cold...' S.D.

Time-Line –

- Britain was desperately short of small arms, rifles, pistols and light machine guns such as might be suitable for use by units such as the Home Guard. Most farmers had shotguns and there were some people with 'sporting' shotguns but shotguns used bulky ammunition which fired small pellets and had only a very short range. In terms of warfare they were paltry scatter guns. Britain's 'Dad's Army' of Home Guard units was reduced to training with umbrellas and wooden dummy rifles. This most unfortunate situation of course provided utterly laughable and wonderful material for Hitler's propaganda machine. Prime Minister Winston Churchill ordered that the British Government should place adverts in the American newspapers and magazines such as *'The Rifleman'* asking for donations of pistols, revolvers, shotguns and binoculars. Our American friends were quick to respond, and very generously so. By 1940 the American National Rifle Association had shipped across the Atlantic some seven thousand rifles plus ammunition on fast ships destined for British Ports. Winston Churchill then arranged for special train services to distribute these weapons to the Home Guard units in every city, town and village.

1940

A Thames Estuary Patrol
May 24th - OPERATION DYNAMO

Skipper 'Bunny' Frost Roberts gave *Sheemaun*'s mahogany wheel a touch to port. 'Bunny' was one of the many amateur yachtsmen who had volunteered to serve on Thames Auxiliary Patrol Service vessels and likewise his fellow crewmen. They all had experience in navigation and small boat handling but had been considered not fit enough or a little too old for active service in the armed forces.

Just now it was approaching low tide. After a busy day *Sheemaun* had completed duties in the Medway Approaches and was punching against the last of the ebb on her way to her berth at Hole Haven, where she would re-fuel and moor up for the night. That week had seen a lot of enemy action. On Saturday 18th the town of Southend had been attacked by two German bombers, several buildings had been damaged including the Nore Yacht Club which had been flattened, ten soldiers had been killed and a number of civilians injured. The many ships lying at anchor in the estuary awaiting orders were tempting targets for enemy aircraft activity, and the frequent bombing and strafing runs were hazardous and very disruptive. *Sheemaun*'s duties for the day had included ferrying relief crews out to four of the moored observation barges along with mail and some supplies and then to put the relieved crewmen ashore at Queenborough. There had been a very unpleasant encounter earlier when they had a lucky escape from a low-flying Messerschmitt that had been strafing the ships. But now they were heading west for their berth at Hole Haven and punching the last of the ebb tide. Ordinarily at this point off the Yantlet sands 'Bunny' would have headed north across the Thames to Hole Haven. This time however the way was blocked by an unusual sight.

An old steam tug puffing out a curling plume of black smoke from its tall smoke-stack, was heading seaward along the Yantlet channel. Streaming out behind her must have been a tow of some sixty or so boats rafted together four or five deep. There were all varieties and sizes varying from open launches and cabin cruisers to small commercial passenger launches. Following in the wake of this higgledy-piggledy tow were another three tugs similarly burdened. *Sheemaun* had to stem the tide and wait until this extraordinary mini Armada had progressed on its way.

On *Sheemaun*, 'Bunny' and his fellow volunteers were quite unaware that in the past week the Tough Brothers Boatyard up-river at Teddington–on–Thames had, on orders from the Admiralty, been requisitioning hundreds of local private and commercial vessels. Douglas Tough together with his colleague Ron Lenthall had then gathered together these River Thames boats into the towable rafts, which they were now witnessing being towed down the Thames to Sheerness. There they would be refuelled, checked over, provided with charts and fitted with essentials such as compasses and binoculars, first aid kits, drinking water and basic rations – being mostly river boats, many did not even have a compass. They were then to be assembled in hundreds at Ramsgate Royal Harbour, from where they were destined to cross the Channel to take part in rescuing the thousands of exhausted men of the British, Expeditionary Force and their French and Belgian army comrades, now all trapped and exposed on the Dunkirk beaches. Small shallow draught craft would be needed to negotiate the shoal waters of the Dunkirk beaches, from where they would ferry the troops out to the hundreds of bigger vessels waiting in deeper water, ready to bring them across the Channel to Dover.

Those little boats were destined to play a major role in

'Operation Dynamo', the breath-taking and unsurpassed emergency evacuation, whereby over a third of a million British, French and Belgian troops, trapped by the advancing German forces, were rescued from the port of Dunkirk and from the beaches for some ten miles Eastward of Dunkirk. The story has been well recorded in the history books and made the subject of several films, but there will be some details that may remain forever unknown.[58]

OPERATION DYNAMO THE DUNKIRK EVACUATION

Almost a quarter of a century later, in October 1964 the Sunday Times published an inspired letter from the late Raymond Baxter OBE FRSA as a result of which many owners from the list of these previously requisitioned vessels were contacted and in 1966 the memorable and prestigious 'Association of Little Dunkirk Ships' was created.

It is known that *Sheemaun* was already in the Thames Estuary area in May 1940 having been chartered by the Ministry of Defence from her then owner Acting Lt. Roy Calver-Link RNVR. And any sea-worthy vessels such as Sheemaun, that might have been within sailing distance of the Thames Estuary and Ramsgate, would have been of particular interest to their Lordships. On May14[th] The BBC had broadcast the following announcement-

'The Admiralty have made an order requesting all owners of self-propelled pleasure craft between 30' and 100' in length to send all particulars to the Admiralty within 14 days from today if they have not already been offered or requisitioned'

---

58. At the time of writing this book, the latest 'Blockbuster' had just been released - the 2017 film *DUNKIRK* by Christopher Nolan.

A post-war analysis of the Dunkirk Evacuation was published in The Supplement to The London Gazette on Thursday 17th July 1947 pp 3295 – 3318.

'…During the course of the operation some 333,000 troops reached safety in England… To those on the French coast, when in the early stages anything up to 50,000 troops were waiting to embark on a 10 mile sea front, the presence of perhaps 20 small warships off shore and 200 small boats spread along the length of the coast… …must have appeared as a feeble effort to tackle this great task… for the first 5 days of the movement, had more beaching craft been available to ferry from the beach to offshore vessels it would have been possible to have evacuated a greater number… the French (number of troops) rose and 150,000 or more was quoted… …It was only due to the foresight of the Admiralty in making arrangements for a continued flow in ever increasing numbers of small power boats and beach craft, which became available on the filth day onwards, that the continued evacuation from the beaches remained a reasonable proposition after the initial 'crisis' had passed… …Meanwhile Vice Admiral, Dover, had asked the Commander-in-Chief, Nore, to send every available shallow draught power boat, capable of ferrying from beaches to ships… A further signal: Please send every available craft to beaches Eastward of Dunkirk immediately…'

It may seem strange that, given this extreme situation, that *Sheemaun* was not directed to join with those little boats and the brave crews who would take them across the Channel to Dunkirk. After-all, the Admiralty already had her details on record. Robert Tough (Archivist to the Association of Dunkirk

Little Ships) settled that seeming anomaly when he confirmed to me that a number of –

'...specific harbour launches did not go (to Dunkirk) because they already had important duties on this side of the Channel.'

1940

The Island of Jersey
A Narrow escape for Stanley and Ellen

'Had we never loved so kindly.
Had we never loved so blindly…'

Lord Byron

itler's forces had invaded Poland and Norway but at the time most Londoners still regarded 'The War' as something that was being fought overseas and in Europe, some in the UK even referred to it as the 'Phoney War' because as Stanley Dodd said –

'It was all happening over there in Europe…'

Although the UK civilian population had not yet been directly affected by bombing and killing, family life was already changed. Lovers and friends, husbands, sons, uncles and brothers had been called up and conscripted by the thousands to serve in the armed forces. There were increasing restrictions and shortages of most commodities. This uncomfortable domestic situation was to change dramatically and for the worse when by another two months Hitler would send his bombers in their hundreds to bomb London and to wreak the dreadful horrors of the 'London Blitz'. Prime Minister Winston Churchill, who had reluctantly come to recognise that the Channel Islands were indefensible, ordered that the British Army on those Islands be quickly and quietly withdrawn along with all equipment.

Stanley Dodd's wife Ellen, who he affectionately called 'Girl', was now three months pregnant. The situation in London was becoming increasingly dangerous and inconvenient. Food and other forms of rationing had been in force since January and in addition to the limitations imposed by the strict rationing, many basic foods and essential goods were anyway becoming scarce. Identity Cards had to be carried, there were army checkpoints at every location and cross-roads deemed of importance. In blissful ignorance of the significance of this deepening and rapidly changing European situation and naturally caring dearly for his pregnant wife, Stanley just wanted to get them both away from it all. He had saved a little money and together they had chosen to go on a holiday to the Island of Jersey which they thought would be a safe and civilised place away from it all. Somewhere that was easy to get to by passenger ferry and would surely be of little interest to Herr Hitler. They even talked about the possibility of staying in Jersey until the war was over. Stanley wrote in his memoirs –

'…The car had long since ceased to be an asset and although I had paid £150 for it by completing the last payment, within a couple of months I was glad to sell it for £40. This I banked…(p 208) …and because of the "mark time" aspect of the war, plus the fact that it looked very much like being the last holiday I would have, we decided to make 'a do of it' and rented a bungalow in Jersey for a fortnight at St Brelades. It was in May 1940 that we got the night train from Waterloo to Southampton and thence by the 'Isle of Sark'[59] to St Helier. It was a beautiful moon light night I remember and we watched the swans all silvery on Southampton Water as the blacked-out vessel left at 03.00 hours. If only I had realised what dangers I was exposing Girl and our unborn child to, I would have

59. Belonging to Southern Railways, the SS *Isle of Sark* Ferry of 2,211 tons. On June 28th she was the last passenger ship to leave Jersey only hours before the Germans invaded the Island. 1942 converted to an anti-aircraft ship fitted with radar and guns. Scrapped 1961.

had a100 fits, but I didn't. It was still peace with us and the war was phoney. We duly arrived at St Helier at 8.30 a.m. and thence by bus to St Brelades. For the record, the Isle of Sark was a two funnel ship, powered by steam and because of the war was painted a uniform grey. We had a cabin on board and made it an occasion. The first week of the holiday was without incident and although it was May there were practically no visitors or holiday makers. In fact we appeared to be the only holiday makers for all that we spoke to seemed to be there to see relatives or fetch someone home… (p209) …But we were on holiday and made the most of it - I even hired a car for the day – a Ford 10 filled up with petrol 12/6[60]. On the second week we noticed lots of unexplained activity during the hours of darkness. Shadowy silhouettes of small ships on the shore, vague figures that vanished in the darkness – in fact in Quaine Bay I'm convinced that I saw the low outline of a submarine far out and the flash of oars as a dinghy was rowed for the shore. The Islands police had instructions to collect any firearms and these were reluctantly handed in, and all the steamers, mail boats and any vessel from the outside world was cancelled and on the second week of my holiday, we were marooned. Fool that I was, fortunately the full implication did not sink in and for just on six weeks I became attached to Jersey Post Office, calling them once a week to collect my wages. In the meantime the Island prepared for siege and as we liked the place so much we were all for it. To spend the duration of the war there would be something. However after nearly 6 weeks of exile, we were rounded up, put on the 'Isle of Sark' again and then we left on the last passenger ship from Jersey. We took 27 hours to get back to England – Weymouth this time, we were escorted

---

60. Twelve Shillings and Sixpence.

by a destroyer and minesweeper and… (p 210) …* I don't think there's any record of this happening. * Inturnment Camp… we were shelled once during the night sustaining a huge dent and hole in the hull. Thus did it sink in to me that this phoney war, was in fact real. For the record, at this time, the delay of 6 weeks or so, coincided with the evacuation of Dunkerque, that Germany had swept through France (for no ships, no papers so we didn't have any news) and that 24 hours after we had left Jersey the Germans invaded and took the Island. All true born Jerseymen were recruited into a labour corps. All "foreigners" especially English were rounded up and transported to Germany to a Wurzach (Concentration Camp) – that is apart from those they threw (into St Helier Harbour) with concrete weights attached to their feet: When we ultimately arrived home by train from Weymouth there was evidence that conditions had altered in London and was more organised on a war time basis…' S.D.

Time-Line –

- On 21st June France surrendered to Hitler's forces. The night of 28th June 1940 saw German Heinkel bombers attacking the defenceless Guernsey and Jersey ports. Among the buildings and vessels damaged was the sole Guernsey Lifeboat which was machine-gunned! Stanley and Ellen Dodd were among the six hundred and forty-seven refugees taken aboard the Southern Railways' ferry the *Isle of Sark* which under cover of dark, and with a destroyer escort, was the last vessel to sail from Jersey to England prior to the German invasion the following day!

1940

HMS *Stork* – Norway May 14th

'When I see the falling bombs
Then I see defended homes
Men above and men below
Die to save the good they know.'

F.R. Scott

In HMS *Stork* - Twelve Hundred Miles North East of the Thames Estuary, Lieutenant 'Peter' Gray RN now found himself engaged in the Norwegian Campaign

May 14th - At eleven and a half thousand tons the MS *'Chrobry'* was a substantial vessel. She had been converted from her role as a luxury ocean-going Polish passenger ship to that of a war-time troop ship. Aboard her were the Irish Guards, a troop of the 3rd Huzzars and a substantial cargo of military equipment and ammunition. She had sailed from Tjeldsundet in Norway escorted by the destroyer HMS *Wolverine* of 1,550 tons and the sloop HMS *Stork*, slightly smaller at 1,190 tons. HMS *Wolverine* although dating from 1918 was capable of 34 knots (39 mph). She had six torpedo tubes, a main armament of four 4.7 inch (11.9 cm) naval guns and two quick-firing two pounder anti-aircraft Pom-Poms. HMS *Stork* carried six 4 inch (10.16 cm) anti-aircraft guns and four anti-aircraft heavy machine guns. Between them these escorts wielded a significant ant-aircraft capability.

The *Chrobry* with her escorting warships was lying in Vestfjord when at about midnight from high above, the unmistakable throbbing drone of powerful Jumo aero engines echoed across the water. Within minutes a formation of twin engine Junkers

88 dive-bombers attacked. Their aim was to destroy the *Chrobry* along with the troops and war equipment she carried. One of Hitler's most versatile aircraft, the Junkers 88, could achieve a fairly high accuracy given a clear run at its target. Bombs screamed down and within minutes there were three direct hits on the *Chrobry*. Bodies, debris and pieces of superstructure were flung high in the air. Scores of men were killed, and many more wounded. The *Chrobry* was set ablaze and ammunition was exploding all around.

Hitler's attacking bomber crews quickly learned to keep above the withering hail of anti-aircraft fire sent up by the armed escorts, but they had achieved their goal and had inflicted severe damage. For the commanders of the surviving ships thousands of feet below them, the priority now was to save lives. Not-withstanding the difficulties and very real dangers, the destroyer HMS *Wolverine* was put alongside the *Chrobry*. In a display of amazing bravery and discipline, seven hundred Irish Guards lined up as best they could in platoon order on the damaged decks of the doomed *Chrobry*. Nearly six hundred were able to clamber across onto the destroyer. Meanwhile Lt. 'Peter' Gray RN on the bridge of HMS *Stork* with his fellow officers minutely scanned the skies and sea for further attack by bombers or U-Boats. Although no enemy aircraft were shot down, the anti-aircraft fusillade from HMS *Stork* succeeded in impeding further bombing attempts and eventually the bombers departed from the scene. 'Peter' Gray then ordered HMS *Stork* to be laid alongside the *Chrobry* and a further 300 men were rescued.

Time-line -

- France was being over-run by Hitler's forces. Faced with either the destruction of Paris by Blitzkrieg or capitulation and submission to German rule, France had little choice other than to capitulate.

By Churchill's orders, on 17th June from a secret airstrip in South East England, a sleek twin engined pre-war passenger plane, a Percival Q6 took off with only the pilot on board. It was destined for a secret airstrip in Northern France. It returned still with officially only the pilot listed as crew, but clandestinely it seems with General de Gaulle aboard and £100K[61] worth of French Francs in gold bullion.

The Franco-German Armistice was signed on 22nd June.

- HMS Stork was the last RN ship to leave Norway after the fateful Norwegian Campaign.
- On 28th July 1940[62] *Sheemaun* was listed in the Admiralty Red Book as one of the 'Minor War Vessels in Home Waters' with RNVR crew and berthed at Hole Haven on the Thames Estuary Essex coast. She would one day be owned and commanded by 'Peter' Gray RN.
- The Chatham Dockyard Muster Bell was silenced.

---

61. Equivalent to £60 million or $80,142,000 in 2018
62. National Archives – Ref AMD208/3

1940

Bombs fall in the Thames Estuary
Skipper Bob Roberts has a Narrow Escape

The late Bob Roberts was a much respected and widely read author and Thames sailing-barge skipper. Indeed, my life-time fascination with boats and the sea was partly triggered by Bob Roberts many years ago when at the age of about ten, I read Bob's thrilling book 'Rough and Tumble'. The true account by Bob of his life at the time and of his ocean girdling adventure in which his boat *Thelma* was wrecked. Sadly, I never met Bob but I have been privileged to meet with a number of 'old salts' and bargees who had known Bob and I have 'trod the decks' of the Thames sailing-barge *Cambria*,[63] which when skippered by Bob was the last engineless barge to trade on the Thames. I have also enjoyed the comradeship of Bob's nephew Mike Roberts with whom some memorable cruising experiences have been shared.

Years later, Bob using his legendary writing skills was to record vividly in his book 'Coasting Bargemaster'[64] his account of the day when for him the so called 'Phoney War' of early 1940 changed and real killing warfare was brought to the Thames. Roberts was then one among several hundred Thames barge skippers who laboured not only to make a hard to-come-by living, but to carry often vital cargoes of a hundred or more tons anywhere between Harwich, the Medway and Thames Estuary, the London Docks and the South Coast as far as Poole... all without the need of precious diesel fuel. Such vessels however were totally dependent upon the wind and tides. If a tide was

---

63. Built in 1906 and still sailing. Now preserved and maintained by the Cambria Trust, and used for training and maritime education and charitable purposes.

64. Seafaring Books 2000 Ch 14 pp 132-134

missed even only partly it could make a difference of a whole day before the cargo could be delivered, and sometimes much more if the weather turned foul. A missed tide would result in the loss of work for the men who would have received and off-loaded the cargo and vice versa for cargoes that had to be loaded. War Emergency Measures had forbidden any movement of vessels in the Thames Estuary at night under penalty of being shot at and every shipping movement on the Thames and in near coastal waters required permission and supervision.

One of the day-time duties of the Thames Auxiliary Patrol Service Boats was to halt and examine any vessel making way through its designated patrol zone. It takes little imagination to see how nearly impossible it could be for a heavily laden sailing barge with only two crew and under full sail, to heave-to[65] in compliance with an examination order. A stoppage that could cost the barge a whole lost day in terms of tide! Not surprisingly Bob had little time for these Auxiliary Patrol Service Boats and there had been some altercations with the RNVR crew of a certain armed Royal Navy Auxiliary Patrol Service Vessel - HMY *Sheemaun*! The following extracts are from Bob's book 'Coasting Bargemaster' -

'I had become used to the nuisance of the Naval Control and had learned how and when to circumvent or disregard the majority of their unwelcome instructions. I had also found that terrific bouts of swearing at naval patrols and examination boats were rather a waste of time…'

Bob expressed little respect for the crews of these boats who he considered were manned by –

---

65. Heave-to, a naval term used to describe bringing a moving ship to a stand-still in open water.

'...ex-bank clerks, barbers, grocers, and the rakings of the offices and counters of the metropolis. A number of whom were so ignorant in a seafaring sense that it paid to answer their questions with a plain 'yes' or 'no' – and then go on our way and take no more notice of what they had said...'

No doubt in Peace Time skipper Bob would have allowed due respect for these his fellow citizens but then it was War Time and those good men had been plucked from their civilian occupations and routines. In fact, they already had pre-service sea experience as yachtsmen. After a few months training they found themselves afloat in all weathers with difficult duties to carry out. They were shot at by low-flying enemy planes, bombed, mined and often sworn at by fishermen and barge skippers. They too were struggling to cope with the war-inflicted changes in their lives.

One sunny day in August, Bob was sailing his barge *Martinet* on an ebb tide down the East Swin with a full cargo of rice bound for Yarmouth, he was later to write poignantly his eye witness account of what became a daily experience for those working and serving in the Thames Estuary -

'...on this particular day, in the August of 1940, the war came upon us in reality. There was a steady droning sound from the south-east which grew louder and louder until it became a veritable roar. The mate sat up and listened. Then the cook came running aft. 'Those are aeroplanes skipper' The boy said excitedly, 'There must be hundreds of them.'

We scanned the sky and there they were almost above us – a great mass of silvery planes heading for the Essex shore. 'They must be Germans' said the mate 'We wouldn't have all those bombers out together.' He was right. He and the

143

cook started counting them – sixty-eight in all they made it. I began to wonder what we had better do. We were the only vessel in sight and there were all those bombers over our heads with six or seven bombs apiece – one of which if well aimed would be quite sufficient to cause the disintegration of the Martinet and her crew.

I ordered the lashings to be taken off the lifeboat and some food and water put in her. Then I went below and put my wallet and the ships papers in my pocket.

I came on deck to see a thrilling sight – and one which I shall never forget. From the direction of the North Foreland came three tiny dots – British fighters flying at a great pace straight for the rear of that formidable mass of planes. For sheer courage and audacity those three pilots exceeded anything I have ever known or seen. I had not realised there were young men in England who could be so recklessly brave. They flew right in amongst the mass formation of bombers and the vicious rattle of machine guns filled the air. A number of German fighters, which we had not noticed before, swooped down from high above the battle to ward off the attackers, but the three British pilots seemed to disregard them and closed with the big bombers. Things happened too quickly for me to keep track of the fight. There were a series of whistling sounds (which were to be all too familiar to British ears in the desperate months to come) and seven bombs exploded in a line off our port beam.

Whether or not they were intended for the Martinet we will never know. More likely I think they were let go by a damaged plane. But it made the old ship shake like a leaf. For several minutes after the last one exploded the barge continued to vibrate violently and we discovered that a concrete box which had been put in her counter to stop a leak had fallen to pieces.

A black aeroplane with German markings came spiralling down and then finished up with a sudden header and a great splash into Barrow Deep. Not far from us a parachute drifted very slowly and I could plainly see the German suspended beneath it. He fell into the water just off our starboard quarter.

I conducted a rapid argument with myself as to what I should do about him. If he didn't want to drown or get killed he shouldn't have come here' I said to myself. 'This isn't his country. And he's only come here to try and kill people with his bombs' This was one of the Germans who threatened to lay Britain's cities in ashes. That meant they would bomb and kill women and children and smash up people's homes. Not long before I had myself been married to a fair maid of Kent; and this German in the water might well have been on his way to kill or maim her and smash up our little home. I watched the parachute settle over him as he hit the water and I could see him struggling beneath it. The killer had provided his own shroud. In its folds he disappeared. I was glad, it served him right." The sky fight had moved away from us and I could see bombs exploding on the shore...'[66]

Time-Line –

- On August 24th, 1940 German Junkers 88 bombers dropped more than five hundred bombs on the Town and Harbour of Ramsgate. Vessels in the harbour were sunk, the town was devastated, and hundreds of homes were blown to pieces. But there

66. This quotation from Bob Roberts' book is included with the kind permission of Jed Lyons CEO of Rowman & Littlefield Inc. who are the copyright owners.

had been just enough warning for most of the population to clamber into the tunnels deep and safe down in the chalk. More than three hundred homes had been lost that day but thanks to the tunnels only twenty-nine souls perished. After that terrible day, for some three hundred homeless families, the Ramsgate tunnels would provide them with a safe, warm and dry place to live in for the next two or three years.

1940

RAF Balloon Command

'...slow moving barrage balloons drift across the misty sky,
Solitary remains of buildings like fingers pointing on the
midnight gloom. Bullets like a thousand fireworks
flickering in the moonlight.'

Bryan Wainwright 10yrs – Friends of Wincoback Hill 2010

Hitler's Blitz of London continued nightly with thousands of people being killed and many more rendered homeless. Whole squadrons of Luftwaffe bombers flew over London dropping thousands of tons of high explosive and incendiary devices[67] as Hitler continued his efforts to paralyse the London Docks and subdue the British civilian spirit. Lone raiders would fly over the Thames Estuary and dock areas dropping magnetic and acoustic mines. One of the counter-measures developed to impede this aerial onslaught was the formation of RAF Balloon Command.

The big balloons were made from rubberised panels of silver painted fabric. They were about 19 meters. (62+ feet) long by 8 meters (26+ feet) diameter, pear shaped tapering from a blunt 'front' to a thick 'tail' on which were mounted three inflatable stabilizing fins – much as for a dart. The balloon filled with hydrogen gas was flown up on a steel wire and there were a variety of wire devices that hung down from the balloon. Some wires might have serrations to better entangle and cut into an aeroplane while others might carry explosive charges. Thus, a serious hazard was presented to any aircraft flying in such an area. As well as being flown over land targets, barrage

---

67. Estimates indicate that about 14,000 tons of German bombs had been dropped on London by the end of May 1941

balloons were flown from barges, drifters and similar vessels in the estuaries and harbours. These Barrage Balloons could be flown up to heights of around 2,438 plus meters (8,000 feet) floating at the end of steel wires. This made it a treacherous game for the German pilots because they had to avoid the wires while at the same time attempting to aim their bombs. It also meant that the bombers had to fly at more predictable altitudes. Referencing on the balloons made it easier for ant-aircraft gunners to anticipate where the bomber would be by the time their shells reached it, and they could better assess the height at which to set their shells to detonate into a cloud of shrapnel fragments. Furthermore, the presence of a score or so of balloons floating high and clustered around a target, while not being a total deterrent would greatly increase the difficulties and risks to which Hitler's aircrews were exposed. Occasionally a German aircraft would become entangled and brought down.

It was essential that the Thames Estuary and London be protected by any possible means from Hitler's aircraft attack and in this the balloons had good effect particularly at night when the German pilots preferred to carry out their air-raids and aerial mine-laying operations, for the balloons were much more difficult to see at night time. Messerschmitt fighter machine-gun attacks on balloons and their mooring craft and crews were frequent but while some balloons went up in flames, a few bullet holes in a balloon usually meant that the balloon slowly deflated and slowly descended. The bullet holes could be easily patched. By May 1940 there were more than five hundred balloons flying to protect London and most of these were in the dockland and Thames areas. One of *Sheemaun*'s duties was to act as water-bus for the Balloon Barge crews and help with supplies and mail.

Thames Barrage Balloon and armed tug on Thames Estuary –
WW2 Picture from the late Stanley Dodd's memoir collection

1940

Rabbit Stew, Belmont - Monmouthshire UK

It was September and the leaves were just taking their autumn hues. Percy Pugsley pulled on his heavy Air Warden's coat, it had large pockets where he ordinarily he kept his big torch, the wooden air raid warning rattle, a note-book and a whistle but just now there was no air raid. Picking up his ash walking-stick[68] he winked at his little grandson and put a finger to his lips ...ssshhh. His grandson, who had called his grandpa Bom-Bom since he was learning to talk, followed excitedly; he knew they were to be off hunting rabbits. Under the shelter of the over-hanging stable roof was a hutch with a chicken wire front and inside was a big heap of straw. At the noise of the retaining pin being pulled from the door latch, the straw burst into activity and a pair of pole-cat cross ferrets emerged sniffing curiously at the air as they stood up on their hind legs. Jack and Jill well understood this routine. Bom-Bom opening his big pocket flap moved close to the ferret hutch and Jack and Jill like quicksilver flowed down into the pocket.

Together the pair set off through the little gate and across farmer Bob Needs' field. Bom-Bom carying a sack slung over his shoulder with the rabbit nets in it. From time to time a ferret stuck its head out from Bom-Bom's pocket. After walking for half a mile, they came to the big rabbit warren by the Duthie Farm copse. The warren was in an earth bank on which were overgrown elders, hazels and hawthorns. Down under their roots were dozens of rabbit holes and signs of new diggings. The warren was only half a mile downhill from the anti-aircraft

---

68. In American jargon - a cane.

and searchlight battery set up on Jack Duthie's farm, as part of the ring of anti-aircraft barrages around Newport Docks. Yet the ear-splitting thunder of the guns and the searing searchlight beams at night-time did not seem to have deterred the rabbits! Bom-Bom took out the purse-string nets and one by one put the nets across as many holes as could be reached, the nets were then pegged down by pieces of stick. Jack and Jill were taken out from the deep pocket and each put by a rabbit hole about ten paces apart. After a quick sniff the ferrets dived into the dark burrow system. Settling down on a grassy tump, Bom-Bom lit his briar pipe and waited... he lifted a finger and pursed his lips... ' Ssshhhh.' His little grandson could barely contain himself with excitement. Lying with an ear to the warm smelling earth he could hear occasional faint bumpings and noises as startled rabbits 'thumped' their warnings and bolted in the maze of burrows deep below in the hard, dry earth.

Suddenly one of the nets with a swish was rocketed into the air, the wooden peg flying away and tangled in the net was a kicking rabbit. Rabbit and net were sent rolling around on the ground. Moving quickly for a big man in his seventies, Bom-Bom despatched the rabbit with a flick of his wrist. No sooner had he done that than another and then another net was flung into the air. It was as if footballs were being kicked hard into the nets. Several more rabbits were soon netted. Bom-Bom only took three, the others were set free to live another day.

'Son – never take more than you need of anything. Always remember that happy is the man who earns a pound and spends nineteen shillings and sixpence. Unhappy is the man who earns a pound but spends twenty shillings and sixpence...'[69]

---

69. A misquote from Mr Micawber in Charles Dickens' David Copperfield.

The three rabbits were gutted there and then. Jack and Jill who had now emerged blinking into the sunlight came bounding over; their treat was the offal from the gutting. After munching their fill, they were quite happy to go back into Bom-Bom's pocket for the journey home. One rabbit went to farmer Bob Needs and his wife Betty, the other two were dealt with by Grandma Pugsley. They would be skinned, washed and hung in the cool larder for two days before being quartered, then slow-stewed in a pot together with parsnip, carrot, potato, and beans and all well-seasoned. Grandma's rabbit stew was delicious. Nothing was wasted; the skins would be scraped, washed, rubbed with salt and alum, then stretched and dried. They would be used for lining hoods and boots, for making fur-lined mittens and the like – this was austerity, this was war time!

Time-Line -

- 1940 September - Out in the Atlantic Ocean German U-Boats were sinking many thousands of tons of Allied cargo ships carrying supplies vital for Britain. Many of their crews going down with them. Back in the UK All food except for seasonal vegetables was scarce and strictly rationed. However, flesh from wild pigeon, rabbit, duck and game was not rationed.

- Adolph Hitler had ordered that all Jews were to wear yellow identity stars. 2000 Londoners had so far been killed in the air raids.

- America agreed to lease some of its destroyers to Britain.

- A German bomb hit Buckingham Palace.

- The 'Battle of Britain' was raging in the skies over the South Coast.

- German bombers had flown over the River Severn
  Estuary to bomb the South Wales Newport Docks.
  One of those raiders, a Heinkel bomber had flown
  into a barrage balloon wire cable at about 7000
  feet and had been brought down. It crashed into
  a Newport residential area – Stow Park Avenue –
  crushing a house. Two young people lost their lives
  along with the crew of the Heinkel.

1940

Rabbit Stew - Whitechapel, in East London

Night after night the German Luftwaffe had been dropping thousands of tons of bombs on London's East End and the Docks. Row upon row of terraced houses lay in dusty smoking ruins and few windows were left unbroken. Many streets piled with rubble were unpassable. At night most of the civilian population slept in shelters or down on the tube station platforms dreading to go home next morning for fear that they would find just a huge bomb crater where once there had been a home. Food rationing was tough, but just as tough was the actual scarcity of food which was exactly what Hitler was trying to achieve. Londoners however were survivors. There was bread, there were still plentiful vegetables available and pigeon meat and rabbit meat were not rationed. Most families had country relatives or country connections in Essex and Kent and so pigeon pie and rabbit stew might often be on the menu.

Bombs last night had fallen on Vallance Road, the smell of high explosive still wafted in the swirling dust along with the acrid smell of burned timbers. Doctor Orpwood-Price[70] looked with horror at the shambles. Doors had been blown out, windows blown out, part of the roof was off, and water still dripped from broken pipes. The Venereal Diseases Reference Laboratory had been badly damaged. Valuable microscopes and scientific apparatus lay scattered and broken, filing cabinets lay broken, their contents partly burned and now soaked by the

---

70. In the 1950s I was privileged to be taught by the late Dr. Orpwood-Price and sometimes stayed with the Orpwood-Price family at their home in Reading. His son David and a good friend was also in my year at the Medical College.

fire-hoses. Putting his hands to his head Doctor Orpwood-Price sighed in disbelief at the devastation. Years of carefully tended research had been wasted and some of that research appeared to have legged it, yes legged it! Several cages had been warped with the doors opened or knocked off their hinges. The inhabitants, a dozen or so rabbits all infected with syphilis or another of the treponemal infectious venereal diseases had vanished.

This was the last thing that the local population needed! Urgent meetings were arranged with local councillors, with the Police and Special Constables, with the Air Raid Precaution wardens and shop-keepers. Notices were posted, and the police toured the streets with megaphones warning people that –

ANY STRAY RABBITS FOUND LOOSE IN
THE STREETS MIGHT BE CARRYING A
SERIOUS INFECTION. THEY SHOULD BE
TRAPPED AND THE AUTHORITIES NOTIFIED

The following day saw streets in Bethnal Green, Whitechapel and Stepney littered with hundreds of discarded dead rabbits. There was no roast rabbit or rabbit stew eaten in East London that week!

1940

A New Life in Wapping,
East London
November

Stanley Dodd's wife 'Girl' was now in the last stage of pregnancy. Wanting to be together with Stanley, 'Girl' had refused to be evacuated away from London to somewhere safer in the Essex countryside, and so the Dodd family stayed with Stanley's father in North London where it was marginally less hazardous compared with the East End and Docks area where a terrible 'Blitz' bombing recurred every night -

'We were no exception, we used to go, Girl, Nellie, Ern, myself and the dog 'Peggy' to my father's place at New Southgate (North London), where we were made most welcome. How we managed I forget, but I think that Girl, heavy with child, and the dog stayed there. Ern and Nellie went to and from Wapping each day and I went to the office. Somehow we all arrived "home" before the dark and the raids continued unabated, as they left the dock area, for it was devastation, they expanded, and so this temporary became a refuge no longer, so ultimately a trickle of us returned. After all, we'd experienced the lot, and had developed a fatalistic outlook – it's the one you don't hear which gets you – and so settled down, if that is the right word – to a life of not anticipating the next second. I don't think any of us were afraid of Death – it somehow seemed insignificant. Maiming yes but death no – just the end of a road which led nowhere anyway. This then was the background to the birth of my eldest son Michael.' S.D.

Her contractions had begun and 'Girl' went into labour on Thursday November 7th. Despite the bomb damage debris strewn everywhere in the streets, Stanley managed to call a taxi and get Ellen to the London Hospital. He helped her to clamber up the wide West Wing staircase to Mary Northcliffe ward. Many of the windows had been blasted out and although the nurses had done their best to tidy and clean the wards there was still dust and debris littered about. The nursing staff were all wearing steel helmets and like everyone else they kept their gasmasks in boxes slung from their shoulders or stowed nearby when the cumbersome things interfered with clinical duties! As 'Girl' was in labour on Sunday November 10th another bomb fell in Vallance Road just at the back of the hospital. The building shook, windows rattled and some shattered. In the labour room the big porcelain basin was knocked partly off its stand held up only by its lead waste-pipe and lead tap pipes. Yet more windows were damaged or blown in. Although not of the Roman Catholic faith, Stanley and Ellen felt that their new baby boy should be Blessed as soon as possible, and the Blessing took place next day in the ward. Priest Father Michael was in the hospital at the time and so a little group of midwives and nurses, all wearing their steel helmets together with the Dodd family gathered around the cot. The new baby was accordingly named after Father Michael.

On Wednesday the 13th Stanley took his wife and their precious new baby Michael home to North London, he recorded -

'He was born 10th November 1940. We were all thrilled to bits and yet dismayed – what was this world he had been born into. On the Monday, I got on my bike and rode to Covent Garden Market early and bought some flowers to take in to her and the child. But what a London and what a ride. Not the London I knew or the London it is today. Just a series of smoking ruins interspersed with roads closed, because of unexploded bombs. Whole roads down and blocked and miles and miles of firemen's hoses to negotiate. I had a special silver St Christopher's medallion inscribed "Ave Michael" and had it blessed by the Roman Catholic father, who I knew, although I was not of that religion. – this was pinned on to his garments – I felt that nothing should be left to chance if there was a possibility of it helping him. So "Ave Michael" - what a world to "Hail" into. And we were lucky. Because of the conditions prevailing and with an eye to covering all contingencies here and "here after" we decided to have Michael christened as soon as practical, and, within a week of leaving hospital.' S.D.

Arrangements were made for baby Michael to be christened at the Church of Saint Peter in Wapping Lane East London. The building of Saint Peter's church had been commenced on St Peter's Day in 1865 since when various further works had been carried out which had been finally completed in the Spring of 1940. On the night of 15th November 1940 however there was yet another night of Blitzkrieg. Hitler's bombers flying high over the London Docks and London's East End homes, workshops and businesses had released hundreds of tons of high explosive bombs, incendiary bombs and napalm[71] bombs all plummeting down to wreak mayhem, damage and death. All around them London's East End lay devastated, whole areas of housing and apartments had been blown to pieces and those buildings that were still standing had all been damaged, few windows remained unbroken. St Peter's Church was among the many hundreds of buildings that had been hit and badly damaged.

On the morning of Sunday the 16th, of St Peter's Church little more than a standing shell remained. It had been reduced

---

71. Napalm – A sticky jellified petrol or kerosene mix that adheres to anything including skin. It burns furiously at a high temperature.

to a charred smoking ruin, but the Dodd family sharing in the defiant spirit of their thousands of fellow London Cockneys were determined not to be defeated by Germany's Fuhrer Adolph Hitler; and so, the Dodd family, their close friends and Father Michael bravely kept to their assignation.

'...Fred Welsh got his right arm blown off and bled to death, a block of flats, empty at the time as the inhabitants were in the shelter, was pranged in the middle as if a giant had taken a vast bite out of it. And St Peter's Church, that was a smoking smouldering ruin. It had been devastated by fire, a Sister of Mercy had been killed, and on this late November afternoon, it reeked of smoke and dampness and T.N.T. The roof had gone and the grey smoke sky looked down into a four walled cavity, the pews charred and smouldering, the altar, stained blackened and cracked in several places, and the font, near the entrance propping up a black smoking wooden beam, with the grey whisks of vapours rising in slow motion towards an equally grey sky. Ted and Phil were God Parents, and Danny, home on leave from the Navy was the other God Parent and between us all we shifted the smouldering beam so that the ceremony could take place. Under the afternoon sky Mike was duly Christened and then back to the flat for a hurried tea, before the next raid...' S.D.

As the terrible raids continued, Londoners did their best to maintain some form of discipline and pride. Those who still had a job tried their hardest to get to work, including Stanley Dodd who worked at the Eastern District Post Office, but getting to work was another matter altogether. There were some bus services still running and the tube lines were running almost normally but many roads were blocked, and some bridges were unpassable. So, travelling around London was mostly on 'Shanks Pony'[72] or by bicycle. Those who lived or worked near to the Thames thumbed lifts wherever possible from passing tugs and other water craft including the River Emergency Service boats. There were times when it seemed the Thames itself was on fire. Stanley Dodd describes the heat being so intense that iron railings melted and pigeons and seagulls flying high above, fell to earth roasted and sizzling –

'Of course, I never went to work – I couldn't – I couldn't get there…(p 217) …even if I wanted to and finally, after about 10 days because the bridges were out of use, the authorities provided a service where you went down to one of the P.L.A (Port of London Authority) piers and literally thumbed a lift from a passing tug, who deposited you at a pier of your choice, in my case Tower Pier. Supplies were brought in by this method and the local hospital – Raines – was evacuated by the same way. But the raids never stopped although we were then not on the receiving end of them. I saw many marvellous sights – two barges blown out of the Thames on to the roof of Butler's Wharf[73] at Rotherhithe. At Gun Wharf, I saw the iron staircase outside the building glow red, then white in the intense heat and then slowly melt and trickle downwards like soft treacle. I saw sea gulls and pidgeons flying perhaps 200 – 300 feet up trying to escape the fire, suddenly burst into flames themselves from the concentrated heat. But the most amazing of all was the Thames. The water was as black as ink from the water used in attempting to reduce the fires – The Thames was as black

72. The Shank Bone or Shin Bone. This slang term refers to having to walk on one's own legs and not to ride or be carried in any way.

73. A six-storey warehouse dating from 1865. Once the world's largest tea warehouse. Since 1980 it has been converted into luxury flats, with restaurants and shops.

as ink with black foam as the tugs thrust their way through it. An approximate colour for the time. Just the perpetual smell of burning and the River Styx. Well as soon as we were able to and communication was established, most of the people would... (p 218) ...leave Wapping and head for the Tube Railway Station, Chislehurst caves in Kent, or relatives not too far away and, at the time, more fortunate, only returning to Wapping during the daylight hours. During darkness it was deserted. We were no exception...'
S.D.

1940

Newport, South Wales UK - 24th November

Sitting at the breakfast table sipping his tea, Godfrey Pell had one ear listening to the BBC news spluttering out from the Bakelite HMV[74] radio announcing that a hundred and forty-eight German bombers had that very night bombed Bristol and Avonmouth, while his other ear listened out for his car which was warming up in the garage. This morning he was tired, rather frightened and feeling that another asthma attack was imminent. He was very reluctant to leave the warm kitchen as he would have to do after a few more minutes. The night of 24th November had been the worst he could remember. At about eleven p.m. the chilling wail of air-raid warning sirens had echoed across the hills. His father-in-law Devonshire born Percy Pugsley and his mother-in-law Margaret Pugsley now lived with the Pell family, having leased their own house to the Council for the use of people evacuated urgently from London so they might escape the terrible bombing raids.

Grandpa Percy Pugsley who was an A. R. P. (Air Raid Precaution) Warden picked up the big wooden rattle used to warn people to get into their shelters, the big torch and pea-whistle, put on his A.R.P warden's helmet and uniform and set off on his bicycle to make sure no houses showed the smallest chink of light from behind their window blinds, and that everyone who should be, was indoors or in their air-raid shelter. All cars had to have light restrictor shades on the headlamps and even the sidelights had to have cardboard shades behind the glass. Front and rear bumpers and the side running-boards had to be

---

74. HMV - His Master's Voice Corp. Bakelite was the first heat mouldable plastic. It was very toxic and contained asbestos fibres.

painted white. Any car with so much as a stray glimmer from its headlights or deficient in other war-time measures would have been stopped.

ARP Warden Helmet in Imperial War Museum – Photo R.P.

A formation of German bombers had flown up the River Severn Estuary using the moonlit waters as their guide. Their targets had been the Avonmouth docks and oil-refinery, and the Bristol City and Newport Docks. The loud droning throb of hundreds of engines in the skies above had kept the family awake and alarmed. From their house up on Christchurch Hill they had clear views north across to the beautiful Usk valley and south across the wide Severn estuary. Just a mile (1.6 km) north-east up the Cats'ash Road where the Ministry of Defence had requisitioned part of the Duthie farm, an anti-aircraft battery had been set up, armed with six powerful searchlights, six Bofors anti-aircraft guns and some 3.7 inch (9.3 cm) anti-aircraft guns. Of course, the German planes flying over Bristol Docks and Avonmouth oil refinery some 21 miles (33.7km) south were miles out of range but Hurricane fighter-planes from RAF Filton aerodrome and RAF Pembrey had been scrambled. A few of Hitler's bombers had been shot down and others no doubt damaged. The bomber formations had been forced to scatter and some had flown north before escaping south-west over the Severn estuary with most of them dumping their bomb loads indiscriminately. Half a mile up the hill searchlights at the Duthie Farm Military Camp had probed and seared the night sky with several bombers being caught in the cross beams. So intense were their carbon-arcs that the heat could be felt reflected. The Bofors and heavy guns had exploded into a fury of activity. Windows rattled and shrapnel fragments rained down, the house shook, and the noise had been deafening. Roof tiles had been broken and dislodged and the greenhouse shattered. Cows and pigs on the Needs' farm just a hundred yards away stampeded in fear.

Godfrey and Joyce Pell, clinging to each other, horrified and frightened, had peered from their bedroom window south across the River Severn estuary for hours, watching the Avonmouth searchlights as they stabbed and wavered into the night sky, while over the City of Bristol and the Avonmouth oil refinery, an ominous flickering orange/red glow lit the sky for miles around. Even at that distance they could hear and almost feel the deep booms and crumps of the exploding bombs. Proof enough of the demoniac destructive and lethal intentions of Adolph Hitler and his acolyte fellow countrymen.

Although he had hardly slept that night, Godfrey had to be up early. He had a routine and following it somehow helped; first, he put the kettle on the anthracite range, then went to the out-house and raked out the central-heating boiler-stove ashes and re-filled it with anthracite. Then he let the chickens out from their hutch and fed them chicken-meal and scraps. Next, he would open the garage, pull out the choke, start the car and go back into the kitchen where Joyce had put together a quick breakfast and had started to dress the children. When the car engine had warmed up, and began to run unevenly, that was the time to set off for work. With a hug and kiss he bade Joyce, his baby daughter Dinah and little son Rodney goodbye, stepped over a broken roof tile and getting into his faithful Austin Ten saloon registration number BDW 677, pushed in the choke and drove off into whatever the day might hold for him.

In the days before this dreadful war, he would have driven down the Royal Oak hill, turned right at the T junction by Morris's Garage, and headed into Newport to the confectionary works and bakery of A. G. Pell & Sons Ltd at 195-196 Commercial Road. But the War had changed all that. Sugar, glucose, fondant, butter, lard, flour, the flavouring essences of vanilla, peppermint, pear-drop and saffron, chocolate etc. and all the necessary raw ingredients for baking and for making boiled sweets were difficult to come by.

Traditional sugar boiling at A G Pell & Sons Ltd Confectioners in the 1950s using the same traditional copper boiling cauldrons as had been used for the previous 100 years
Photo - Courtesy Nigel Pell

Food rationing had been introduced and was strictly enforced. All foods except vegetables and wholemeal bread were rationed. The allocation per person per week was - bacon eight ounces (227 g), sugar 16 ounces (452 g), butter eight ounces (227 g), margarine four ounces (113.5 g), meat one pound (454 g), one egg four ounces (113.5 g), and fish the same. Milk a quarter pint

(0.142 L). People could only buy according to their Ration-Book coupon allocation. Confectionary businesses were being hard hit and the severe petrol and fuel rationing added great difficulties to the matter of supply and delivery of goods, but the Pell business was less unfortunate for they supplied the South Wales Coal Mining Pithead Shops and the coal miners defined as an Essential Workforce, received extra rations. As Prime Minister Lloyd George had said –

'In peace and war King Coal is the Paramount Lord.'

As an essential war production worker, Godfrey received a just adequate petrol allowance for his daily commute, but instead of turning right at the bottom of the hill to go west into Newport as he used to, now he turned east towards Chepstow. His father Arthur George and his older brother Clifford were left to run the reduced business. Clifford's older son, also named Arthur, had been conscripted into the Royal Navy and was serving on the aircraft carrier HMS *Vindex,* battling through the Arctic seas as one of the Murmansk convoy escorts. John the younger son with poor eyesight and had been allowed to continue in the business. Under the Military Training Act of April 1939 Godfrey, suffering from asthma, had been found unsuitable for active service but his administrative skills were recognised, and he had been appointed as Personnel Officer at the Dinham Propellant Factory just east of Chepstow.

Dinham was a massive organisation, employing some thousand plus workers and contained within a perimeter fence enclosing over a thousand acres (404 Hectares) of land set on a hillside. The key product was cordite, the explosive propellant charge for ordnance, which included anything from small arms ammunition to the huge naval guns. Save that huge quantities of water and sulphuric and nitric acids were used in making the nitro-glycerine. Godfrey knew little about the chemical process, but the fumes greatly aggravated his asthma!

Three shifts day and night were worked, and numbers of workers lived on-site. There was a very active social and recreational theme including dances, talks, table-tennis and film shows two or three times a week. Godfrey who shared with his brother Clifford a keen interest in cine-photography had been appointed as the 'honorary' projectionist. Tonight, the film was 'Sunny Side Up' a two-hour American movie with soundtrack. The large works 35 mm projector was very different from the little Paillard Bolex 16mm silent film projector he was used to although the principle was the same.

The film was popular with the audience and it brought a welcome relief from the pressure of war and work. The workers particularly liked to laugh and join in with the double-entendre saucy song 'Turn the Heat Up' and when a curved banana held up by a pretty girl straightened itself! But it was stuffy and hot in the confines of the projection booth given the heat from the carbon-arc lamp, heat from the motor and the stuffiness of the Assembly Hall Many in the audience were smoking and the projection beam flickered and stabbed through a blue/grey haze of tobacco smoke. Despite the irritation to his chest Godfrey too was enjoying the film but when he moved he felt a strange tickling and swishing sensation around his ankles. Feeling down he was aghast to find he was standing in a 'pool' of cine-film, which having failed to take up properly on the lower spool had been winding and slithering around on the floor like sea-foam being blown around on the beach. As it was the last spool he decided to let it run to the end. But afterwards it took him a very long time to re-wind the film by hand. Strict security meant no 'phone call home and that night he returned very late to an overwrought wife!

Joyce told him how that same day their son then a few months short of his 4th birthday had been playing in the neighbouring field. Their little boy had found a strange black metal thing with two large round things like big tins and a strap. It was heavy, but he had managed to drag it home.

A Kreighoff Rheinmetall MG 15 7.92 mm machine gun.
Manston Spitfire Museum - Photo RP

Proud of his find he had been upset when his mother screamed and told him to put it down carefully. She had called farmer Bob Needs who was also a Special Constable. Bob didn't like the look of it and contacted the Commanding Officer of the Gloucester Regiment encamped a few hundred yards away across the road. Regimental Sergeant Major 'Biff' had been sent over to assess the matter. He identified the strange object as a German MG 15 machine gun. There were live rounds in it and it must have been jettisoned from one of the bombers, perhaps being pursued by a Hurricane fighter. Rodney was praised for his efforts but told very firmly that if he ever again found anything like that, not to touch it, but to tell a grown-up about it at once. R.S.M.[75] 'Biff' took it away. Godfrey, upset and deeply worried by the

75. Regimental Sergeant Major

previous night's events then made urgent arrangements for a sunken air-raid shelter to be built deep in the garden and with a stout anti-blast wall across the entrance.

I vaguely remember dragging that machine gun through a gap in the hedge. That was when I began to realise that this war, with all the searchlights, bangs, excitement and soldiers driving around in Bren-gun carriers and big tanks, was not a game like Cowboys and Indians where you shouted *'Bang Bang you're dead!'* and then everyone got up and went in for buns and orange juice. This was real, and those bullets had been in a plane flown with the pilot and gunner having every intention of killing those below them, mummies and daddies, families and friends. I began to understand that fathers, uncles, brothers, relatives and friends were being killed somewhere every day, killed never ever to come back to their families. Now I knew why so many of my mother's friends sometimes cried so much. Mercifully I hadn't pulled on its trigger.

That morning the milk-cart[76] was late as farmer Bastin had such difficulty with catching and harnessing his frightened cart-horse!

Time-Line –

- The Town of Coventry was destroyed by Hitler's bombers. Franklin D. Roosevelt was elected for a third term as President of the USA.

- 24th November 1940 - My Grandfather Percy Pugsley ARP Warden, was patrolling the Christchurch Parish north of Newport Docks

---

76. Milk was delivered in metal churns carried on a horse-pulled cart. There were no milk bottles, the house-wives took china jugs out to the cart to be filled with the fresh milk. There was no refrigeration, the jugs would be put on a stone slab in a cool North-facing still-room with a fine wire mesh instead of glass at the window.

during a heavy bombing raid. On that same night another Devon Pugsley, Commander Anthony Follett Pugsley RN was aboard the destroyer HMS *Javelin*, one of a flotilla of destroyers operating under Captain Lord Louis Mountbatten. They were on a night patrol off the South Devon coast. They met with a force of three German destroyers and in the ensuing battle HMS *Javelin* was torpedoed. Only half the ship remained afloat! Commander Pugsley survived and went on to command the 14th Destroyer Flotilla. Known as *'The Destroyer man'* (Title of his Biography) he was later to be made a Companion of the Order of the Bath and awarded the Distinguished Serviced Order. He was eventually promoted to the rank of Rear Admiral.

- *Sheemaun* was serving in the Thames Estuary as an armed Auxiliary Patrol Boat, crewed by volunteers. One day many years away I would put my hands to her wheel.

1941

A Requisition is Served

In the early part of WWII, the Wrens[77] were trying to buy available stocks of Navy serge from which to make their trousers. It is said that a Naval C-in-C made the following signal –

'Wrens clothing is to be held up until the needs of seagoing personnel have been satisfied'

From 'The Sailor's Little Book' by Basil Mosethal 2000

Under her amateur volunteer crews *Sheemaun* had been patrolling in her allocated area. The Ministry of Defence provided sufficient fuel for the purpose and there was an allowance of tea, bread, butter and jam, tins of baked beans and corned beef. The crew doing shifts of two weeks on and two weeks off. While on duty they lived and slept aboard as Hitler's bombing raids were having a very disruptive effect on road and rail travel.

In the previous day's patrol, they had rescued a British airman who had bailed out of his Hurricane and was fortunately not badly hurt. They had taken supplies and mail to the moored observation barges and had checked and inspected several Thames barges and a fishing boat and narrowly missed being hit by a strafing German fighter-bomber. A careful log of all events had been kept including sightings of enemy aircraft and anything that seemed out of place. With *Sheemaun* moored at her Hole Haven Berth, skipper 'Bunny' Frost-Roberts and his crew of volunteer yachtsmen were tidying ship, sorting out warps and stores, dipping the fuel tanks and generally making sure all was in order.

By now *Sheemaun's* white painted hull was beginning to look

77. Wrens - Women's Royal Naval Service

a bit tatty, there were big black marks and scuffs caused by the old lorry tyres that were generally hung off the docksides as fenders. In peace-time the little ship would have been treated to a good clean up and re-paint, but this was wartime. Almost every day vessels somewhere in the Thames Estuary were being machine gunned by such of Hitler's Luftwaffe that happened in the vicinity some had even been bombed. The last thing needed of *Sheemaun* was for her to present herself on a plate as a gleaming white target! Ah, yes… their rifles needed cleaning and oiling and the deck, which was rather slippery, could well do with a few buckets of sea-water and a stiff brush. The crew who in pre-war years had cherished the ways of the backwater creeks and saltings, now greatly appreciated moments of quiet which even in this war did still occur.

A lone grey heron that had for some time been standing sentinel-like at the water's edge, suddenly launched itself into the air as a black Humber Snipe car pulled up on the sea-wall at the head of the jetty. A uniformed Naval Lieutenant alighted, descended the ladder and making straight for *Sheemaun* he stopped alongside.

'Is the Skipper aboard?'

'Bunny' who had been rubbing rather ineffectually at one of the dark scuff marks on the hull straightened up and as he had his cap on he felt it right that he should salute the officer who reciprocated the gesture.

'Well you could say I'm the skipper, although I'm not the owner.'

The officer strode forward and handed 'Bunny' an envelope marked 'Ministry of Defence'. 'Bunny' opened it and took out the letter, his eyes widened as he read it .

Department of War Transport

T.W.5074/41/S.P.C.2

EMERGENCY POWERS (DEFENCE) ACT. 1939.
DEFENCE (GENERAL) REGULATIONS. 1939.

NOTICE OF ACQUISITION

WHEREAS, the M.B. "SHEEMAUN" has been requisitioned 535(8)

NOW THEREFORE, pursuant to the provisions of paragraph (2) of Regulation 53 of the Defence (General) Regulations. 1939, the Minister of War Transport hereby gives notice that he has acquired the said vessel in pursuance of the said regulation 33.

Signed by authority of the Minister this twenty eighth day of August, 1941.

W.G. Hynard

Lt. L.A. Golding, R.A.,
65, Conduit Street,
London, W.1. (Per registered post.)

The Lieutenant smiled –

> 'You've all been doing a great job and appreciated by the Admiralty but now the Royal Navy is to take over. I realise this may come as a bit of a shock but at least you won't have to clean off all those black scuffs now!'

He went on to explain that the original papers were already with the registered owner Acting Lt. Roy Calvert-Link RNVR but who had expressed concern for his dedicated volunteer colleagues currently serving on *Sheemaun,* had asked that they too might see a copy of the requisition and be given time to disembark along with their few belongings. After checking their green Identity cards, the Lieutenant handed 'Bunny' an envelope.

'There are the warrants to cover your bus or rail fares. A Naval Volunteer Reservist Crew will be arriving shortly.'

With that done he saluted, thanked the crew again for their splendid voluntary efforts and departed. The driver was already turning the Humber around as the Lieutenant clambered back up the ladder. 'Bunny' looked at his fellow yachtsmen

'Well gentlemen that was interesting but to be expected. Poor Roy, he must be upset at losing his pride and joy. So, let's get our gear off and head for home. Maybe our applications for Reservist positions will come through… who knows!'

Rolling gently *Sheemaun* curtsied as her erstwhile crew of volunteer amateur yachtsmen jumped down onto the jetty with their canvass ditty bags. There was certain sadness in the air and one by one they patted the old boat's gunnel and then set off for the bus station. The following day an hour before low water, a crew of two reservists boarded *Sheemaun* lowered her masts, gunned her engines, cast off and took her on the flood tide up the Thames to a boatyard at Teddington. There the little ship had different type of re-fit. The main mast was taken off, the rifles taken out, and her hull was painted a dull wartime grey.

A pair of menacing Hotchkiss machine guns were mounted on the foredeck. A grey Carley[78] style float was mounted on the after deck and a rifle rack installed in the saloon, and the 'Red Duster' ensign[79] was replaced by the Royal Naval White Ensign. Within a few days *Sheemaun* had been made ready to return to the lower Thames in her new and official Ministry of Defence role as HMY[80] *Sheemaun*. She had become one of the twenty Royal Navy Thames Auxiliary Patrol Service Boats to be assigned to full War-Time duties in the Thames Estuary area and would fly the White Ensign of the Royal Navy.

Time-Line –

- HMY *Sheemaun* was listed[81] as a Royal Naval Auxiliary Patrol Vessel armed with two Hotchkiss machine guns and based at Hole Haven between 1/9/40 and 2/11/41. She was then based at Cliffe Fort from 9/11/41 to 15/7/45. After the War from 15/7/45 she was placed with the Department of Sea Transport

---

78. Named after its American Inventor - Horace Carley 1838 -1918).

79. 'Red Duster' is a slang term for the British Red Ensign which was proclaimed by King Charles II in 1674 to be flown by English Merchant Vessels and now is also used by privately owned British leisure yachts.

80. His Majesty's Yacht *Sheemaun* - as recorded at the Imperial War Museum and confirmed to me by Maritime Historian Nick Hewitt.

81. From Lorna Reid at Ministry of Defence Records Department Portsmouth, 2/3/10

1941

Sandwich time at Cliffe Fort Naval Jetty

'I went into a French restaurant and said to the waiter
Have you got frog's legs? He said "Yes," so I said,
Well hop into the kitchen and get me a cheese sandwich'.

Tommy Cooper

The Luftwaffe had again been determinedly active and effective with dropping magnetic mines into the Thames and its estuary, already more than a hundred vessels of some hundreds of thousands of tons total had been sunk by those unseen but lethal weapons in only the first three months of the war. Today there was a lull and HMY *Sheemaun* was moored up while her crew of trained Royal Naval Volunteer Reservists crew took a brief rest, tidied ship, re-fuelled and had a 'brew up'. Taff went ashore to get some stores. Mike was helping Andy to strip and oil the twin Hotchkiss machine guns mounted on the foredeck. Although the design dated from before the First World War it was still a deadly piece of machinery. This naval version consisted of two guns bracketed together and mounted on a tripod. Each fed from a 30-round magazine clip and with a combined firing rate of some 220 rounds/min. The fire rate was relatively slow in comparison to more modern weapons of the time but the 13.2 mm shells, which could include tracer and armour-piercing rounds had a range of some 4,140 yards (3,800m) and at half a mile a direct hit could pierce the armour of a light tank.

The men were proud of the twin Hotchkiss, but the guns were prone to jamming. When in action, a portion of the explosive gas was diverted from the barrel chamber through a small port into a piston chamber so actuating a mechanism that expelled the spent case, loaded the next cartridge and cocked the firing pin. This gas pressure had to be regulated carefully for if the recoil piston failed to fully return, then the cartridge case ejection pawl would not operate, and the gun would jam. On the other hand, if too much gas was let through the resultant vibration would spoil the aim. There were several recoil springs that could fail at a critical moment and so all this had to be checked, cleaned, oiled and any worn or suspect parts replaced.

Un-noticed by the men, a group of three officers had been approaching along the jetty pausing sometimes to study more closely some of the various little fighting ships berthed alongside. Behind HMY *Sheemaun* was the *Navigator* but ahead of her was a gap where the lovely former motor yacht HMS *Aisha would* have been berthed but the *Aisha* at 98 feet (29.8 meters) and with a steel hull had been sunk when on 11th October having triggered a magnetic mine just north of the Isle of Sheppey. Fortunately, her crew had time to abandon ship without loss of life. Although injured they were rescued by a passing tug. The incident had been a solemn reminder of the ever-present dangers lurking in the seemingly familiar estuary waters and had been a particularly sad moment for those based at Cliffe Fort for HMS Aisha had taken part in the Dunkirk Beaches Evacuation only five months earlier.

The trio of officers who had now arrived alongside HMY *Sheemaun* were observing the men as they busied themselves with the guns. The tall officer coughed. Stanley and Andy looked up, sprang to their feet and saluted. The officer stepped closer to get a better view, just as Skipper Buckie stepped out from the wheelhouse clutching in one big hand mugs of steaming tea and in the other hand a basket of sandwiches. On seeing the officers his face reddened. Buckie jerked to attention, even if he had been wearing his cap, with his hands so full to have saluted would have been impossible. The two shorter officers glanced at each other but the tall man smiled…

'At ease sailor, please don't let us stop you.'

Buckie paused, his mouth opening and shutting… then the words came out…

'Will ye no hae a mug o' tea Sarr?'

The two shorter officers again exchanged glances.

'That's most civil of you. Yes, indeed I will, permission to come aboard skipper?'

Buckie stood aside as the tall officer stepped aboard, HMY *Sheemaun* curtsying gently to his weight. Clasping the mug of steaming tea, the officer looked over the Hotchkiss complementing the lads on keeping it in good shape. His eyes fell on the basket of sandwiches in Buckie's hand. Buckie's lips worked silently then he found his voice…

'Will ye no hae a san'ich Sarr… they're best plum jam?'

The tall officer had a sandwich in his hand almost before the two standing on the jetty had exchanged looks, the older one clearing his throat in disapproval. Handing back the mug the tall officer stepped back down onto the jetty. Buckie now had his cap on and the crew saluted smartly, the tall officer returning the salute. As the three officers walked away the tall one turned around -

'Thank you, gentlemen that was a really delicious sandwich.'

A few minutes later the staff car was a speck in the distance. The three fore-deck crewmen looked at each other in amazement.

Buckie grinned.

'Ma auntie Evelyn she makes the jam, she picks thae wild plums hersae but tae sugar's hard tae come by sae she chucks in plenty o' rum. I'll noo say where tae rum comes from!'

A bellowing guffaw came from aft, it was the skipper of the *Navigator* –

'… Hey d'ye know who that was?'…'I'm not sure… but I reckon that tall bloke was… well… I reckon that was the Earl of Winchilsea!'

Buckie's mouth worked overtime in silence.
Andy recovering his presence of mind put on his history school-master's face as he looked at his mates –

'Buckie makes a great sandwich… but…well do you know why we call them sandwiches?'

His mates looked back with almost pitiful expressions. Buckie made murmuring noises about men in white coats. Taff rounded on Andy…

'Don't be daft… that's what they're called… it's simple."

Andy grinned

"Oh is it… O.K. then well what's the Welsh for sandwich?'

Taff's jaw dropped and his head tilted as he thought for a moment, frowning at the quite unexpected turn in the conversation. Then straightening his head he laughed…

'What a daft question... I had to think a bit... well the Welsh for sandwich is...er ... brechdan... Why?'

Andy beamed - 'There you are'.
He was enjoying this game, but a growling noise came from Buckie...

'Och Aye... so whae' s a sandwich?'

Andy who still held a sandwich in his hand, peeled it open and explained.

'Well... you see this talk about Earls reminded me of a story about the Earl of Sandwich. Apparently in the Eighteenth century the then Earl of Sandwich was a heavy gambler. Rather than leave the gaming table to eat, he ordered his servant to put slices of meat between two slices of buttered bread and bring it to the gaming table... other gamblers soon followed his example and that's how the sandwich got its name...'

The three listening heads nodded appreciatively then Buckie scowled...

'There'll be noo gambling on this boot while Aa'm at'ai helm...'

Time-Line -
* 1941 The Earl of Winchilsea was an Acting Officer with the Royal Naval Volunteer Reserve section serving in the Nore Division Thames Estuary Area. His pet bulldog 'Funf' was the mascot of the Thames Estuary Armed Auxiliary Patrol Service. It was claimed that all 'Funf' desired was to be

allowed to test his teeth on Herr Adolf Hitler's ankles!

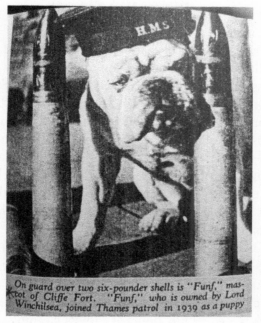

On guard over two six-pounder shells is "Funf," mascot of Cliffe Fort. "Funf," who is owned by Lord Winchilsea, joined Thames patrol in 1939 as a puppy

Thames Armed Auxiliary Patrol Boat Service's Mascot 'Funf' 'RNVR' Photo - *Illustrated Magazine* November 1942

1941

Pie in the Sky

It had been a dull grey November day the chill wind occasionally pulling some spray off the tops of the rolling swells and it was getting dark. A couple of coasters had been checked, given the flag code for that day and sent on their way westbound for the London docks. Clouds obscured the sky above, but they did not diminish a familiar but ominous throbbing and droning that was felt in the chest as much as it was heard in the ear. Almost certainly hundreds of German Junker 88s and Henkel bombers returning east after pounding London… God help those poor buggers in London! But at least in these conditions they would not be dropping mines in the Thames Estuary.

Rolling in the heavy Thames swell HMY *Sheemaun* ploughed on towards her Cliffe Fort berth, Buckie cursing under his breath as the wheel fought his grip. Taff Jones the gunner also swore quietly, the salt spray soaked across the twin Hotchkiss machine guns which would require hours of wiping, cleaning and oiling. As he peered through the windscreen and looked at the dripping guns he saw something grey under the gun mount. It was a pigeon and clearly exhausted. Must be knackered poor thing, somehow, it's landed on the deck, Taff mused to himself. Leaving the shelter of the wheelhouse Taff went forward but the pigeon jittered away from his grasp. Half flapping and half flying it scuttled back down the heaving side-deck and then fluttering through the open wheelhouse door, brushed past Buckie's broad shoulders and down the companionway into the saloon where it perched on the rifle rack, bedraggled and panting.

With the outline of Coal House Fort coming up on the North bank they would now bear South West for Cliffe Fort and their berth. The engines, reliable as ever, were purring smoothly as HMY *Sheemaun* breasting the swells aside, cleaved her way to the jetty. No time now for pigeons. Buckie throttled back on both and HMY *Sheemaun* carrying way nosed up to the jetty. With a short burst of astern on her starboard engine Buckie brought the boat gently alongside port-to. On deck Andy and Taff deftly hurled the mooring warps, lassoed the mooring bollards and made fast. HMY *Sheemaun* lay quietly rolling a little to the swells coming in. Time now to complete the day's patrol, to log the engine hours, strike the ensign at sundown, pump the bilges, refuel, 'water ship' and put on the Hotchkiss cover to protect it from the dew.

Acting Lieutenant Clive Baker RNVR settled himself at the writing desk completing the day's report. Taff below in the hot engine room busied himself checking filters, sump oil, cooling water, belt tightness, battery water and generally wiping down and making sure there was nothing that might come loose in heavy seas. Satisfied with his endeavours Taff heaved himself up into the wheelhouse, closed the engine-room hatch and wiped his hands on some old rags.

Buckie lit the Rippingille® stove burners and started to sort through the WD (War Department) victuals… tins of baked beans… carrots… Spam®[82]… dried egg powder… dried milk… tea… condensed milk… powdered potato… dried peas… tinned butter… dried onions… tinned tomatoes… bags of flour… and there was a little bacon still left, a few bangers, a bag of potatoes and a loaf of bread. Well they were hardly going to starve but this

---

82. A tinned meat product Invented by the American Hormic Food Co in 1937. Millions of tins of SPAM were issued to the Allied Forces in WW2. In a 1970 Monty Python TV sketch a restaurant served Spam (unwanted) in every dish on the menu – it was "Spam, Spam, Spam, Spam…" with everything and many years later un-wanted emails would become known as Spam! Spam is now a national delicacy in South Korea. Some say that Spam is short for Special American Meat – but no one really knows.

was not exactly appetising. Looking aft into the saloon where Lt. Baker was completing the log and where Taff was wiping down the table Buckies' eyes fell on the pigeon. That would do nicely, pan roasted along with a little bacon and sausage, seasoned and served with tatties and peas.

Sitting huddled on the rifle rack its little eyes hooded under little grey lids the pigeon appeared to be asleep. Buckie putting his head around the saloon door whispering his intentions and nodded to Stan to grab the pigeon and pass it to him. Taff who had almost forgotten about the bird took another look at it.

'Hey! That's no ordinary wild pigeon… Look… it's got something on its leg… looks like a little aluminium tube.'

Lt. Baker started up from the table -

'Yes, you're right. That's a National Pigeon Services Homing Pigeon it may have an urgent message. We'll have to get it to the C.O. at once.'

A suitable box was found, the pigeon gently but securely placed inside and Acting Lt. Baker RNVR having scrambled ashore with it, set off at a pace. Half an hour later he returned.

'We were quite right, it was a messenger pigeon that could have come from anywhere, Holland, Germany, France or Belgium. Possibly even from an Allied scout plane or bomber. The C.O. sends his congratulations for bringing it safely ashore with its message.'

Acting Lt. Baker went on to explain to the gaping crew that homing pigeons were an important means of sending wartime messages. He knew of this because his uncle kept homing pigeons and had told him that hundreds of pigeon-lofts up and down the country were involved in the National War Effort. He explained how a pigeon flying at sixty or seventy miles an hour could cover three to five hundred miles or so in a day, depending on the weather and while carrying a tiny canister strapped to its leg. A pigeon would be able to rest and feed itself as it might need. To bring it down was an almost impossible task other than for a predator such as a hawk. Homing pigeons generally flew fast with a definite direction of flight. If you saw just one or perhaps two pigeons flying fast and in a recognisable direction, then most likely a message was being carried. In contrast, wild pigeons tended to gather in loose flocks, sometimes of a hundred or more birds and their flight pattern was usually random. This knowledge was drummed into farmers and agricultural workers so that they could identify the homing pigeon and avoid shooting at it. Our special agents behind enemy lines used pigeons to send messages[83]. Many ships had a pigeon-loft and even some Allied bombers carried with them pigeons in a water-tight basket that could be released in an emergency such as might happen if the bomber came down in the Channel or worse, behind Enemy lines.

Buckie turned down the burners and picked up the tin-opener, the crew ate Spam that evening.

Comment – In 2009 an exhausted homing pigeon landed on *Sheemaun*'s deck as we were cruising in the lower Thames. It then fluttered through the wheelhouse door and down the companionway into the saloon where it perched on a shelf. It seems that *Sheemaun*'s wheelhouse and open door can easily be mistaken by a pigeon for its pigeon loft!

---

83. The messages were written in a code which enabled information to be sent with the minimum of characters. However, a minimum of two pigeons were needed. One pigeon carried the alphabet for a specific code and the other pigeon carried the encrypted code message. Two back-up pigeons might be used as well so a single message could require four pigeons. The BBC's John Maguire reported on 26/12/12 that a message had been found on the remains of a WW2 pigeon -…DHFP FOVFN WYYND CMPNW… etc. Attempts to de-cipher it without the corresponding Alphabet Code have so far failed.

1941

HMS *Stork* Makes a U-Boat Kill
19th December

'O voyagers, O seamen,
You, who came to port, and you whose bodies
Will suffer the trial and the judgement of the sea
Or whatever event, this is your real destination'

T. S. Eliot

Heading north at a point midway between the Azores and Lisbon, convoy HG76 consisting of twenty-two ships was homeward bound from Gibraltar escorted by the armed sloops HMS *Deptford* and HMS *Stork* and seven corvettes with support of the aircraft-carrier HMS *Audacity* and the destroyers HMS *Exmoor*, HMS *Blankney* and HMS *Stanley*. The escorts did their best to fight off repeated attacks by a pack of nine U-boats. Over ten days four U-boats had been sunk variously by the efforts of the escorts and aircraft from HMS *Audacity* although at the cost of one aircraft lost.

Now with six U-Boats stalking the convoy, on the night of December 19th some 330 miles West of Lisbon at 04.15 hours, struck by two torpedoes the destroyer HMS *Stanley* suddenly exploded and quickly went down. The weak moon must have been just enough to outline a ship sufficiently for a luckily positioned U-Boat to take aim at it. Almost immediately the escort vessels responded by firing 'Snowflake' rockets into the sky. The 'Snowflake' rocket was designed to explode at height of around 1,200 feet (365 m) and release a 300,000-candlepower magnesium flare which as it descended slowly on a parachute would brilliantly illuminate the area below and for a third of a mile (0.48 km) around.

There, exposed in the harsh magnesium glare, starkly revealed, lying low on the surface with its decks being washed over by the waves, lay the menacing low outline of the U-574 commanded by 27-year-old Oberleutnant Dietrich Gengelbach. The officers on the conning tower of the U-574 were effectively blinded and knew it would be only moments before salvos of shells came their way. The U-Boat's siren sounded... Alaarm... alaarm... alaaarmm... True to well-honed discipline and practice, almost as the orders for a crash dive were being shouted, the buoyancy tanks of the U-574 were being blown. Oberleutnant Gengelbach and his officers scrambled down from the conning tower into the U-Boat's control centre slamming shut and securing the hatch after them. The U-574 quickly sank under the waves as the powerful electric motors cut in. However, once 'in the cellar' as it was termed her submerged speed would be at most 7 knots (13 kph) and her dived range was limited.

On the bridge of HMS *Stork* and with good ASDIC echoes pinging back from the submerged U-574, Captain 'Johnnie' Walker[84] would again live up to his reputation of being Britain's ace 'U-Boat Killer'. At his side was Lieutenant 'Peter' Gray RN. Two depth charge runs were ordered to be made over the U-Boat's estimated location. The first run at 15 knots when five depth charges were dropped set to 50 feet (15.24 m). The second run was at full speed. This time ten depth charges were dropped set at 50 and 140 feet (42.6m.)

Deep below the surface all the crew in U-574 could do was hold their breath in fear as the sound above of pounding propellers became a crescendo. Then they were subjected to the deafening thunder and crashes of the depth charges. The U-574

84. Captain Walker's Old Boy's Association 1938 – 1945 held their last Re- union on Saturday 10th July 2004 at the Pier Head Liverpool.

as taken in a giant's hand was smashed and thrown about, lights faded and went out, machinery and equipment was dislodged and then the fearful sound of hissing and gushing water pervaded the silence. The flickering emergency lights soon revealed that the U-574 had been severely shaken and damaged. Her pressure hull was cracked and leaking, the starboard electric motor had burned out and was on fire and the mountings of the port one had been badly damaged.

Recognising the hopelessness of their situation, Oberleutnant Gengelbach had decided against surrender and had instead taken the decision to go down 'Bravely and Honourably' with his crew. Engineer Oberleutnant Laurenz however refused to countenance this and drew his 7.65 Mauser pistole. He had reported the severe electrical and hull damage to his Captain but had also reported that both diesel engines were unimpaired and there was still compressed air available. The battle of wills was resolved when Oberleutnant Genglebach relented and ordered the U-Boat to be surfaced. Although badly damaged and no longer capable of operating submerged, her diesel engines were unimpaired and the propeller shafts intact. When on the surface the U-574 could not be pinpointed by the warships' ASDIC. It would be dark and while the enemy would of course fire flares to illuminate the area, with a moderately heavy sea running the slim outline of the U-574 speeding away at 17 knots would make a difficult target. Gengelbach agreed that there was still the chance of making a run-for-it. He ordered the tanks to be blown. But when the U-574 surfaced, to their utter horror it was found that the rudder was jammed, and all the U-Boat could do was make a circle around to port.

Up on the bridge of HMS *Stork*, Captain Walker and 1st Officer 'Peter' Gray, being quite unaware that this strange manoeuvre was due to a jammed rudder, were now faced by the puzzle of a surfaced U-Boat racing at close to 17 knots in a wide circle but too close for the Stork's guns to be depressed low enough to bear. It was soon apparent that a moment would come when at a critical tangent of the circle the U-574's deadly bow torpedo tubes would be aimed directly at HMS *Stork*! Captain Walker barked an order that the helmsman must match the U-Boat's turning circle. A tense game of 'Dance Macabre' now ensued with HMS Stork and the U-574 circling together. At almost full speed HMS *Stork* was only just able to keep abreast of the sleek and powerful U-Boat. The two warships circled each other in the flickering dazzle of the magnesium flares.

From the perspective of Captain Walker and 1st Officer Gray on the bridge of HMS *Stork* there was every indication that the U-574 was still very much a fighting vessel. But after some three complete circles the U-574 stopped and lay rolling in the seas. Men could be seen clambering onto the deck and there was real concern that the U-Boat's gun would be brought into action. Unable to depress their guns low enough to target the U-Boat the officers and gun-crews on HMS *Stork* were limited to impotently shaking their fists and shouting abuse.

Gasping in the foul air as he waded through the pungent swirling mix of oil and water down in the bowels of U-574, Oberleutnant Laurenz was opening the sea cocks and valves in order to scuttle the U-Boat; he then shot himself. Commanding Officer Oberleutnant Gengelbach who had also decided to remain and to go honourably to his grave with the U-Boat withdrew to his cabin and lay on his bunk to await the inevitable finality which would be on him in only minutes, but which must have felt as a lifetime.

Meanwhile up above in the fresh cold spray driven air on the bridge of HMS *Stork* Captain 'Johnnie' Walker and his First Officer 'Peter' Gray surveyed the grim scene while deciding what the next move should be, quite unaware of the tense and final life and death drama that had been played out down there in the

U-574 with its hopelessly jammed rudder, the dead and dying and its sea-cocks open to the chill Atlantic waters. 'Peter' Gray then raced out onto the bridge and heaving a Lewis machine-gun onto the bridge coaming and aimed a withering hail of .303 (7.9mm) bullets into the conning tower of the U-Boat. Captain Walker shouted across to his First Officer -

'We'll ram them now Number One... better hold tight.'

The helmsman was given orders to swing HMS *Stork* away from the U-574 and then to come back on a course to ram. Orders were shouted to secured shut all water-tight compartments. Moments later one thousand two hundred tons of HMS *Stork* juddered as her steel stem bit into five hundred tons of U-Boat on its starboard quarter just for'ard of the conning tower. Spent Lewis gun shell cases rolled and clattered up against the bridge deck weather shield. The U-574 shuddered and rolling over was held for a moment caught on the ASDIC dome which protruded forward beneath the bow stem of HMS *Stork*, then with loud creaking and grinding sounds the U-574 rolled free, a deep gash now visible in the mid-starboard ballast tank. Captain Walker gave orders for a pattern of depth charges set 'shallow' to be fired as HMS *Stork* carried way on past the U-Boat. A series of thunderous impacts shook HMS *Stork* as U-574 disappeared under the welter of huge geysers of water flying skywards, the heaving cascades streaming and sparkling rainbows in the harsh magnesium flare light. Captain Walker and his First Officer exchanged glances. Grim smiles of satisfaction could not be supressed, but this was not a time for exaltation and celebration, this was war, deadly war but both men knew that below them were terrified fellow sailors who also had been obeying their orders. Below them were sons, brothers, sweet-hearts and husbands never to be seen again.

With HMS *Stork* now hove-to close by the fatally damaged and wallowing U-boat, First Officer 'Peter' Gray scrambled down into the ship's boat that had been quickly lowered and was taken across to the sinking U-Boat. His highly dangerous task was to get into the U-Boat's conning tower and down into the control room, seize whatever papers and documents might still be there and then get out quickly before the U-Boat finally went down.

Clambering up to the slippery and listing conning tower was a difficult exercise even for the fit 'Peter' Gray. With pistol in hand he tumbled down into the devastated control room almost choking on the foul air that greeted him, air tinged with a distinctive smell that he knew could only have come from a recently discharged firearm. From deep below came the ominous gurgling and swishing sound of water, as the U-Boat rolled sluggishly in the swell, she was sinking fast.

Grabbing whatever documents and books he could reach, including a wooden box containing a sextant and then burdened as he was, 'Peter' Gray scrambled up from the U-Boat interior, clambered down from the conning tower and tumbled back into the waiting tender. The coxswain gunned the engine full astern and they pulled clear of the U-574 just as the cold Atlantic waters began to close over its decks for the last time. Out of a crew of 43 only 5 men from the U-boat survived to be plucked from the sea and only twenty-five survivors from the crew of 173 on HMS *Stanley* were found alive with one more to die from his injuries the following day. Lieutenant 'Peter' Gray was later awarded the Distinguished Service Cross for his actions.

The sextant proved to be a magnificent Carl Plath Kreigsmarine sextant, stamped with the Kreigsmarine Eagle and Swastika emblem, its serial number and that it had been made in Hamburg. Plath sextants and navigational instruments enjoyed a world-wide reputation for quality and accuracy. This

Greigsmarine sextant along with its poignant memories would come to be treasured by Lieutenant 'Peter' Gray. It would later accompany him when he transferred to others of His Majesty's warships and as his naval career progressed. Scientific instruments of course have no political or sovereign bias, but ironically its superb qualities when used to check future navigational positions would bring its readings to bear with a disadvantage against other vessels of Hitler's Kreigsmarine!

The Karl Plath Sextant retrieved by Lt 'Peter' Gray RN from the sinking U- 574. These two photographs by courtesy of Nicholas Gray,[85] son of the late Rear Admiral 'Peter' Gray CB. DSC. Nicholas Gray kindly demonstrated the sextant to me.

Seventy-eight years later, one can but shudder as one imagines the scene in the U-574. Oberleutnant Genglebach exhausted and finally defeated and dejected, but still too proud to give himself up or too afraid to bear the shame of surrender; lay himself down on his damp smelly bunk with those tenderly cherished family photographs close-by, mostly now with smashed glass and stains.

---

85. Nicholas Gray in his youth cruised with his father on *Sheemaun*. Nicholas is known for his sea-faring books. 'Last Voyages' and 'Astronauts of Cape Horn'. That Plath sextant has safely guided both Admiral Gray and his son Nicholas over many thousands of miles of the world's oceans.

The terrible noises around him of grinding metal, concussions and shouts, bilge-pumps throbbing uselessly as the in-flooding Atlantic waters swirled ever deeper above the deck plates. He was no longer the Kapitan of anything save for a few more minutes his sinking steel coffin. Did he see himself as a brave hero? Did he finally come to see himself as just one more statistic amongst the hundreds of those others young men, many of whose deaths he had been responsible for as they were blown to smithereens, concussed, burned alive and otherwise sent to their drowning, choking deaths? Did he finally feel it had all been worth it or did he have last minute doubts? Did he have doubts about his tyrannical Fuhrer? Did he have reflections about the futility and ghastliness of war? How terrifying it must have been as the cold oily waters closed over his face and he could no longer hold his breath? Did he have a last-minute panic and regret that he had not scrambled up that ladder to the open air?

Probably he took the quick way of ending the impossible and ghastly situational experience he found himself in - with the help of his 7.65 mm Mauser.

We will never know.

The time would come when in his retirement 'Peter' Gray, by then Rear Admiral Gray CB, DSC, would come to own and widely cruise in a little ship called *Sheemaun* and the sextant would accompany him.

Background reading –
Uboat.net. U-Boat Archive - Interrogation of Survivors of U 574. Record provided by Tony Cooper and Roger Griffiths. Daily Telegraph - Obituary of Rear Admiral G.T.S. (Peter) Gray CB. DSC. Personal communication - From Nicholas Gray son of the late Admiral Gray.
Nicholas Gray crewed extensively with his father on *Sheemaun* in the 60s and 70s.

1941

Christmas Day at Hole Haven

'And in despair I bowed my head:
There is no peace on earth, I said
For hate is strong, and mocks the song
Of peace on earth, goodwill to men.'

Henry Wadsworth Longfellow

B ut now it was cold, damp and dull. A dense fog swirled
slowly across the water as the world around HMY *Sheemaun*
put on its own peep-show. One moment all that was visible
would be the pontoon and the bow of the vessel aft and the
stern of the vessel forward of them. Then a sudden wafting
clearance would reveal other nearby vessels variously berthed
and moored close nearby, their masts nodding slowly and their
mooring chains occasionally rumbling. All the rigging, the guns
and decks were dripping with condensation. Oily water slurped
against the hull leaving a foul gunge, wafts of tar and chemical
smells drifted down from the Coryton oil refinery just upwind
to the west, those bulky storage tanks blatantly advertising themselves as a very tempting target for Hitler's bombers. For once
though this Thames 'Pea-Souper' brought a welcome respite as
there could be no river traffic and Hitler's planes would have
to wait for better raiding conditions. The great river was quiet,
and no wailing air-raid alarms could be heard. Although 'on
duty' there was no way that HMY *Sheemaun* would be able to
put out in these conditions and which looked set for a day or
more. Skipper Buckie and his crew with an eye to the weather
had made some 'contingency seasonal preparations'. Stanley and
Taff who had been granted Christmas leave would be with their

families, so their duties had been taken on by fellow RNVR servicemen, 'Chalky' White and Paddy Doherty whose usual vessel was undergoing maintenance.

A sprig of evergreen had been put over the compass in the wheelhouse and a few coloured paper cut-outs were hung up in the saloon. They had some non-regulation bottles of beer aboard and a flagon of very non-regulation Essex rough cider. 'Chalky' had bagged a couple of duck. Tim's wife had made a fruit pie[86] well soaked with a rum ration that one of the observer barge crew hadn't wanted and 'Paddy' had brought his tin whistle. Potatoes, carrots and swedes were not in short supply there on the Essex farm-land shore. The Rippingille® stove had been lit and well warmed up and while the duck roasted in the oven and the vegetables steamed in the pot, the crew took it in turns to telephone home from the 'Press button **A** then Press button **B**' of the black coin-box in the red GPO[87] kiosk just over the sea wall down by the historic Lobster Smack Inn.

Buckie returned with a solemn face. He had met up with one of the crew of a sister patrol boat who had just lost a relative. Yesterday the town of Shoeburyness had been bombed. From HMY *Sheemaun* they had seen the vapour trails of the German bombers up high and of their escorting Messerschmitt's and the attacking spitfires, even at that distance they had heard bark of cannons, the crackling of machine guns and the thud, thud, thud of the anti-aircraft guns but there had been several heavy explosions that had reverberated in the solid hull of HMY *Sheemaun* almost before they could be heard. They knew that those heavy explosions could have only resulted from large bomb

---

86. Government Wartime recipe No 168 – Baked Fruit Pie – Fresh or bottled fruit, 4 slices stale bread, 3 tablespoons water, I tablespoon sugar. This could be improved by adding extra fruit and bread and for those who could get it, some naval rum.

87. The General Post Office – Under the Post Office Act 1969 the office of Post Master General would be discontinued.

or mine strikes. But then out in the Estuary their hands had been full enough with the business of chasing after and checking the many barges, small coasters and the occasional fishing boat that were daily transiting between the East Coast and the Thames, relieving the Observation Barge crews and delivering mail. Buckie explained that on Saturday 20th and Sunday 21st Hitler's bombers had dropped land-mines over Shoeburyness. These were fiendish devices loaded with between 1000 lbs (453.5 Kg) and 2000 lbs plus of high explosive. The ordinary high explosive bomb which plunging at hundreds of miles an hour would generally bury itself deeply in the ground, as a result, its explosive blast would make a large crater and most of the blast would go skywards. In contrast the 'Landmine' had a parachute and was set to detonate at or just above ground level. The blast going sideways would totally flatten buildings for hundreds of yards around. It would blow off rooves and blow in windows for up to half a mile away and cause considerable injury and loss of life. A lot of damage had been done and with many injured. There were also reports of more parachute mines having been dropped in the estuary. They would be either magnetic mines or acoustic or both. These would now have to be located and dealt with as soon as conditions allowed.

Berthed nearby was a fellow Patrol Boat *Navigator*. Like HMY *Sheemaun* the *Navigator* had also been launched in 1935 and she had originally been named *Aberdonia* but some reason the Admiralty had seen fit to change her name when she was requisitioned for patrol services. At forty-eight feet in length she was a little longer than HMY *Sheemaun* but built by Messrs Thorneycroft Ltd at Hampton-on Thames as a river/estuary cruiser she was of much lighter construction at twenty tons. HMY *Sheemaun* lurched slightly as boots scuffed on the deck.

'Permission to come aboard?'

Buckie clambered up the companion way into the wheel-house and found Jim the skipper of *Navigator* and his mate Pete grinning through the windscreen -

'Yes... ye 're welcome aboard lads, come and join us.'

Jim and Pete followed Buckie down into the saloon and from a canvass bag pulled out a stone flagon of Kent scrumpy[88], a fresh crisp dumpy loaf and some cheese. Traffic on the river Thames after dark was not only forbidden but under the Emergency Powers (Defence) War Act 1939 any vessel seen underway after dark would risk being fired on and that duty of interception fell also to the armed boats of the Auxiliary Patrol Service. However, tonight the rolling fog would ensure that nothing could move so they might as well make the best of it. The six men settled themselves comfortably around the saloon table. Naturally, given the madness and atrociousness of this war families and friends were foremost on everyone's mind. Glasses were raised and Andy, jokingly, proposed a toast.

'To Sweethearts and Wives - May they never meet'

For which paltry effort at humour he received a withering scowl from skipper Buckie. Glasses were again raised, this time solemnly-

'To our wives and families and to all our fellow countrymen fighting in this dreadful war wherever they might be ... may it soon end with us the Allies victorious.'

As volunteers with previous yachting experience they had all given up their various trades and occupations and all had been through the necessary training course for their roles in the

88. A strongly flavoured cider.

Royal Naval Auxiliary Patrol Service. Back on shore everyone's family had been in some way affected. Some families had been evacuated to safer towns and villages in the West and North of the country. Cousins and brothers had been called up and were now on active service abroad. Some had lost their homes and businesses to Hitler's bombs. Several families they knew of personally had received that dreaded telegram informing that a loved one was missing or missing believed killed.

Out on the Thames Estuary they were experiencing almost hourly reminders of the awful conflict. Merchant ships would come in through the defence boom to gather a dozen or more at a time for re-fuelling and to receive orders, many of them damaged from aircraft attack and some near to sinking. All with tales of how they had survived while other vessels in their convoys had been sunk by U-Boat torpedo attack or air attack and usually with loss of life. A steady flow of naval vessels, corvettes, destroyers, mine-sweepers and armed tugs trafficked in and out from Sheerness and Queenborough harbours. Almost daily there would be strafing and bombing by German fighters and bombers and whenever the weather and moon was propitious German bombers; power gliders and fast E-Boats would lay their deadly magnetic and acoustic mines. Merchant ships with their precious cargoes could not risk sailing up to London or to return down-river until the latest 'sowings' of mines had been located and dealt with. There was much talk about the tricky navigation conditions in a wide river with strong tides, and with many obstructions and dangerous sandbanks that at low tide were exposed or lurked just under the surface.

A half cable east of them was the Lobster Smack Inn which Andy had visited a few weeks earlier. He described how having rowed across to the earthen flood defence dyke and tied up the tender, he had been amazed to find the roof of the inn so far below the level of the top of the dyke, confirming that a major part of Canvey Island was in fact well below sea-level ...

'They only serve half- pints... it's regulations they say, pints aren't allowed but it's a lovely old pub, very historic and there's a nice warm log fire.'

Still smarting from Buckie's withering scowl, Andy feeling a need to redeem himself, went on to explain...

'They reckon Charles Dickens wrote about it in Great Expectations, in that part where Pip, Madgwick, Herbert and Startop rowed down tide from the Temple steps in London intending to catch a steamer to the Continent. Anyway, they'd arrived about level with where we are now, the tide had just turned, and it was getting dark. They thought they were lost but seeing a roof and a light, they rowed towards it, put the boat ashore and found the light was from a pub window. That pub could only have been the Lobster Smack Inn, people reckon it's over six-hundred years old. Mind you, the sea wall then was nothing like as high as it is now and there weren't miles of barbed wire set all along it.'

Andy, whose home town was nearby Basildon, then recalled how his history teacher had loaned him some books and persuaded him to write an essay on Canvey Island. In an amateur way he had been interested in history ever since -

'Yes, you're right Pete, the whole place reeks of history. About three hundred years ago a Dutch fleet sailed into Hole Haven creek and plundered the local farms. In those days the Dutch and English were at war with each other because both competed for the same sea-trade, but the low-lying Canvey Island often flooded and later when the two countries were at peace the Canvey Island farmers invited the Dutch engineer Cornelius Vermuyden[89] to drain the land and build a sea wall or dyke. In return the Dutch could have a third of the land they reclaimed from the sea. Over many years since, the dyke has been built higher and higher and as we can see is now well above the roof of the Lobster Smack Inn. There are still some Dutch cottages and some of the street names are Dutch such as Haarlem Road and even now some of the locals have Dutch names.'

Buckie, fascinated by what Andy was relating momentarily stopped chewing...

'Well... ye would'na half credit that... good on ye Andy... just goes tae show there's more to life than this bloody war... An' talking about history I reckon we're in the middle of it ourselves right now... is there any o' tha' fruit pie left?'

Pete glanced through the porthole...

'It's still a 'pea-souper' out there... we'll not be seeing any action tomorrow I reckon... It won't be foggy out in the Atlantic though... I wonder how those poor buggers in the Atlantic and Arctic convoys are managing...?'

---

89. Named after the famous engineer, the Cornelius Vermuyden School on Canvey Island was opened in 2012

Time-Line –

- There was plenty of seasonal wild and farmed fruit available to those who lived in the countryside, but sugar was strictly rationed. Fruit was bottled into Kilner jars and a Camden preserving tablet added. The tablet released sulphur dioxide which killed the yeasts and bacteria so saving both on sugar and the fuel to boil the fruit!

1942

HMS *Stork* and HMS *Vetch*
Another U-Boat kill

'Also pray for those who were in ships, and
Ended their voyage on the sand, in the sea s' lips
Or in the dark throat which will not reject them
Or wherever cannot reach them the sound of the sea bell's
Perpetual angelus'

T.S. Eliot

Convoy OG 82 consisting of seventeen ships bound for
Gibraltar was out in the Atlantic heading south a few
hundred miles west of Ireland. The escorting warships were
under command of the legendary 'U-Boat Killer' Commander
F. J. 'Johnnie' Walker RN commanded the sloop HMS *Stork*
with his First Officer 'Peter' Gray and supported by the corvettes
HMS *Penstemon* and HMS *Convolvulus*.

Meanwhile on March 30th the U-252 had set off on patrol from
Helgoland under command of Kapitanleutnant Kai Lerchen.
His first assignment had been his secret voyage to Iceland where
on April 6th he put ashore the German espionage agent Ib Riis.
That mission having been successfully accomplished, he was
then ordered to head south for the eastern Atlantic area used
by the Allied convoys. Only three days out from Iceland on
April 9th Lerchen had sighted what was to be his first 'Kill'.
It was the Norwegian merchant ship *Fanefjeld* of 1,335 tons
carrying a cargo of salt and the ship was alone. The U-252 had
surfaced and one torpedo was all that was required. The defenceless *Fanefjeld* sank quickly with the total loss of all aboard. Her
Captain Haakon Naess, his crew of twenty-one, her Icelandic

Pilot and a civilian British passenger all went to the bottom. For Lerchen who had just celebrated his thirty-first birthday it was a good omen and he had high hopes of adding to his list of Allied shipping 'Kills'. Patrolling on the surface at night allowed him to keep the U-252's batteries fully charged and the U-Boat well ventilated. Under diesel power she could make seventeen and a half knots (just over 20 mph) but was limited to about 5 knots when submerged and running on batteries. He planned to join up with one of the eastern Atlantic U-Boat 'Wolf Packs' or to do whatever it might be that Admiral Doenitz would order. There was always the chance that a lone merchant vessel or better still a convoy might be detected by careful observation and use of the sensitive hydrophones. In the right conditions a ship, silhouetted by moonlight made an easy target to be sent to the bottom of the ocean. His birthday now quite forgotten, Kapitanleutnant Kai Lerchen scanned ahead into the darkness, for some hours now, his hydrophone operator had been reporting the ever-closer sound of a convoy which must be almost within striking distance.

That night it was dark, but HMS *Vetch* was equipped with the new 10 cm Type 271 centimetric radar and which had revealed an echo at 7,500 yards range. Lt K.M.B. Menzies RN on HMS *Vetch* discretely signalled news of the contact to his Commanding Officer on HMS *Stork*, then calling for 'Full Steam Ahead' and with the engineers taking her triple expansion engine to its limits Lieutenant Menzies raced HMS *Vetch* at 16 knots in the direction of the echo. He ordered 'Snowflake' rockets to be fired. Moments later a dazzling display of burning magnesium revealed a low grey outline on the sea ahead of them, just where the radar was pin-pointing an echo. It was the U-252! With her bow wave creaming as she raced towards the U-Boat HMS *Vetch* opened up with her main armament of 4-inch naval guns and her 2-pounder gun as the target came on bearing, but the warship was pitching and rolling which made accurate aiming almost impossible.

For those young Kreigsmariners on the U-252 conning tower the blackness of night suddenly burst into blinding light as the flares above slowly descended on their parachutes. Kapitanleutnant Kai Lerchen, quite unaware of the 'all-seeing radar' now carried by the Corvette HMS *Vetch*, had been taken completely by surprise. The close presence of several Allied warships – feindfahrts - and a substantial convoy was also revealed but within seconds the seas around U-252 began to erupt huge fountains as shells from the corvette struck close-by ... too close. Lerchen just had time to aim his U-Boat at the fast approaching corvette and fire off two torpedoes, then there was no other option but to crash-dive. *'Alaarrmm... alaarrm ...alaarrm'* screamed out from the speaker system as the U-252 made an emergency crash-dive. But there was no comforting distant explosion, the torpedoes had missed and now the warships' thrashing propellers could be heard above coming louder and louder.

On the bridge of HMS *Stork*, gripping the cold steel coaming to steady themselves, Commander Frederick 'Johnnie' Walker RN and First Officer 'Peter' Gray RN peered through their binoculars into the harsh magnesium-lit theatre of war ahead. At her full speed of 18.5 knots (just over 21 mph) HMS *Stork* would join up with HMS *Vetch* in less than ten minutes. Meanwhile the latest echo-location equipment on HMS *Vetch* plotted an accurate contact with the submerged U-252. Between them the two warships in coordination, dropped a spread of 45 depth charges each with 300 lbs (136 Kg) of high explosive.

Below them the hunter-killers were now the hunted. Forty-four fit young German men clenched their sweating hands in fear and hardly dared to breath. This was to be their terrifying first and last experience of blechkoller, the much-feared claustrophobic hysteria so graphically reported by those few U-Boot Fahrers (submariners) who had survived the terrible ordeal of being depth charged. Now for those men, the crew of the U-252 trapped deep under the waves down in the 'cellar', this most dreadful experience of blechkoller was on them and all around them. A terminal experience, that for them, and mercifully, would only be experienced for seconds.[90]

As the boiling waters subsided HMS *Stork* and HMS *Vetch* hove to and a boat was lowered. The ships' searchlights were directed on the area while a search was made for survivors but the 796 tons of the U-252 along with her Kapitan and crew of 43 had been pulverised. All that was found was a mess of 'oil, wood, blood and guts and a human heart and lungs, complete but penetrated by splinters'[91] which were retained by the medical officer of HMS *Stork* and preserved for later research.

90. In WW2, of the 40,000 brave young German sailors who served in Hitler's ill-fated Untersee Boot fleet, 28,000 were killed. That's almost three out of every four men.

91. This detail per the late Clay Blair's book - *'Hitler's U-Boat War'* 1986

1942

A Visitor Book is purchased
March

'You never write your signature for yourself,
it's always for other people'

M. Dresbold

It opened evenly and comfortably in the hand, weighed one
and a half pounds and the solid covers were made of leather
bound fibreboard. The pages, lightly ruled and cream coloured,
were of dense linen rich paper neatly stitched with best waxed
linen thread and with gold leaf finishing. At nine and a half
inches by seven and a quarter and one inch thick it was a perfect
Visitors Book, hand crafted to last for years and would hopefully see out this awful war. Lt. Cmdr. 'Peter' Gray DSC RN
duly paid the Tyneside bookseller the agreed price of one pound
seven shillings and sixpence[92], put the book into his carrycase
and hailed a cab to take him to the docks where his ship, the
Hunt Class destroyer HMS *Badsworth* was nearing completion
of major repairs. She had suffered severe damage at Malta when
a huge hole had been blown in her bow by a mine.

Peter Gray had for some time desired to have a 'Visitors
Book'[93]. A book that he would keep close by him and a book
that as time and circumstances granted, would come to record
the names and signatures of those who would visit and receive
hospitality on whatever vessel he might at the time be serving.
And so, when only a few days later the Commanding Officer
of HMS *Badsworth* entertained some fellow officers. Peter Gray

---

92. At 2017 values that would be £60!

93. It was usual for the captains of Royal Navy ships to carry a visitor book.

produced his Visitor Book having written at the top of the first page the heading -

HMS *Badsworth*

The first signatures entered on the third of March 1942 were –

Eng. Rear Adm. John Wildish -	*Staff Adml. WA Liverpool*
Cmdr. John Falcon Steward -	*HMS Tenacious*
Reg. C.F. Depward -	*Merchant Navy. N.S.Dept. Bath.*

Over future years, the page headings would record the various naval vessels on which 'Peter' Gray came to serve and later, in his retirement years came to own. There would follow a series of several hundreds of signatures until the twenty ninth of September nineteen hundred and ninety-one. Amongst those hundreds of signatures would be found those of the Lord

Hailsham (First Sealord), the Governor of Malta, the Prince of Russia, Lord Brougham, various Admirals, Commanders, Captains, Naval Attaches, celebrities such as 'Professor' Jimmy Edwards BBC broadcaster and comedian etc. etc., and amongst the list of distinguished vessels which would proudly carry this 'Visitors Book' - would one day be a small and historic wooden boat –

Sheemaun

Time-line –

- On Tuesday March 3rd - One hundred and seventy-three civilians lost their lives at Bethnal Green Underground Station which was being used as a bomb shelter.

- At the same time, two hundred and thirty-five Allied planes bombed the Paris factory of Renault which with France under Hitler's domination was supplying hundreds of lorries to Hitler's forces.

- In Singapore the Japanese were holding 80,000 British, Indian and Australian prisoners. Japanese fighter aircraft machine gunned the Australian Town of Broome killing 88 people.

- December 7th The Japanese Navy Air Service bombed Pearl Harbour inflicting huge losses on the American Fleet.

- December 11th The United States of America declared War on Germany.

1942

A lucky 'Visitor' signs the book during an Arctic Sea Battle
May 3rd

'Out of a fired ship, which by no way
But drowning could be rescued by the flame,
Some men leap'd forth, and ever as they came
Near the foe's ships, did by their shot decay,
So all were lost, which in the ship were found,
They in the sea being burnt,
they in the burnt ship drowned.'

John Dunne 16th Century

Convoy PQ15 consisting of twenty-five merchant steamships was on voyage from Iceland to Murmansk with essential supplies, fuel, ammunition and the spare parts desperately needed on the Russian Front in the fight against Hitler's Axis Forces. That this was an important convoy was reflected by the accompanying massively armed escort of twenty-five warships. An escort which included the Battleship USS Washington, the Aircraft Carrier HMS *Victorious*, several cruisers, numbers of destroyers, smaller armed escorts, armed trawlers and four submarines! Among the merchant ships were the SS *Jutland* of 6,153 tons laden with ammunition and military stores, the SS *Botavon* and the SS *Cape Corso* of 2,388 tons commanded by Capt. W.C. Montgomery, and among the escorting warships and destroyers was HMS *Badsworth* commanded by 'Peter' Gray.

Inevitably this massive but heavily defended convoy of more than fifty ships attracted the serious attention of Hitler's Kriegsmarine U-Boats, his Luftwaffe Junkers 88 bombers and his newly formed geschwader of Heinkel torpedo bombers. Two hundred and fifty miles South West of Bear Island in the Barents Sea the heaving waters were bitterly cold. Ice encrusted the ship's railings, decks and rigging causing concern about the stability of the vessels. Then on the 2nd May Convoy PQ15 came under heavy attack from above by six Junkers 88 bombers combined with attack from below the surface by deadly U-Boats. However, the capacity of so many escort vessels to throw up a formidable and effective anti-aircraft (ack-ack) barrage resulted in one Junkers being shot down and forced the remaining Junkers to back off and take a largely defensive and reconnaissance role.

At close to midnight in the grey Arctic half-light the visibility was variable to about four miles. Captain Harvey Crombie DSO. RN[94]. Commander of HMS Bramble described[95] how six enemy aircraft flew in low and dropped torpedoes. A hail of Ack-ack fire from the escorts resulted in two aircraft being hit, one crashing in flames and the other almost certainly went down later. Some of the torpedoes however found their targets. The SS *Botavon*, SS *Jutland* and the *Cape Corso* were all hit. The SS *Jutland* crippled and rolling in the seas, dropped out from the convoy. The *SS Cape Corso* laden with ammunition blew up with the loss of most of her crew. The crippled SS *Botavon* also dropped out of the convoy and began to settle by her bow.

With escorts patrolling and depth-charging the area no further U-Boat threat was evident, and the escorts were able to send in rescue ships. Between them HMS *Badsworth*, HMS *Chiltern* and several armed trawlers rescued a hundred and thirty-seven survivors. HMS *Badsworth* alone taking aboard from the SS *Jutland* eight passengers, fifty-three crew and her Master John Henderson MN.

---

94. Distinguished Service Order. Royal Navy.

95. Letter of 8th May 1942 – Ref ADM 199/721

Captain Crombie recorded that aircraft could be heard circling above the clouds but observed –

'They appeared frightened of coming through. One Ju88 was shot down. No further air attacks took place'.

Of the SS *Botavon* Captain Crombie wrote –

'I ordered *Badsworth* to sink her by gunfire.'

On the bridge of HMS *Badsworth* Captain Crombie's signal was handed to 'Peter' Gray. The order to sink the SS *Botavon* came as no great surprise but it was a painful and distasteful matter for one of His Majesty's destroyers to be ordered to fire on a British vessel flying the red ensign. The vessel had been evacuated and would probably sink in time, but the convoy had to continue its voyage and they could not allow the risk that the enemy might be able to seize the SS *Botavon* and benefit from its cargo. Furthermore, to sink a substantial vessel by gunfire alone was no easy matter. HMS *Badsworth's* main armament of Mk XVI quick-fire naval guns was readied. Each capable of firing 15 rounds/minute and able to project a thirty-eight and a quarter pound (17.35 Kg) high explosive shell almost twenty thousand yards (18,150 m). It would need a half dozen waterline hits to open the poor old *Botavan's* hull to the freezing waters for the last time. From as close a range that would enable good accuracy while not so proximate as to endanger HMS *Badsworth* should the *Botavon* explode violently. All three twin gun turrets were brought to bear and the command was given - 'FIRE'. A broadside of six four-inch naval gun barrels erupted.

Down below in 'Peter' Gray's cabin the Visitors Book tucked in the bookshelf juddered as shock waves from the broadside reverberated through the *Badsworth's* hull. Two seconds later a series of flashes and explosions tore away great shreds of steel from the SS *Botovan*'s water line sending up cascades of water as if in a last salute. It took only a short while for the SS *Botovan* to roll beneath the waves her red ensign defiant to the last. Grim faced, 'Peter' Gray gestured a salute and ordered his helmsman to set course to re-join the convoy.

There in the bitterly cold arctic conditions of the Barents Sea with a large Allied fleet of armed vessels engaged in a life and death battle with shadowing Axis enemy aircraft and U-Boats; any attention to the recording of names in a Visitors Book is the last thing one would expect! Yet there is in 'Peter' Gray's Visitors Book kept carefully on-board HMS *Badsworth*, a signature written on that very date the 3rd May 1942, when the SS *Botovan* went to the bottom of the Arctic Ocean!

John Henry Smith… Stamford Lincs

It was imperative that the convoy[96] carried on to Murmansk, the SS *Jutland* would have to be left to her fate, sinking slowly, abandoned and rolling in the grey seas.

Shadowing Convoy PQ15 was the Kreigsmarine U-251 under command of Kapitan Leutnant Heinrich Timm. Now on her third wartime patrol, the U-251 displaced 769 tons when surfaced and had only been launched ten months earlier. With her diesel engines she could make almost 18 knots (33.3 kmh) – easily fast enough to overtake the slow convoy, but submerged she had at best a range of 80 miles at only 4 knots. Convoy PQ15 however was strongly defended. Her escorts carried depth charges and had the benefit of ASDIC with which a submerged U-Boat could be detected and located but anyway while submerged there was no way the U-Boat could overtake the convoy. The escorting warships also had the benefit of radar accurate enough to detect and range even a periscope

Down under the bitterly cold waves in the control station of U-251 Heinrich Timm could hardly believe his luck when at periscope depth he spotted the lone SS *Jutland*. This was a decent sized vessel which his records put at over six thousand tons, and with no escort vessels in sight. Aware of the earlier airborne torpedo attack on Convoy PQ15 Kapitan Leutnant Timm felt this was unlikely to be a trap. He ordered U-251 to be surfaced. Finding that the target was not moving greatly simplified the aiming calculations. The order to fire was given,

---

96. My cousin, the late Arthur Pell served as an AB on the HMS *Vindex*, a 'Flatiron' Aircraft Carrier that escorted the Murmansk convoys. As crew hammered and axed away the ice that clung to the ship's superstructure, Arthur had to struggle in sub-zero temperatures to repair and service the fabric covered Fairey Swordfish Biplane torpedo aircraft. The crews on HMS *Vindex* were ever appreciative of the comforting presence of heavily armed escorts such as HMS *Badsworth*.

torpedoes leaped from the bow tubes and sped on their course. From the SS *Jutland* came two flashes and dull explosions with cascades of water. Minutes later she slid under the waves. Feeling well satisfied Kapitan Timm gave orders for the U-251 to head West in the expectancy that he might find another convoy steaming eastwards. If he could be in the right area, then with the U-Boat lying a-hull low on the surface, they would not reflect the underwater ASDIC pings and might get a chance to sink another freighter. There was always the worry that the Allied warships with their centimetric radar might 'see' the U-251[97] but with a moderate sea running and with the hull low in the water, it was quite likely they might escape detection – but lying a-hull meant rolling and pitching which would be very uncomfortable and some crew would be badly seecrank (sea-sick). In the event over the next many months spent patrolling the bitter Northern waters and despite having joined up with organised 'wolf-packs' the U-251 failed to sink any more Allied vessels.

When ashore in Murmansk Port 'Peter' Gray had to intervene at great risk to himself, when a Russian soldier threatened to shoot a British sailor who had given chocolate to a Russian sailor. Fraternising was strictly forbidden by the Russians!

---

97. In July 1945 the U-251 would be blasted to smithereens in a rocket attack by eight fast Mosquito fighter bombers, of the 43 crew only 4 survived. The sunken hull is now a 'Dive Site' just off the Danish Island of Laeso. (u-boat. net).

1942

Madagascar - Operation Ironclad
May 7th

'Chance yoked us, yes. For the rest
It was all desire and capitulation
To it, white flag, hands up and all:
Honourable surrender but complete conquest.'

Steven Payne

The French Colonial Empire which at one time had been spread across the world, was still second only in size and dominion to the vast British Empire. Situated four hundred and fifty miles off the East African coast, and under French Colonial rule; second only to Australia in being the next biggest island on Planet Earth, the huge thousand-mile-long island of Madagascar lay at a geographically strategic location on the shipping routes between Australia, India and the Dutch East Indies, Cape Horn and Great Britain. But, following Hitler's invasion and conquest of France, Madgascar had come under the control of the Vichy[98] French Government. It became urgently necessary from the perspective of the Western Allies that a strategy was produced that would bring Madagascar under allied control – accordingly Operation Ironclad was put into action. One of the warships involved was the light cruiser HMS *Dauntless* on which the Ship's Surgeon was Surgeon Lt. Commander Leslie Gordon Percival Shiers FRCSE RNVR.

British naval and land forces after fierce fighting had largely

---

98. July 1940 – Northern France had surrendered to Hitler's Military control. Per the Franco- German Armistice of July 1940 a 'Vichy' French Government was allowed to govern the southern part of France but was in all essence a 'Puppet' government effectively under Hitler's control.

taken control of the northern part of the huge island, but there remained defiant a Vichy French garrison of some eight thousand men defending the critical deep-water Port of Diego Suarez. The natural harbour of Diego Suarez was so huge that it could have contained the entire British Fleet with space for almost the same again, but this garrison town was still holding out despite now having to face a powerful Royal Naval force that had been assembled at sea just a mile or so off shore. A force that included the battleship HMS *Ramillies*, two aircraft carriers, two cruisers, eleven destroyers, a dozen or more minesweepers, corvettes and auxiliaries.

With the intention of parleying for a bloodless conclusion, the head of this substantial Royal Naval Force, Commanding Officer Rear Admiral Edward Syfert signalled to the Governor of Port Diego Suarez -

'We have arrived as friends, we ask you to surrender so that blood-shed may be avoided.'

But arrogant and defiant, the Governor General Armand Leon Annet refused –

'My honour will not allow me to surrender.'

The next morning Admiral Syfert signalled again but still the Vichy French Governor-General refused to surrender; and so, it was decided to send ashore a negotiating party in a boat flying a white flag and led by Captain Hewitt the Commanding Officer of HMS *Dauntless*. But there was an unexpected difficulty when it came to producing a white flag –

'Well of course Royal Navy Warships didn't carry a white flag... the very thought is preposterous... Admiral Lord Nelson would have had a fit in his grave! But anyway, a white flag now had to be produced… so I suggested they used one of my white operating theatre drapes… this was agreed, and a flag was soon made up and bent on to a pair of wooden oars…'[99]

A Picket Boat was duly despatched with white 'flag' flying but the Vichy French opened fire with a machine gun and the boat was forced to turn back. The Vichy French commander making it clear that it as a matter of honour the Garrison would not surrender without a fight!

In the brief battle that ensued, a shell fired by a Royal Australian Navy destroyer demolished one of the French Garrison stone towers, where on the top of which a French Tricoleur was being run up. The explosion killed the man who was hoisting the Tricoleur and sent out a cloud of flying splinters and stone fragments one of which wounded the French Commander in his arm. Now with Honour satisfied, the French Commander surrendered the garrison and the local hostilities ceased. The wounded Vichy French Governor General was taken aboard HMS *Dauntless* where his wound was treated by the young Acting Surgeon Lieutenant, Leslie Gordon Shiers FRCSE, RNVR[100] who was to recall to me –

'Well he was a stubborn fellow but a decent enough chap at heart… just needed some stitches and dressings… Then after that little palaver we had to sail into the port to establish an administrative authority and set up defences… I thought it was a great honour to be on the leading ship.

---

99. Conversations held in *Sheemaun's* saloon with 'Doc' Shiers as we both relaxed and reminisced over an excellent bottle of the 'Doc's favourite Claret. No one had to drive home afterwards! 'Bob' Shiers' comfortable ketch *Ann Too* was moored only yards away from *Sheemaun*.

100. Fellow of the Royal College of Surgeons Edinburgh. Royal Naval Volunteer Reservist.

Much later I learned that HMS *Dauntless* had been selected to lead the fleet in because as the oldest ship, if she should be sunk by a mine then it would be less of a catastrophe than if a newer ship was sunk!' [101]

Acting Surgeon Lt. Surgeon Leslie Shiers RNVR – who shared with Lt. 'Peter' Gray RN a dislike of his first name, was known as 'Bob' to friends and colleagues or just as 'The Doc' to most others. After the War 'Bob' Shiers set himself up in private practice in London's prestigious Harley Street and then became the inventor of the world's first knee replacement hinge prosthesis. 'Bob' refused to patent his invention as was then fashionable for medical inventions. Instead he freely demonstrated the prosthesis and the necessary surgical technique he had developed, inviting other surgeons to further develop and improve on his invention. He would later become an established and well-known London orthopaedic surgeon and a recognised High Court Expert Witness.

The amazing tapestry being woven in the 'Loom of Time', would in future years come to link together 'Doc' Shiers FRCSE and Rear Admiral 'Peter' Gray CB. DSO. with *Sheemaun*. The 'Doc' too would one day put his hands to *Sheemaun*'s wheel. 'Doc' retained his love of the sea and wooden boats to his dying day.

Sheemaun salutes her old friend 'Doc' Shiers

Time-Line –

- Major Harry Emory Chubb OBE, M.I. Mech. E., had just been appointed Deputy Superintendent at the Hertfordshire Constabulary – an unpaid voluntary post. He would one day come to own *Sheemaun* and sell her on to Vernon Haydon, Proprietor of Branksome Towers Hotel, Dorset.

---

101. In conversation with Bob.

1942

A Maunsell Naval Fort
is towed into the Estuary

'...Built with sweat, and tears, determination
Shall no one try nor succeed to break
Integrity, honour and for all at stake
Lessons learned from painful past
Of enemies who destroy en masse...'

Marinella Marie 2012

June had been a cool month, with a tendency for early-morning mists which burned off as the sun climbed. Across the channel in Europe the war was raging. Across the South of England and over London especially, there were bombing raids on most nights despite the barrage balloons, the batteries of anti-aircraft guns and brave efforts of the defending night fighter pilots. German bombers were still managing to drop mines into the Thames at night, and at any time, day or night, the fast German Schnellboots, or Enemy Boats, would streak across from the French and Dutch coasts and shoot up or torpedo such Allied vessels as they came across, and those E Boats would also lay mines in the shallow waters of the Thames Estuary. They couldn't penetrate the Defence Boom, but their sudden unwelcome appearances in the outer Thames Estuary presented a constant hazard to any Allied vessel be it a warship, a merchantman or just a small coaster or sailing barge.

The Auxiliary Patrol Service boats had received orders that on Saturday 27th that there would be significant tug movements and heavy towing operations. Taking advantage of the ebb-tide on Saturday the 28th a towing of a huge and cumbersome structure would be taken seaward from the Northfleet wharf in North Kent. A clear all-round zone of a cable (200 yards/185 metres) would have to be maintained and a pair of armed auxiliary Patrol vessels were to proceed ahead and two would follow astern of the tow, to ensure that all small craft and shipping complied. In addition, there would be a Royal Naval fast motor gun boat in attendance.

Skipper Buckie of course knew that part of the Thames well. The wharves at Northfleet being on the Kent or southern bank almost opposite the Tilbury Docks on the north bank but this was one of the narrow parts of the tidal Thames, the ebb tide would be sluicing around Stoneness Point to flow North East for a mile, then sluice around Broadness Point picking up even more turbulence as it turned ninety-degrees to flow South-East for a mile down to the Northfleet Reach. There the waters would tend to pile up against the Northfleet Wharf as they were forced through forty-five degrees and be sent East on their way out to sea. Given that this was such a relatively narrow section of the Thames. Any major towing operation setting out from Northfleet could be a tricky exercise. The huge tow would have to be cast off for a departure timed for a half-an hour before high-tide slack-water, that would give the optimal conditions for a difficult manoeuvre and then the ebb tide would set in and assist with the task of getting the huge construction safely out to sea.

HMY *Sheemaun* would have to be on station in good time for the cast-off. Buckie put the chart on the table and picked up the dividers. Northfleet was five miles upstream of Cliffe Fort jetty and HMY *Sheemaun* would make about seven knots with a weakening flood-tide under her of about one knot average. So, they would need to cast-off about forty minutes ahead of high-water time at Northfleet. It was very unlikely that any vessels would be heading up-river against the ebb but small coasters and Thames sailing barges seeking to ride the ebb seaward might set out from small creeks and from any number of anchorages or moorings. The sailing barges however were a nightmare to the Patrol Service because without engines they could be a law to themselves and usually with a surly skipper to deal with, but if a barge had to be towed away, then that was what would be done. HMY *Sheemaun* would not be alone. She was one of the twenty armed Auxiliary Patrol Vessels based in the lower Thames Estuary and today this was a duty she would be sharing with three other Patrol Vessels.

It was Saturday 28th June, the early morning swirling mists had cleared away and the small flotilla of Patrol Boats cast off from Cliffe Fort Jetty to set off upstream. Buckie's guess as to the early morning traffic had been right, in that there would be no inward-bound vessels until the next flood-tide. As they approached the Northfleet Wharves an incredible sight confronted them. Towering above the cranes and warehouses was a huge concrete creation. The massive concrete base on which it floated looked like a lozenge shaped barge, from which arose two stout tubular towers joined across their tops by a massive building with three rows of windows. On top of this building was another single storey building bearing radio aerials, searchlights and look-out windows. On either side large guns were mounted. At one end of the platform there was an open frame-work with flights of stairs and atop that was a crane. The whole structure was painted in confusing camouflage colours and patterns. It looked to be at least a hundred feet high (30.5 metres) and must have weighed thousands of tons.

Massive hawsers ran out to two steam tugs positioned ahead and pointing down-stream; and two more behind pointing up-stream to assist with manoeuvring and to act as brakes. The huge floating assembly, looking dangerously top-heavy, was being gently eased away from the background of the wharf where it had been built. When away from the wharves it looked even larger.

The role of HMY *Sheemaun* was to patrol the Essex bank ahead of this large tow flotilla and to make sure no small craft got in the way or attempted to cross in front of the tow flotilla. Taff had already prepared the signal flags likely to be needed –

Code Flag **T** – vertical red, white and blue panels

DO NOT PASS AHEAD OF ME

Coode Flag **K** – vertical yellow and blue panels

STOP YOUR VESSEL INSTANTLY

To reinforce the meaning of any flag signal messages, or, for that matter any other instructions given out by the crew of HMY *Sheemaun*, there on the foredeck were the very persuasive Hotchkiss machine guns!

The ungainly convoy gradually pulled clear into the main channel and it began its course seaward with the strengthening ebb tide. The tugs' tall funnels belching thick smoke as their big screws churned the water, and hoisted to their signal yards were conspicuous black balls above and below a black diamond shape signifying –

VESSEL RESTRICTED IN ABILITY TO MANOUEVRE.

With the ebb flow gradually increasing to nearly four knots, the Essex and Kent shores slipped silently by. A laden Thames barge that had anchored off the East Tilbury Marshes, no doubt also awaiting the ebb, looked as if it might be about to cast off. Buckie gave the wheel a touch to port thinking to hail the skipper and Taff ran up the K flag, but there was no need, the barge skipper and his crew of two were standing staring awestruck at the huge monstrosity making its progress seaward between the silently steaming tugs. They had clearly decided to let this lot get well past before casting off and they just gave a wave as HMY *Sheemaun* motored past.

Loud shouts came across the water. From HMY *Sheemaun* the crew could see men on the two aftermost tugs gesticulating and pointing. There in the direction they pointed to could be seen a red buoy slowly rotating and drifting with the tide. It must have been torn from its mooring by the concrete monster. One of the up-stream Auxiliary Patrol Service boats was already making for it and would take it in tow to secure it to the nearest convenient mooring or jetty. That was one of the many tasks that not infrequently fell to the Thames Auxiliary Patrol Service boats.

To port lay Coalhouse Fort, an obsolete nineteenth century fort that had been hastily re-armed in 1940 with two Naval 5.5-inch guns from HMS *Hood*. Although designed in 1913 the guns could fire shells of 82 lb (37.2 kg) at twelve rounds a minute. But so effective was the Thames Estuary Defence Boom and the integrated gun defences in preventing any enemy vessel from penetrating into the Thames, that they did not fire at any vessel in anger during the Second World War.

When this strange flotilla reached the Medway Channel Approach the escorting Auxiliary Patrol Service vessels had orders to break away and to resume their normal patrol duties. The crew could see a Royal Navy corvette and armed tugs forming up ready to escort the huge contraption through the Defence Barrier. Buckie throttled back, and the crew watched as the group of tugs with their enormous and strangely shaped tow continued towards the Defence Boom gateways, then he spun the wheel to head HMY *Sheemaun* westwards into the now weakly ebbing tide. Taff put down the binoculars and passed them to Andy –

'Well what d'ye make o' that?'

Buckie pushed his cap back and scratched his head

'Dunnoo ne'er see'd the likes afore... but those big guns right at t' top... however they're going tai aim those wi' that thing swaying around? Beats me...'

Andy joined them on the bridge-deck –

'You know they've been worried about those E-Boots charging in the dark from out at sea and letting off at everything then disappearing fast... and... the bombers coming in high over the estuary and dropping all those mines... well I reckon they're going to anchor that out in the estuary where the shore batteries can't cover... like a sort of concrete fortress. It'd be much cheaper than a ship, it wouldn't need to move and would be almost unsinkable... and with that height they could shoot down on any E-Boats or subs.'

Buckie pulled his cap back on and scowled –

'Well... we can'na know but ye could be right... one thing's for sure... we ain't seen anythin' and we don't say nothing... when we're back ashore...'

Taff pointed South across to the now uncovered Blyth Sands towards the little inlet known as Egypt Bay –

'Look there's a barge aground... he must have tried to nip across on the ebb, but he misjudged and got stuck. He'll be in trouble when he floats on the flood... and if he's caught moving after dark he'll risk being fired on...'

Buckie grunted –

'Silly fella tae try that… but… whae if he's got something he should'na hae in his boat like a camera? Whae – if he's an agent or got an agent aboard? Whae did he sneak across there where no-one else could follow an' jus' when the towin' job was on?'

A detailed report was entered in the log and Buckie nudged the throttle levers, he wanted to get back to base in good time to hand in the report. Meanwhile the observation barge crews would keep an eye on the stranded trading barge and one of the Chatham based Patrol Boats would get into a position to intercept it when it floated off. Meanwhile the discussion turned to other matters closer to home, but sharp eyes were scanning every creek and inlet on the way.

Time-Line –
- January 1942 - HMY *Sheemaun* was listed by the Admiralty as based at Cliffe Forte on the Isle of Grain. The construction of those huge concrete fortresses commenced February 1942 at Red Lion Wharf Northfleet under the supervision of their designer, engineer Guy Maunsell. This one, known as Fort U3 Naval Fort was of re-enforced concrete construction. Huge hollow 'barge' bases 148.5 feet (45.2m) long by 14 ft (4.3.m) deep by 85 ft (26m) wide on which were two 24 feet (7.3m) diameter hollow concrete legs surmounted by deck 75feet (76m) above the barge base which housed a gun platform with radar control. Living quarters, storage and ammunition was accommodated in the hollow circular legs. They had generators, fuel &

water tanks, search lights and two 3.75 anti-aircraft guns and two 40 mm Bofors guns on the platforms. Crew numbered about 60 and served duties of 2 weeks on and 2 weeks off.

- Fort U3, the Naval Fort, was towed out to Tongue sands 6.3 miles off Margate on Saturday 27th June 1942 and the base flooded to let it sink to stand securely like a towering concrete fortress in the shallow waters on the sea bed at the southern end of the area known as E-Boat Alley.

- Six other Maunsell forts, some of a different design but all based on hollow concrete floats, were likewise sunk onto the seabed in the Outer Thames Estuary. Their crews successfully shot up and generally discouraged the German E-boat incursions, they fired on a German U-Boat causing it to be scuttled, they made it very hazardous for German bombers to overfly the outer Thames Estuary and they shot down a significant number of enemy planes and numbers of the V1 flying bombs.

1942

The Illlustrated Magazine reports on the Thames Patrol

By W. J. Passingham 7th November 1942

One of the most dramatic stories of the war lies behind the activities of what is now called the Royal Naval Auxiliary Patrol, London. This has acted as guardian of the Thames Estuary since it was first formed under the direction of the Port of London Authority during the summer of 1938.

Throughout the first days of alarm in 1938 the vital importance of the Thames Estuary - Gateway to the Pool of London – became obvious. And an entirely volunteer force called the River Emergency Service was formed on the lines of the A.R.P organisation ashore.

In those early days, the personnel of the River Emergency Service wore grey flannel trousers, reefer jackets and yachting caps.

These men faced the first of the great enemy air raids over the estuary and the London Docks, and they performed acts of great heroism that were unsung- almost unseen.

For, in the beginning they were nobody's baby, and a request for recompense on account of services rendered was regarded as an impertinence.

As 'amateurs' they dragged blazing lighters loaded with petrol, ammunition and high explosives worth half a million sterling to the country, to safety – shot down enemy raiders with out-of-date guns and circled round areas of the river where mines had been dropped, thus preventing shipping disasters of major magnitude in the very fairway of London's river.

Today, the importance of their work cannot be over

emphasized. In the case of an enemy invasion they would be defenders of a broad gateway leading straight to the Empire's capital which is also mother of markets to the whole world.

Recently, I saw much of the work of the Royal Naval Auxiliary Patrol, which ranges from the Poll to Southend. I saw motor patrol boats, armed tugs, drifters, barges, hoppers and repair vessels all at their endless task of guarding the estuary. The day was clear, sunlit, and over the broad bosom of the Thames were a bewildering variety of craft whose work only experts could explain.

A haze hung low over the distant Pool of London, and the green of the Kent and Essex shores made an animated scene not easily forgotten.

At noon, the Thames estuary was as busy as any great thoroughfare in the heart of London.

To the outsider there appeared to be no signs of defenders up and down this vital approach to the Empire's capital.

Yet eyes there are which see everything – every incident – which trivial to the uninitiated, may be of significance to the guardians of this broad highway.

The moment a ship enters the estuary her progress is reported from point to point down river, and the unseen eyes of those who watch are the Thames Patrol. She may have wounded aboard, sickness, or injury from enemy air attack.

And the Thames Patrol is there with medical assistance, salvage experts, engineers, stores – and a suitable anchorage according to the ship's condition.

Throughout the night this work of patrolling London's river goes on. Thames Patrol is responsible for ensuring that the Admiralty's lighting regulations are complied with everywhere.

It also maintains a comprehensive programme of training – in gunnery, small arms, and all work necessary for defending the great highway to London.

There are four men who keep a constant watch for the location of enemy mines. They face a life of dull routine, and the rigours of winter out in the broad estuary at all hours of the day and night – relieved only by the Thames Patrol Boats which bring them the necessities of life.

So much is there to see in the Thames Estuary nowadays that the defences of the river rarely appear at all to strangers. A merchant ship may be making her way towards her anchorage in the Pool, and to all outward appearances nobody takes the slightest notice of her.

Yet she is not only in constant communication with the shore, but perhaps, miles away, preparations are made to receive her and deal with what may be a precious cargo.

Today, the Thames is a river of secrets, showing a peaceful front to the world which conceals the heaviest defences London has ever known in her long history.

And in all the riverside inns where seafarers forgather a curious silence – a frosty stare for the nosey stranger with a load of pointed questions.

You may never know the exact nature of the objects you stare at in the estuary and perhaps in no other spot the world over are secrets so well guarded.

The Thames Patrol is constantly required to assist in the regulation and control of merchant shipping in the river, especially when the Southend anchorage is congested and the progress of ships must be stopped.

The Patrol Boats give warning to ships in forbidden anchorages – which is not an easy task when the river is fogbound.

Because of enemy mine-laying activities, all navigation must be prohibited in certain areas.

All outward-bound shipping is logged by the duty watch at Tilbury and details telephoned in code to headquarters. Those whose duty it is to seek out a ship berthed among hundreds of others in the Thames have only to telephone the Thames Patrol, who keep a list of all craft in the river from Barking to Sea Reach – a distance of twenty miles.

Information of this kind is constantly passing up and down river, from section to section of the Royal Naval Auxiliary Patrol.

There are ships bound for the Port of London from all parts of the world, and each carries a balloon it wants to get rid of when it the vessel enters the Thames Estuary.

A Thames Patrol Boat is there waiting to relieve them of the appendage, to see it is properly inflated before it is handed over to another outgoing vessel.

Supplying rations, rum and tobacco to men
on an observation barge

This work of servicing ships with kite balloons is carried out entirely by the Thames Patrol. It often involves overtaking merchant vessels as far as three miles above or below Tilbury Docks.

More than fifty balloons are frequently handled in the course of a day, and when the weather is calm a Thames Patrol tug may be seen speeding out with five of them attached to itself.

Whatever may be said of this or that great city in any part of the world, London is still the greatest prize of them all – an invader's dream of conquest.

Its approaches from the sea are guarded by officers and men of the Royal Naval Auxiliary Patrol.

These are the same men who stood by at Dunkirk, who have been standing by ever since. They are an unassuming crowd and so quiet that their great services to the nation are apt to be overlooked.'

The above is copied from the war-time press cuttings carefully kept by the late Stanley Dodd RNVR

Time-Line –

- On completion of her repairs and following satisfactory sea-trial under the command of Lt. 'Peter' Gray HMS *Badsworth* sailed to re-join the Londonderry Escort Force and then to proceed to escorting the Arctic Convoys to Murmansk

1943

HMY *Sheemaun* Close and Personal with Hitler's Magnetic and Acoustic Mines

'...A furious billow, rolling deep, Engulfed them in
Oblivion!'

Emily Dickson

Whenever the weather was suitable and the moonlight sufficient, Hitler's Luftwaffe bombers dropped mines by the
score into the Thames and its Estuary. In the relatively short
period of a month several hundreds of mines had been laid
with the consequence that within the first months of the war
more than a hundred ships were sunk and many were damaged.
Inevitably many of their crewmen were killed and many were
injured. Mines released by the bombers would descend under
dark parachutes swing like large pendulum bobs as they came
down. As the parachute was swung by its heavy mine, air would
be spilled from under the edges of the canopy with a soft chufff
chufff sound like a slowly moving steam engine, as Stanley Dodd
described -

'...This was a large canister of high explosive weighing
around 2000 lbs. It was dropped on a blackish green parachute so that it was invisible and as the mine fell, it would
swing pendulum fashion and spill the air out from the
parachute in a rhythmic chuff! chuff! Like a steam shunting
engine on the railway...' SD

Trained observers would listen for this ominous sound and
take reference sights on the splash-down so that next day the

232

Estuary Patrol Services could be directed to where the mines lay on the river bed. As afore-mentioned, the mines laid in the relatively shallow waters of the Thames were generally of two types – Magnetic or Acoustic and both were deadly.

The magnetic mine contained a sophisticated magnetic compass mechanism. Any steel or iron ship passing over it of sufficient mass to cause a slight deviation in the magnetic field would trigger the mine to explode. The acoustic mine however was designed to be activated by sound waves passing through the water such as might be generated by the engine vibrations of a passing vessel or the noises from its churning propeller. Magnetic mines could be made to explode themselves by towing electric cables nearby while passing a big electric current through the cables. The current had to be sufficient to cause a local disturbance of the natural earth's magnetic polarity. Named after their physical configuration, such devices were known as 'Double L' electrical sweeps. The cables however were often destroyed by the mines they activated and the vessels that towed the sweeps did not always go unscathed. At other times the mine might be made to self-destroy by placing a delayed action explosive charge close to it.

Acoustic mines could be made to self-destruct by exposing them to loud vibrations such as could be generated by a pneumatic Kangol® 'Jack Hammer' similar to those used to dig up the roads. Such hammers were mounted on cantilevers at the bows of a ship and when lowered into the water they sent powerful vibrations through the water ahead of the ship in order to detonate any acoustic mine lying on the sea bed ahead of the ship. Alternatively, a machine gun could be used to pepper and agitate the water ahead, but that necessarily used up a lot of ammunition. HMY *Sheemaun* sometimes put her machine guns to this task, aiming far enough ahead to keep a safe distance away from where a mine might be exploded, and where possible firing was done while aiming down at an angle of greater than ten degrees to reduce the risk to others from stray bullets ricocheting dangerously.

Stanley Dodd recalls this experience –

'...Then I had a spell of mine sweeping Double "L" sweeps for magnetic mines and a stripped Lewis gun for acoustic mines... (p 232)... all very interesting and inspiring when they went off. A mound of whitish green sea water would quite slowly rise higher and higher until it topped 200 feet[102] and then just as slowly – almost slow motion – would subside in a glistening cascade of turbulence, while the surrounding sea would be littered with all the fish you could imagine. We used to pick out the best and what we couldn't eat, we would sell and drink the proceeds.

(One thing you will have gathered – Stan Dodd was no camel).

Then there were the magnetic mines – the method of clearing is perhaps of interest. These mines are essentially for use in shallow water – up to say 6 fathoms.[103] We used a small motor launch, because it could be thrown clear even if overwhelmed and that, being largely of wood, had little magnetic attraction apart from the engine. We generally had 5 personnel, a coxswain, a seaman, an engineer (me) a diver and assistant to work the pumps. The area to be swept was precisely charted and you would station yourself in the point of start. Then a sinker would be lowered to hold the boat and the diver attached to an aluminium chain (non-magnetic) would jump over the side and walk to the furthest extremity of the retaining chain. Then take... (p

102. 61 metres
103. 11 metres

233)... one step "inwards" to give some slack and then walk in a circle around the sinker. If the chain caught on an obstruction, you felt your way along it and investigated. Nine times out of ten it proved to be a rock on the sea bed but on the tenth it would be a mine. Then you would mark the mine with a buoy and sail slowly over it towing a miniature double "L" sweep which if switched on at the right moment, altered the polarity of the firing mechanism and the whole lot would go up with you just outside the danger zone and riding on the crest of a wave like a surf rider. This magnetic detonation method was also used by the obsolete Wellington Bomber and consisted of a large circular coil which created a magnetic field and produced a detonation. They would fly at almost sea level and produce the same result, but it wasn't fool proof – ours was, as we literally walked over the entire sea bed area. This job took me about 6 months and during that time, to relieve the monotony we used to take it in turns to do each other's jobs. So I went diving. That's not all it's cooked up to be. The sea is for the most part very murky and you could only work at dead high water or dead low water when the water was relatively clear. Also you could not walk precisely in the strong currents, But it was... (p 234) an experience and one which I would not have missed.'

Stanley Dodd RNVR.

An interior view of the for'ard port side in *Sheemaun's* foc'sle.
Photo RP

Secured under the square-headed bolt, an iron re-enforcing plate lies against the Oak frame. The Oak frame it is repairing had been cracked by an explosive impulse. In War-Time it would have taken only an hour or so to bolt on the plate, whereas in Peace-Time the vessel would have been taken out of the water and a new piece of Oak skilfully scarfed in; a job that would have taken several days.

1943

ON HMS *Badsworth* - The Visitor Book is shaken by a Naval Salvo

'...I was the staunchest of our fleet
Till the sea rose beneath our feet
Unheralded, in Hatred past all measure...'

Mary Pollock

Operation Torch was planned by Prime Minister Winston Churchill and President Franklin Roosevelt as a joint action in which the British and American Forces would cooperate to liberate the French Colonies of Morocco, Algiers and Tunisia from Hitler's grasp. British troops had landed in German occupied Algiers and were fighting their way West to Tunis but for the first two months the superior airpower was held by the German and Italian Axis Forces. The Allied Eastern Task Forces had come under sustained and heavy attack by German Junkers 88 fighter bombers and the Italian Savoia bombers that paid special attention to the Bone Airfield. As a result, numbers of Spitfires and Hurricanes had been damaged, the airfield buildings and runway had been damaged and a fuel dump of 20,000 gallons (90,922 L) of petrol had been blown up. Supplies, fuel, ammunition and spares were desperately needed.

HMS *Badsworth* was engaged in escorting the convoys of ships carrying those supplies vital to the Allied troops in Tunisia. There was constant risk of attack from U-Boats and from strafing and bombing aircraft above which had to be fiercely fought off and a sharp look-out had to be kept for the ever-present menace of mines.

It was the 22nd April 1943 the escorting duties had been

successful and the convoy, relatively unscathed, was closing on the harbour of the city port of Bone, now known as Annaba, where it nestles under the hills in the North East of Algeria. Suddenly HMS *Badsworth*'s hull was violently concussed by a huge explosion aft, her stern heaving up as a column of seething white water hurled skywards, the quarter deck had been peeled open like a sardine can and whole ship shuddered. In 'Peter' Gray's cabin the bookshelf contents including the Visitors Book lay scattered about on the floor. The whine of her Parson's turbines faltered dramatically, and the usual mechanical vibrations and noises of a fighting ship quickly died away to be replaced by shouting, the clatter of hurrying feet and alarms sounding.

HMS *Badsworth* had been struck by a mine, quite probably by a magnetic mine but whatever type of mine it had been, the ship was in serious trouble. Badly damaged aft with the quarter deck almost separated and the propeller shafts knocked out of alignment but still just able to turn, she was taking water fast and some crew had been injured. In moments the damage control reports began to come in to the Bridge Command and they were alarming. The warship was sinking and could be in danger of capsizing. Commanding Officer Lt. Cmdr. 'Peter' Gray lost no time. He arranged for rapid transfer of most of the crew to another vessel then with a selected 'Skeleton Crew' he had the sinking destroyer run hard ashore in the sandy shallows near the City Port. The pumps were barely able to keep up with the inrush of sea-water but now aground the ship could not settle any deeper. Together with the Chief Engineer, the First Officer, Damage Control Officer and electricians, Lt. 'Peter' Gray led an inspection of the damaged stern area. It was a grim scene; Damage Control had already seen to it that all water-tight doors and hatches had been closed. The distortion aft was such that some of the water-tight doors and hatches had been rendered useless.

The hull compartments forward of the extensively damaged area had been isolated and were being pumped out but it looked as if the ship would still become a total loss for the damaged aft compartments were effectively open to the sea. Down there in the bowels of the listing ship oily, smelly debris strewn water swirled and slopped back and forth. A wooden crate containing only smashed wine bottles bobbed slowly around in circles as the sea washed in and out through the gaping breach in the hull, a couple of bobbing corks added a surreal irony to the scene of destruction. It was obvious that there was nothing that could be done now to restore buoyancy...... or... was there?

A man who knew and enjoyed his wine, 'Peter' Gray was aware that a major export of this part of Algeria was high quality cork and that the Cork Oak flourished abundantly on this fertile coast. An idea flashed into his mind and after a quick consultation with his First Officer and the Chief Engineer, a plan of action was laid. Boats were lowered and leading a sortie of armed men. 'Peter' Gray located a cork warehouse, and where despite much protesting by the proprietor he purchased by demand, on behalf of His Majesty King George VI, the entire stock of raw, unprocessed cork planks. It was arranged for the cork planks to be delivered to the beach from where they were ferried out to HMS *Badsworth*. The crew then worked feverishly for a week packing as much cork as it was possible to push down into the warship's flooded compartments. They secured the remaining watertight doors and made good the job of sealing and closing all other relevant avenues of leakage such as electrical conduits, piping and ventilation ducts.

After the remaining compartments and bilges had been pumped out HMS *Badsworth*'s keel lifted just clear of the beach! No longer in a condition capable of fighting a war against Hitler's forces, she was now fighting internally for her own survival. But thanks to the stroke of genius which had enabled a sufficient restoration of buoyancy, she was hauled off the beach and towed, ignominiously but proudly, into Bone harbour by the minesweeper HMS *Clacton*.

Returning later to his cabin 'Peter' Gray rescued his Visitor Book from amongst the debris strewn across the floor, picked up his few personal belongings, then packed his bags and prepared to hand his ship over to the care of the salvage crew. After a re-fuelling stop-over at Malta the Royal Fleet Auxiliary Tug *Jaunty* then towed the badly damaged but floating, one might venture to say, now almost unsinkable, HMS *Badsworth* to Gibraltar for further provisional repairs, arriving there on the 17th June.

At the subsequent Admiralty Board of Enquiry in London Lt. Cmdr. 'Peter' Gray found himself being given a tough gruelling by the Lords of the Admiralty. Their lordship's made very clear their apparent displeasure at his having not only fouled a mine, but then compounding the situation by wasting good tax-payer's money on an unauthorised and frivolous expenditure on... of all things... tree cork! An unpleasant meeting which was to rankle in 'Peter' Gray's mind for years to come.[104]

Seventy-five years later, it seems to my mind that was a sad reflection of some of their Lordship's fossilised and isolated thinking at the time.

---

104. As told to me by Admiral Gray's son Nicholas.

1943

The story of a Lancaster Bomber Pilot, the Night Bombing of Germany 1940 - 1945

'But alas for the Germans when the tide did turn,
and it was their turn to burn,
As Dresden was bombed and Nature helped,
To destroy this evil the Fatherland had whelped.'

Tom Barker 2005

B ritain together with most of non- German Europe had been suffering greatly from Hitler's Blitzkrieg onslaughts. The London Docks had been brought almost to a standstill and major cities and ports up and down the country had been heavily bombed, with nearly forty-five thousand civilians killed and thousands more injured. The savage destruction of merchant shipping by sea and air had brought the losses of many thousands of tons of essential supplies and the further sacrifice of thousands of lives, but the pendulum was swinging. Prime Minister Winston Churchill had urged for every effort to be made to boost the War Effort and in response British households had surrendered thousands and thousands of aluminium cooking pots and pans. Furthermore, thousands of obsolete machinery, miles and miles of municipal park iron railings, thousands of iron gates and tons of every scrap of removable iron and aluminium were being collected and re-processed for use by Britain's armament factories. The British armament manufacturing machinery was now focussed on producing thousands of heavy bombers and fast fighter-bombers and this huge effort was being mirrored in Canada and the USA. The resulting huge task force of bombers would be masterminded by Bomber Command, headed by Air Chief Marshall Sir Arthur (Bomber) Harris.

The intention was to mirror Hitler's plan and so turn the tables to bring about the collapse of Hitler's aggression by neutralising the German capacity to build war-machines and supply the munitions and fuel that they needed. Accordingly, plans were drawn up to bomb not only the German factories and munitions efforts but also the infrastructure of roads, canals, rail lines and power distribution systems, furthermore by wiping out large residential areas and rendering the German workforce homeless, the factories would in turn be starved of labour. For obvious reasons this was on humanitarian grounds a very controversial policy as there would inevitably be great risk to the civilian populations, but the times were desperate; it was a destroy or be destroyed situation.

One hundred and twenty-six British Bomber Squadrons were created, of which fifty-five were Lancaster Squadrons. Most of those heavy bomber squadrons were based at airfields created in Britain's flat eastern countryside ranging from southern Yorkshire down to Essex and from where sorties were flown across the southern North Sea to penetrate inland over Hitler's Axis forces in Germany and Eastern Europe.

Earlier bombing sorties by the Wellington bomber had been little short of disastrous as the fast and heavily armed German Messerschmitt fighters shot down so many of them. It quickly became obvious that in day-light the heavily loaded bombers were virtually sitting ducks. So instead Bomber Command made a strategic switch from day-time bombing to night-time bombing of Germany. Night bombing however brought with it the increased difficulties of accurate navigation and the problems of locating the target areas in darkness. These difficulties were largely overcome by the Path-Finder Force. Motto –

The PFF used lightly loaded Wellington bombers and the fast de Havilland Mosquito fighter-bombes. Those aircraft, crewed by experienced pilots and navigators, were equipped with hyperbolic radio navigation instruments. The PFF would fly out ahead of the main bomber formations in the dark and in all weathers. They would accurately drop incendiary bombs and coloured flares onto the targets. The following formations of often hundreds of heavy bombers would then bomb the marked areas. It was an effective strategy and it prevailed, but at great cost not only to the unfortunate recipients of the attacks, but also to the heavy bomber squadrons which suffered significant losses of both aircraft and crews.

Prime Minister Winston Churchill proclaimed that –

'The fighters are our salvation, but the Bombers provide the means of victory.'

The four-engine Avro Lancaster Bomber or 'Lanc' was Bomber Command's work-horse, With its four Merlin engines producing over 6,500 hp and a wingspan of 102 feet (31 metres) it could easily carry bomb loads of more than 12,000 lbs (5443 kilos) and depending on the bomb load could fly up to 28,000 feet (7.6 kilometers) with a top speed of around 300 mph (482 kph) and a cruising speed of just over 210 mph (338 kmh) with a range of 2,530 miles (4071.6 km). The 'Lanc' carried a crew of seven and it was said that without its load of bombs and with a very experienced pilot at the controls, it could out-manoeuvre a Messerschmitt and was so strongly built that in a spiralling power dive[105] it could withstand G forces that would rip the wings from a fighter plane!

---

105. A manoeuvre termed 'A Corkscrew' by the crews who had to do it.

Some 'Lancs' were modified to carry the massive 22,000 lb (10,000 kg) 'Tall Boy' and 'Grand Slam' bombs, designed by engineer Barnes Wallis, which were used against Hitler's U-Boat pens and his heavily armed battle cruisers hidden in Norwegian fjords. As a last means of communication should the worst happen, some of the 'Lancs' carried homing messenger pigeons, to be released with coded messages in the event of that 'Lanc' being shot down behind enemy lines. A small number of 'Lancs' were specially modified to carry the 'Bouncing Bomb', also designed by Barnes Wallis, that was used with such effect against the Edesee and Mohne dams

Between 1942 and 1945 Bomber Command 'Lancs' flew 156,000 sorties and dropped 608,612 tons of bombs. Understandably, Hitler's generals had organised a strong defensive network with one hundred and fifty thousand anti-aircraft guns clustered around prime targets. The many batteries of guns relied at night on powerful searchlights to reveal the bombers flying high over-head. In each group of searchlights there would be one which was radar directed and which could home-in on the otherwise invisible bombers. Those searchlights had blue beams and when a plane was illuminated, the other searchlight beams could be homed in onto the target. The release of clouds of thin aluminium ribbons, known as 'chaff', did to some extent 'blind' the radar, but when a bomber was caught in the dreaded 'Blue Beam' it was very difficult to escape.

On the nights of 25th and 26th July 1943 some six-hundred Lancaster bombers destroyed the Krupps armament works at Essen and most of the City of Essen. In four waves of attack in February 1945, seven-hundred and ninety-six Allied bombers destroyed more than a hundred factories in the City of Dresden and raised most of the city to the ground in a fire-storm. On many of those dreadful raids some of the crews took with them a 'Lucky Mascot' such as a teddy bear. 'Gallows Jokes' were often made such as –

'Well old man… if I don't make it back… you can have my bacon and egg breakfast…'

and last letters would be left addressed to loved ones –

'If I don't come back… well… would you make sure that this letter gets to… Thanks old man.'

Out of the 7,377 'Lancs' that were built 3,249 were lost in action. Of the 125,000 men who flew with Bomber Command 55,573 lost their lives – a 46% death rate. In addition, over nine thousand were taken prisoner and more than 8,000 were wounded bringing the total number of operational aircrew killed, injured or taken prisoner to a horrifying 60%. Furthermore, when a 'Lanc' was shot down it proved to be a difficult plane from which to make a parachute exit, especially for the rear-gunner, and only some 14% of crew successfully parachuted from stricken 'Lancs'. The crews were all young men aged between 19 yrs and 25 yrs of age and unquestionably courageous. Those who flew on the dangerous bombing missions had all volunteered to do so, every one of them being fully aware that each sortie flown had a greater than 50/50 chance that it could be his last alive day on this earth.

There can be no doubt that those terrible night-bombing raids greatly hastened the end of the war in Europe. But the 'Lanc' could also bring food and warmth. After Germany capitulated, and only a few weeks after making those devastating bombing raids over Germany and German occupied Holland, the same bombers then engaged with dropping food, clothing and chocolates! Later they would be fitted with bench seating and would re-patriate the thousands of prisoners released from Nazi prison camps.

The reader might well ask –

'But what can this have to do with *Sheemaun*?'

Well, Thomas William Humphreys Burton was aged 22 yrs when on 3rd September 1939 Prime Minister Neville Chamberlain declared that Britain and France were now at war with Germany. Thomas worked with his father in the family's modest Butcher's Shop in Norfolk and was expected to follow in the family business. But Thomas's head was often 'In the Clouds', for he had an ambitious adventure streak running in his veins. He had saved up and learned to fly in the then ubiquitous air-trainer, the de Havilland Tiger Moth biplane and on 11th October 1936 at the age of 19 years he received his Pilot's Licence from the London Aeroplane Club. Thomas Burton would come to play a significant and dangerous role, in being just one amongst those many hundreds of brave bomber crews who nightly risked their lives while striving to bring the awful war to an end.

BURTON, Thomas W½ Humphreys,   14602

69 Lupus Street, S.W.1.

Born 12. 1. 1917   *at*   Nottingham
Nationality British
Rank, Regiment, Profession   Butcher
Certificate taken on   D.H.82 Tiger Moth, Gipsy Major-1X
At London Aeroplane Club
Date   11.10.36.

Thomas Wm. Humphreys Burton aged 19 yrs

After War had been declared in September 1939 Thomas volunteered to serve in the Royal Air Force. He underwent training as a bomber pilot at the Ministry of Defence Elmdon airport (now Birmingham Elmdon Airport) from where he was transferred to Bomber Command to fly as a Lancaster Bomber pilot. Some idea of the terrors and stresses that he endured can be imagined from the preceding account of the Lancaster Bomber raiding sorties in the Second World War. Thomas endured all those terrible stresses of flying at night over the heavily defended German cities and factories, the blinding searchlights and explosive ant-aircraft flack, the tensions while being shot at by Messerschmitt fighters and shaken by mid-air explosions. Many were the times that he landed back in England, sometimes with his 'Lanc' riddled with bullet holes and shrapnel damage and with bits hanging off it.

Every time Thomas flew his bomb laden 'Lanc' and his six fellow crewmen up into the unknown night, he was fully aware of the risks and the emotional over-load in his head as he held the controls and studied the dimly glowing instruments arrayed before him must have been numbing.

Conversely, each time he brought his big 'Lanc' safely down again, now empty of bombs, the sheer relief must have been overwhelming. But, behind the exaltation and relief of returning home alive from a bombing raid, for those young men, who themselves all had families and kindred, there was always the nagging knowledge that they had left behind them terrible injuries, death and destruction. Thomas Burton would one day come to find in *Sheemaun* the freedom, space and peace of mind that he sought.

1943

Bournemouth Sunday 23rd May

'In the lonely afternoon say a prayer
For Lance Bombardiers Norman and John
Up on the roof of Beales department store,
Aiming well their triple Lewis guns
Engaged a pack of Focke Wulf fighter planes
And shot one down in Bournemouth Bay.
At dusk remember Unter Officier F K Schmidt;
No victory over death. One end to war.'

Poet Laureate for Bournemouth Poets

Genteel south-facing Bournemouth with its bracing air and lovely sea-shores and views, had for decades attracted the comfortably-off and retired gentlefolk. But now, as had every other town and city in Britain, Bournemouth had been transformed by the war. The sandy beaches had been put strictly out-of-bounds and were littered with anti-invasion devices, observation posts and tank-traps. No longer could holiday-makers take a day-tripper outing in a pleasure boats, there was no bathing or amateur fishing allowed and only vessels with orders or permission could set out to sea. Guns and machine-gun posts covered the beaches and cross-roads and anti-aircraft guns had been mounted on the rooves of some buildings. It was an offence to throw away paper and cardboard that might be recycled, almost every consumable was rationed and there was a virtual curfew after sun-down. There was no street lighting and no lights could be shown from windows or vehicles.

Bournemouth town had been designated as an ideal location for the resting and convalescence of exhausted aircrew and troops, many of whom were also recovering from injuries. The Hotel Metropole had been requisitioned to provide accommodation for some hundreds of Canadian airmen who were convalescing or on temporary rest-leave. Likewise, Australian air-crews were accommodated at the Central Hotel. Most of the other larger hotels and in many streets rows of guest-houses had also been pressed into service to accommodate and give respite to exhausted aircrew, many of whom were also recovering from injuries. On any sunny day the delightful Pleasure Gardens would be thronged with convalescing air-crew and troops. At Bournemouth Central Station the platforms were constantly crowded as each day the passenger rail-services brought in exhausted men by the hundreds and took away as many to return to fight where they were desperately needed in the air or on the front-lines.

The townsfolk of Bournemouth had become accustomed to this 'invasion' and to the threatening squadrons of German bombers that nightly droned and throbbed high overhead in the night sky, on their way to and from bombing the factories in the industrial Midlands. From time to time bombs had been dropped randomly on Bournemouth, the bomber crews lightening their bombers to make them faster and more manoeuvrable as the Hurricane fighters and Spitfires pressed home attacks. Generally, as the early warning and radar systems detected the approaching German bombers, the dreaded, mournful wail of the sirens usually gave about to fifteen to twenty minutes warning before the planes were overhead. But for Sunday 23rd May, Hitler had ordered a deliberate and direct attack to be made on the town and this time it was in daylight. The fighter-bombers came in fast and low, arriving almost as the first sirens sounded, leaving people frantically scrambling to get into their Anderson shelters or to down into the deeper municipal shelters as the bombs and bullets rained down. This time it was people, not factories or airfields that were Hitler's targets.

On that fateful morning of Sunday 23rd June, the blue skies and warm sunshine made for perfect flying conditions as twenty-six single seater Fokke Wulf 190 fighter-bombers took off from German occupied Caen airfield. Capable of speeds up to 370 mph (590 kph) they would be over their target in less than half an hour. Their target was the British seaside town of Bournemouth.

For 22-year-old Unter Officer Friedrich Schmidt it was his first operational sortie. He had impressed his senior officers with his ability to fly the fast Fokke Wulf, and now he was proud and excited to have been selected for this daring sortie. The raid had been meticulously planned, they would avoid radar detection by flying low across the Channel and all had memorised the maps and reconnaissance photographs of Bournemouth Town. Their brief was to put Bournemouth 'out of action' as a rest and convalescence centre for Allied troops. They were to bomb the bus and rail stations and as many of the hotels as they could target. People on the ground were also to be machine gunned as most of those would be resting or convalescent soldiers and airmen. Rows of houses were to be bombed and machine gunned.

They wave-hopped low over the Channel waters at times their powerful slip-streams whipping foam from the wave-crests. As they rapidly bore up on the target, Unter Officer Schmidt's apprehensions turned to cold alertness. Taken quite off-guard, the British had not yet scrambled their defending Spitfires and Hurricanes and the coastal gun defences appeared to be silent. The surprise had been total, it was to be 'Ein truthahntrieb'[106]

They would not be acting randomly. So as not to waste time and ammunition, each pilot had his targets and after only five minutes heavy bombardment and strafing, they would be away

---

106. 'A turkey shoot'

and heading back to Caen when, much too late, the Spitfires and Hurricanes would be scrambling into the air.

Unter Officer Schmidt was enjoying himself. To aim his bomb precisely at this low height would be easy. The risk of collision had been impressed into all the pilots, so he kept a careful eye open for his twisting and whirling colleagues as he pulled the Fokke Wulf's nose up and swerved to strafe the Pleasure Gardens, aiming for the fleeing figures. Next to bomb the East Court Hotel and then to strafe the rows of houses before turning back to Caen.

But just as Freidrich Schmidt lined the hotel up in his sights, he was startled to see the flashes from a machine gun on the hotel roof. In the same instant his Fokke Wulf was shaken by a juddering vibration, the engine spluttered and died and the whole plane shook as propeller thrust and torque was suddenly lost. Now the only noise was that of the rushing air, but he was too low to bail out. The few seconds of paralysing fear that gripped him ended in a blinding flash, a flash for which there would be no memory left to record it.[107]

From Air Chief Marshall Hermann Goering's perspective, the raid had been a success. In minutes the Hotel Metropole had been reduced to a ruin and most other hotels likewise. The Fokke Wulfs machine-gunned civilians and the convalescing troops alike as they scrambled for cover in the Pleasure Gardens. They strafed open populated areas and bombed and machine-gunned rows of houses. The Central Station was directly hit and badly damaged. As a result, at least a hundred and fifty people were killed with many hundreds more injured. Over three and a half thousand buildings were damaged and Bournemouth's valuable function as a 'secret' accommodation and rehabilitation centre was effectively negated.

---

107. Unter Officer's Fokke Wulf crashed onto the St Ives Hotel. He died on impact. The bomb was still in its rack. Per Nick Churchill - Dorset Life Magazine April 2013.

The hitherto peaceful town of Bournemouth was now in Hitler's gunsights and by the end of the War, Bournemouth would suffer some fifty air-raids and be hit by well over two thousand bombs. A thousand or more people would be injured, another two hundred killed and more than thirteen thousand buildings damaged, most rendered uninhabitable.

The Branksome Tower Hotel, which had somehow managed to avoid being requisitioned by the Government and had escaped Hitler's attention, stood on the Eastern outskirts of Bournemouth. There the management and the few remaining staff were doing their best to keep the hotel running under the most difficult of conditions. Food was rationed as everywhere in England, all consumables were difficult to obtain, petrol and fuel was severely rationed, heating was restricted, and no light could be shown from any window or in the grounds after dark. Money was short and travel restricted. Most of the male staff considered fit enough to fight, had been conscripted to serve in the forces. Air-raid precautions had been implemented. Basement rooms had been fitted with steel plate Morrison shelters and corrugated steel Anderson type shelters had been dug into the outside grounds.

On that fateful Sunday morning, Hotel manager Vernon Haydon, looked out across Bournemouth in alarm. Fast German fighter-bombers were criss-crossing low over the town, their machine guns stuttering as bombs exploded and columns of dense smoke and flames billowed into the blue sky. Yet, there had been no sirens! Shouting to his staff and the few guests to get into the shelters, Vernon as 'Captain of his ship', the Branksome Tower Hotel, was the last to scramble down into safety just as the sirens started to wail. They sat there in stunned silence but within half an hour the wailing sirens sounded the one tone 'All Clear'. They scrambled out from the damp, musty underground shelter and blinking into the daylight, set about finding news as to what had happened. A shaken Vernon hastened to get to his Home Guard unit on Brownsea Island.

At the outset of the War Vernon along with some of his staff and other local men had joined up with the Home Guard. Vernon held the rank of Lance Corporal and proudly wore his First World War pilot's wings badge, but an old war injury that affected his sight had excluded him from being called up for active service this time. However, as an active member of the Brownsea Home Guard unit he was well placed to over-see air-raid precautions at Branksome and to ensure that staff and guests always went into the shelters whenever the air-raid sirens sounded, and Vernon also made sure that a .303 rifle and WW1 army issue revolvers were close to hand. Vernon Hayden would one day skipper *Sheemaun* and he would take with him an army revolver.

1943

Captain Kitt and Smuggling

'O lovely Pussy! O Pussy my love,
What a beautiful Pussy you are,
You are,
You are!
What a beautiful Pussy you are!'

Edward Lear

It was late in May; the blackberry bushes and elders were flowering and now in the twilight HMY *Sheemaun* was lying to her berth at the Cliffe Fort jetty. It had as usual been a busy day and there had been an unpleasant 'hit and run' machine-gunning low pass by a German Fokke Wulf fighter-bomber. Fortunately, no damage had been sustained but the near misses had been very alarming. Stanley had gained some feeling of satisfaction when they had fired the Hotchkiss in anger and hopefully had punched a few holes in the attacker, but the fighter-bomber had come across low and fast and it was out of sight in no time. It certainly made an interesting highlight in the day's log!

They had intercepted and examined four sailing barges, as ever a thankless task, and towed one damaged, engineless barge to a jetty. They had been provoked into aiming the Hotchkiss across the bow of a fishing boat that had failed to respond to the flag signal order to heave-to. Taff had been very reluctant to aim the twin guns across the bow of another British vessel, but the aggressive gesture had the desired effect and the surly skipper of the fishing boat had cut his engine. For his trouble he had been made to open some wooden cases found in his cabin. They contained tins of WD (War Department) stamped butter to which he had no right. The fisherman's claim that he had found them floating off the Lower Hope was probably quite true. The crates were taken aboard HMY *Sheemaun* to be handed over to the naval stores ashore.

The most unpleasant task had been finding the bloated body of a German airman. It would have been very difficult to get the corpse aboard so instead it had been secured with a line in preparation for towing it carefully to the intelligence unit at Sheerness. Much to Buckie's annoyance one decent ash boat-hook had been broken and another one lost in the process. Faced by this very unpleasant and smelly reality the crew were sombre-faced, well-aware that somewhere over there in Hitler's Germany a family would be devastated when the news was received of a husband or brother or son who would never return. It was one thing to watch an enemy plane trailing flames and smoke as it spiralled down into the Thames... a good reason to grin and punch the air in exultation... however, it was quite another thing to be confronted with a body that had only a short time before been a young man flying overhead in that bomber.

But now as it was getting dark, a blackbird had suddenly flown out from the bushes chattering its warning 'cheeps' to the world around. Looking across to where the bird had flown from, Stanley had a strange feeling that they were not alone, that something in the bushes across the jetty was watching. Taff laughed at the suggestion but agreed that from the perspective of security those bushes deserved attention. The large flashlight was produced and after a quick scan of the sky for aircraft, its beam was briefly directed shoreward. Two un-blinking bright eyes shone back.

Stanley who was fond of cats pursed his lips and made some encouraging noises.

'Pus pus... come on there's a good pussy...'

He went below and came back on deck with a saucer on which he had paced some Spam* then moving gently he approached the bushes, put the offering down and returned to the boat. A few minutes later a splendid tabby cat came from the bushes, cautiously ambled up the jetty and sniffed at the Spam. It didn't at first eat but sat looking towards them blinking slowly, then daintily ate the Spam and afterwards sat and washed its face and whiskers. Stanley sitting quietly then extended his hand and whispered

'pus… pus…'

The cat looked at the boat for some time, then with its tail up it trotted across and jumped up onto the deck bedside the men. This was no feral stray; this splendid fellow was affectionate and was seeking human company. He particularly liked being stroked; he had a deep rumbling purr and liked rubbing his head against his new human friends. Over the following days a routine developed where the cat would be waiting for HMY *Sheemaun* at the jetty and would happily come aboard. He didn't seem to be concerned that sometimes the crew might change as duties demanded and it wasn't long before he had his own sack to sleep on, his own bowl and a sand-tray. It was agreed that while everyone including the cat knew who 'Pus Pus' was, somehow a stronger name was needed. After discussion over a tot of rum it was resolved that 'Pus Pus' would be promoted to Captain Kitt.

Captain Kitt was duly fitted with a collar bearing four wavy rings as indicative of his senior rank and had now definitely moved in as the Ship's Cat. Mostly he went ashore when HMY *Sheemaun* set out on patrol duties, but he did sometimes do duty afloat and was quite happy to curl up on a bunk although he never settled to the percussive explosions of mines or the deafening staccato of the Hotchkiss.

A time came when Stanley was due for a week of shore leave, and it was deemed appropriate that Captain Kitt would probably be better off if re-homed with the Dodd family. Accordingly, for the journey to London a strong cardboard box was fitted out with breathing holes and a comfortable little blanket. Captain Kit was not pleased at the prospect of being shut up in a box but after a struggle he settled down grumpily and the box was secured with a strap.

Strict security meant that every movement into or out from the Naval Jetty involved a stop at the barrier and Guard House. The duty Guard on this occasion viewed the box with suspicion and insisted that it be opened for inspection. He was so surprised when a very upset tabby cat leaped out and raced off back down the jetty that he almost dropped his rifle. After that performance it became customary for the Cat Box to be nodded through the security check often with a wink and jokes made about

'Not letting the cat out of the bag!'

Andy explained that was an old naval term from the dark days of strict discipline and flogging. He related that the special whip used for those cruel floggings consisted of a short hempen bound leather shaft with nine leather whiplashes at its head like the Medusa's head of serpents. Each whiplash had a knotted end to add weight and make it cut into the miscreant's skin. This sadistic and vicious weapon of punishment was called a 'Cat o' Nine Tails'. It would be kept usually in the Bosun's bag but when required for administering a flogging it was taken out of the bag – hence the term –

'Letting the Cat out of the Bag'

Rumour has it that Captain Kitt was not always present in his ventilated cat box as it was 'nodded through' security – instead his place there might sometimes be taken by a little rum or other item less available in civvy street, and vice versa some items arrived on HMY *Sheemaun* that might otherwise have been excluded!

Captain Kitt continued with his seafaring life until the end of the war when he transferred happily enough to civilian life at the Dodd family home in London.

HMY *Sheemaun*'s Four Striper Tabby Cat – Photo RP

1944

A Messy Job

'Some men are pink or yellow
And some are black as coal
The rich man has the money
And the poor man has the soul.
Keep rolling anti-fouling
Antifouling roll,
Keep rolling anti-fouling
Ant-fouling roll.'

Merv Lilley

Despite being under-way and on patrol duty almost every day for month after month, HMY *Sheemaun* had been gathering an unsightly skirt of green weed around her waterline and hull. The Auxiliary Patrol Vessels of course were regularly inspected and serviced, but the underwater hull could only be checked if the vessel was out of the water.

For this all that was necessary was to place and secure the vessel at high tide between sturdy posts – known as scrubbing-off posts then wait for the water to ebb away and there would be a few hours when the vessel was high and dry, in which an inspection could be made and routine maintenance such as changing the anodes or anti-fouling the hull could be carried out. Now the Naval Administration at Cliffe Fort had listed HMY *Sheemaun* for her turn between the posts. Her crew were not exactly overjoyed, for there would be no 'Day-Off' and they would be the ones who had the task of scrubbing down the hull, changing the anodes and doing any minor repairs and touch-up jobs.

As the tide reached its full height Buckie eased the boat

between the strong wooden posts and the crew made her fast. The day had been carefully chosen so that the tides were 'making'. In other words, it was in the period coming up to full moon and tomorrow's high tide would be higher than today's. Had the task been scheduled at or after full moon the tidal heights would have been decreasing each day and there would have been risk of the boat being stranded for may be three weeks until the next high 'spring' tides. Today the weather was fair, the tide was right and gradually as the tide ebbed away HMY *Sheemaun* came to lie like a stranded whale secured upright between the posts. Jokes were made but smiles faded when Buckie asserted that as Skipper his job was to supervise; then Stanley held that as mechanic it was his duty to check all had been done properly. Taff Davies now looking alarmed expressed the view that as gunner his was a skilled post. The three crew-members then stared hard at Able Seaman Andy Travers – who was not amused.

Buckie laughed -

'Och we're just teasing ye… we'll all get it done taegether…'

By just over half an hour they had scrubbed the weed off and the hull was revealed to be in good condition. Stanley bolted on new anodes and then they attended to the drum of 'Anti-Foul' which the Navy had supplied. Prising off the lid revealed a rather vile looking light blue/grey coloured grease which they would have to wipe all over the underwater hull with long handled stiff brushes. Andy sniffed at it –

'That's disgusting …'

Stanley laughed, he had seen all this before -

'That's 'Crab Fat'… it's Naval Grease… sticks like s**t to the boat and everything else yet the weed and barnacles just slide off… they say it also protects the timbers from worms and the like…'

Taff looked disbelieving –

'You mean they make that from crabs?'

Stanley grinned –

'Nah… it's a strange story though… Well y' know how it is when a ship puts into port… the sailors go ashore to have a 'Good Time' and of course some come back on board with lodgers… y' know… pubic lice… crabs… the medical orderly gives them stuff called Blue Unction to put on which kills the lice. It looks very like Naval grease which some blokes, not wanting their names to be recorded in the book, have tried, and they found that Naval Grease kills the crab lice just as well… and so to sailors this muck is known as Crab Fat!'[108]

Andy the ships amateur historian then chipped in –

'Talking about names for things reminds me… y' know when we take the kids of rum ration out to some of the ships… have you ever wondered why it's called a kid?'

The other shook their heads and looked at Andy expectantly.

'Well it's from pre-Biblical times… when thousands of years ago in the East they used the skins of goats as containers for carrying water and wine… a kid goat was about the right volume. Even now we refer to a small barrel as a Kid.'

---

108. The 'Crab fat' story was told by Stanley to his son Mike.

Buckie grinned –

'Well d'ye hear tha'… so tha's whae at means when we say a bloke's had a skin full! But talking 'bout skin fulls if any o' you guys are seen poking about wi crab fat where ye should'na… it's t' cat o' nine tails I'll be having at ye!'

With the job done and greasy hands wiped off on old rags, the incoming tide was beginning to lap around the keel of HMY *Sheemaun*. The drum of 'crab fat' was returned to stores, the crew swilled the mud off their boots, had a final wipe-down themselves. The last thing anyone wanted was to take any of that foul mess back on board where they worked and lived. After another hour and a half HMY *Sheemaun* began to stir, then she was buoyant and the tethering warps were coming slack. The engines were started and after Stanley had checked that cooling water was flowing from the exhausts, Buckie helmed her back to the Cliffe Fort jetty.

1944

Human Error and a Major Thames Estuary Disaster

'I dip and I surge and I swing, In the rip of the racing tide,
By the gates of doom I sing, On the horns of death I ride.
A ship-length over side. Between the course and the sand,
Fretted and bound I 'bide. Peril whereof I cry.
Would I change with my brother a league inland?
Shoal! Ware Shoal! Not I.'

Rudyard Kipling

A massive Convoy - HX 301, of merchant ships had departed from New York on 25th July 1944 bound for Great Britain and escorted by destroyers, corvettes and an aircraft carrier. They would sail more than three thousand miles for instead of heading directly east across the Atlantic, a route which would have taken them through a vast area of ocean still dangerously patrolled by Hitler's U-Boat 'Wolf Packs', they headed north to Halifax. At Halifax yet more vessels joined the convoy bringing it to a total of 130 merchant cargo carriers, creating almost an armada of ships. Then taking the North-East route and fighting through an Atlantic gale the convoy made its way to Liverpool. Carrier based planes were able to scout way ahead of the convoy and the accompanying heavily armed escorts ensured that there were no losses due to enemy action.

The convoy included tankers laden with urgently needed fuels, merchant ships with cargoes of food and commodities, ships carrying cargoes of tanks and weapons and ships laden with 'general cargo'. Among these ships was the American Liberty Ship LS 243756 carrying some six thousand eight hundred tons of explosive munitions destined to be off-loaded at the Normandy Coast of France. The cargo of high explosive munitions was needed by the American Divisions of the Allied Forces who were now, following the successful D-Day invasion, steadily pushing Hitler's Axis forces in Europe evermore eastwards.

Convoy HX301 duly arrived at Liverpool unscathed on 8th August where many of the ships discharged their cargoes, some took on new cargoes and other ships joined them to form a new convoy No FS 43. Convoy FS 43 then headed north around the top of Scotland and south wards down the east coast of England threading their way through the mine-fields to arrive at the destination assembly area in the Thames Estuary on 15th August. After passing through the Thames Boom Defence some vessels would proceed up river to discharge their cargoes in London and others would discharge at Sheerness and Chatham, but most would remain to refuel and refresh before taking the still treacherous route westwards through the English Channel to the now established Normandy Beach-Head and to the port of Cherbourg where their cargoes, vital for the Allied European Offensive action against Hitler, would be offloaded.

The Defence Boom straddling the Estuary effectively shielded any vessels within its vast area, from hostilities as might come from Hitler's fast torpedo and gun carrying Schultzboots. Formidable defence back-up was provided by the batteries of guns on the Essex coast, on the Isle of Sheppey, by the Thames Estuary Maunsell gun-towers and a variety of armed vessels. In addition to these man-made hazards, Old River Thames provided her own defences that had been laid out and honed over thousands of years, namely the treacherous tides and sandbanks which fan out eastwards like fingers on a hand. The ebb and flow of turbulent tides further complicating this natural impediment to safe navigation. Covered by water at High Tide in fair weather this vast area of the Estuary can appear as a placid expanse of water. At low tide however, it takes on a quite different appearance for much of the bulk of these great sandbanks are exposed and become the feeding grounds for hundreds of birds and the resting grounds for hundreds of seals. Other areas of sandbanks lie just beneath the surface where they form deadly traps for any unwary vessel. Tidal variations as between Spring Tides and Neap Tides and which can vary the volume of ebb and flow by huge amounts, add their own special complications as do changes in the atmospheric pressure and wind strength and direction.

But now there was almost an electric energy in the air. The vast area of water between Southend to the north and Garrison Fort on the Isle of Sheppey to the south teemed with many scores of anchored vessels and there were hundreds more anchored or berthed in the Medway River, at the Sheerness and Queenborough harbour jetties and variously in the twelve miles or so of navigable estuary as far as Chatham. In addition to the moored and anchored vessels there was constant movement of shipping between those anchorages and the docksides. Warships in the form of destroyers, corvettes, mine sweepers, armed tugs and various fast torpedo and motor gunboats transited the Defence Boom 'gates' so frequently that the gates were open most of the time.

HMY *Sheemaun* was taking a course North East as she exited the Medway Approach Channel and picking her way carefully between the anchored ships. Stanley Dodd RNVR who was on deck checking the twin Hotchkiss machine guns glanced up at the skies. Tonight, there would be a waning gibbous moon which meant they were coming off springs, but the tides were still flowing fast in the estuary as they had discovered when earlier in the day's patrol work they had to 'gun' the engines to better punch against the flow. It was Saturday morning 19th August. Among the seven huge American built 'Liberty' Ships lying there at anchor was the SS *Richard Montgomery*. Wind and tide rode, she was lying with her bow pointing North East. She was so massive that even the heavy swell failed to make her roll. Buckie headed HMY *Sheemaun* towards the Nore Swatch channel. They had letters to deliver and post to collect for the crews of some of the static moored observation barges. Glancing astern 'Taff' Davies agreed that anchoring such a big ship in those shallow waters was questionable.

'Well I've seen some daft things but I suppose those officer boyoes in the Admiralty Harbour office know what they're doing... she's got big guns so I suppose she's got a big anchor too...'

A backward glance at the SS *Richard Montgomery* revealed worryingly that she did not seem to be moving with the water but their attention was then switched to a laden sailing barge.

It was a blustery grey day, the Easterly wind pushing against the last of the ebb made for a vicious choppy swell. The War in Europe had moved on and these days there was much less threat from enemy sea and air action than there had been a couple of years ago. The Luftwaffe still attempted to fly raids over this wide area of the Thames Estuary, however now with the Maunsell Forts in position and heavily armed with searchlights and guns, the Outer Thames Estuary had become almost a 'No Go' area for Hitler's planes since significant numbers had been hit and damaged and some brought down. The heavy guns on a Maunsell Tower Fort further out in the estuary had damaged a U-Boat so badly that it had to be scuttled and abandoned. It seemed that England's enemies were at last learning some hard lessons.

Stanley stood by the Hotchkiss as skipper Buckie at the wheel, carefully brought HMY *Sheemaun* alongside the lee of the barge that had just taken the tide in through the Defence Boom gate. The barge skipper was not too pleased at being requested to heave-to his engineless vessel for inspection -

'We're all in this together mate… wot the 'ell d'ye think I've got 'idden in 'ere… bloody Adolph 'itler? I… got better things to do like getting this cargo to Conyer…'

Turning his face leeward the disgruntled skipper spat and swore, then beckoned to his crewman to drop the stays'l and spinning the wheel he brought the barge head to wind, the great main'sl flapping as she came up into irons[109]. Although he had been politely requested to heave-to this was wartime and the barge skipper knew that the machine guns on the foredeck of HMY *Sheemaun* were not there just for decoration!

As the barge lay rolling in the swell, Stanley fended off while Taff Davies attired in naval cap, dark blue jersey and with pistol holstered belt made a nicely judged leap aboard. HMY *Sheemaun* stood off while he made his checks and looked at the skipper's papers. All had been in order, a hundred tons of coal to be shovelled out at Conyer Creek jetty and exchanged for a load of bricks to be carried up to Lu'non. They bade the barge skipper a safe journey but the cheery salute that Stanley had given him was returned by a scowl and another spit to leeward. Buckie put them on course to take the tide up to their berth at Cliffe Fort jetty. En-route they collected packets of mail from some of the anchored ships and there were kids of rum to be delivered to some smaller naval vessels and mail for the Observation Barge crews.

Stanley had picked up the binoculars and was scanning the murky South shore…

---

109. A nautical term referring to the situation where a sailing vessel is pointing directly into the wind and so is virtually at a standstill.

'Look... there's... the London Stone...'

He passed the binoculars to the others...

'Can't say I see much... just a lot of mud and a thing like a column sticking up...'

Stanley smiled -

'Yes, It's an ancient historic marker[110] of the lower limit of the authority of Guilds and Liveried Companies of the City of London held over the Thames... there's another stone opposite on the North side... called the Crow Stone... they're something to do with fishing rights and permits...'

Buckie sniffed –

'Yer mean it' aad summart t' do wi taxes and dues...'

Taff laughed ...

'Yes... everything in some way has to do with someone grabbing what they can off someone else... even killing... this bloody war is all about grabbing and killing...'

Stanley grinned -

There's a U-Boat in the Medway it's...'

---

110. In the Reign of Henry VII an Act of Parliament decreed that the London Mayor "Shall have the rule of the River Thames from Staines to Yenlade which today is known as the Yantlet. This limit was marked on the Essex shore by a Boundary Stone inscribed with the date 1285 now known as the 'City Stone' or the 'Crow Stone' There is a similar stone on the opposite Kent shore by the Yantlet known as 'The London Stone'. The area was renowned for its richness of oysters and tasty little flat fish called flounders.

He was cut short by a worried looking Buckie -

'It's nae possible... It could'nae get past the Defence Boom... could it?'

Buckie scowled at the cormorant that was struggling to take off into the air ahead of them, it was so full of fish that it had to paddle frantically with its feet for a bit of extra lift.
Stanley continued -

'I was going to say... that nothing's new in this war business. The Medway sub wreck's been there since after the First World War when some surrendered Jerry U-Boats were taken there to be scrapped. That one broke its tow and ended up on the mud at Humble Bee Creek... it's been there ever since... but we've had the Dutch invasions and there's been the Vikings and the Romans... the weapons and the science has changed but it's war just the same... needless killing, stealing and suffering... we Brits have been no better.'

Andy looked up from the chart –

'Talking about Humble Bee Creek an' all that, makes me wonder at those names on our charts. The name of Humble Bee Creek is fairly obvious as is Slaughterhouse Creek and Deadman's Creek and Shivering Sands, but what about the Columbine, the Spaniard, Pan Pudding and the Woolpack?'

Stanley interrupted, grinning -

'Yes, and what about Stangate Creek, I reckon I can lay claim to that one!'

Looking across at Stanley, Buckie scowled –

'Tha's enough o' this daft talk. It's a serious bus'ness we're in. Next time we drop anchor hook in Stangate Creek, ye'll be the one on th' end o' th' chain if ye don' watch out.'

Aside from the rumble of the engines and slapping burble of the bow cutting through the water... there was silence for some time. Then Buckie, always in tune with his inner man, broke the silence -

'Ah'm hungry, d'ye think farmer Jason's got any rabbits?'

A couple of hours later they had moored HMY *Sheemaun* at her Cliffe Fort berth, oiled and covered the Hotchkiss, logged the engine hours, checked oil and fuel, written their reports and handed them in with the mail from the ships and observation barges.

After clearing with the Duty Sentry at the gate hut Taff went across to the nearby farm of Jason Epps while Buckie lit the Rippingille stove. They were lucky, the evening meal would be a thick vegetable stew with rabbit. Daylight was turning to twilight and the long shadows were fading. HMY *Sheemaun's* watch had finished but some of her Medway based sister patrol boats would still be working their evening watch - one could never predict barge and fishing boat movements – and the estuary holding area was teeming with shipping. At least now that it seemed that the Allies had Jerry[111] on his back foot in Europe, the air raids had noticeably eased and tonight for the moment the sky was quiet. Stirring the pot from which delicious aromas wafted into the saloon, Buckie turned his head -

---

111. A slang name for the German enemy.

'Wha'd'ye think o' that big un that's stuck on the Middle Sand?'

Stanley looked up and sucked on his teeth, the corners of his mouth set grimly -

'...phew... I don't like the look of it... the tides are falling off and I doubt she'll re-float for another two weeks unless they can off-load at least half the cargo... wouldn't like to be her skipper!'

Buckie gave the pot a couple of stirs and reached for the ladle -

'Oocchh we've got tae early turn t'morrer so we'll be seein'... all tha'... if there's noo a big bang tonight...'

Taff looked up startled -

'I hadn't thought of that... Gee if that lot goes up it won't be like a mine going off... I could end up back in Pontypool[112] all in a flash and worse still with you lot beside me!'

Meanwhile out in the anchorage just off the Medway approach channel, most of the skippers and captains on the other vessels at anchor near the SS *Richard Montgomery* were well aware of the risk of grounding. As the making tide strengthened and the wind backed northerly the SS *Richard Montgomery*'s anchor chain could be seen stretched out bar taught then suddenly it would go a little slack, only to come bar taught again amid little showers of rust. For a ship at anchor this was every seaman's nightmare, this anchor was dragging across the sands and the huge ship was creeping in ominous little saltatory jerks towards the middle sand bank. In this instance of a huge ship laden with ammunition

---

112. Taff's home-town in Wales 156 miles (250 kms) west of where they were.

and explosives, close amongst other anchored ships and not far from the towns of Sheerness and Southend, a scenario of the worst possible nightmares was unfolding.

It was now dark and surely the Master and his officers and crew must have become aware of their predicament, after all no experienced seaman could mistake the weird intermittent grumbling and graunching sound that a dragging anchor creates! But no response or even evidence of human activity could be seen aboard the big ship. Unknown to the nearby watching crews the exhausted commander of the SS *Richard Montgomery*, Captain Wilkie, was asleep while his Chief Officer was on watch-duty. Oblivious to the dangers of this shallow murky sea with its hidden shoals and sand-banks, he had been told not to disturb his Captain. Under orders of strict radio silence and orders forbidding the showing of any lights, all that the other vessels could do was to sound their whistles and sirens. Still no response came from the SS *Richard Montgomery*.

Then at just before daybreak on Sunday morning 20th August a dreadful disaster was enacted. The stern of the SS *Richard Montgomery* wedged deep into the Sheerness Middle Sandbank and as the tide ebbed the big ship became firmly embedded laying stranded across a wide hollow in the hard, treacherous sands. Captain Wilkie and his crew were now awake and fully alerted to this predicament but there was little that they could do, it was already too late for preventative action. Anyway, the ship's boilers had been partly stood down and while there was enough steam pressure available for 'domestic' purposes it would take hours to raise steam enough to operate the big triple expansion engine and auxiliary machinery. They would have to wait for the next spring tides to re-float the ship but that would not be for another two weeks.

But time and tide wait for no man. The minute hand on the clock of fate was ticking inexorably. Nothing could now re-script the lines of history about to be written. As the powerful tides ebbed and flowed, sand was scoured away from under central part of the great keel, and as the tide ebbed, such massive strains were being applied and re-applied to the grounded hull that steel plates began to fracture with sounds like gunshots. When a plate fracture occurs in a ship built with a riveted hull, the fracture can generally go no further than to the edge of the plate or to the next rivet, but with an all-welded steel hull, a fracture can spread across the welds of contiguous plates, with the result that the hull can break apart like an egg-shell. The fate of the SS *Richard Montgomery* was now sealed. Lifeboats and emergency floats were launched and the crew abandoning the stricken ship scrambled down into them to be taken aboard the various tugs and vessels that had gathered around.

Much later it would be revealed that there had been a tense human personality battle at HMS *Leigh* the shore-based Naval Thames Control Centre on Southend Pier. The Naval Harbour Master had ordered that the SS *Richard Montgomery* be told to anchor where she now was. But the Assistant Harbour Master, horrified at what he regarded as dangerous error of judgement, had tactfully suggested that the position might instead be allocated to a vessel of shallower draught. The Harbour Master didn't agree and insisted that the mooring position was to be allocated to the SS *Richard Montgomery* as he had directed. The Assistant Harbour Master apparently then refusing to signal the order unless ordered to do so in writing. In the ensuing stand-off the superior officer at HMS *Leigh* (Southend Pier Admiralty Offices) sided with the Harbour Master and the Assistant Harbour Master was relieved of duty and re-deployed to another post two days later!

The Duty Schedule for HMY *Sheemaun* 23rd August included service runs to the moored Observation Barges and Balloon Barges in her area as well as the routine of intercepting and examining any incoming smaller coasters, barges and smaller vessels. That there were no reports of the Germans having dropped more mines was a relief to all. Whispering and 'idle talk' was strictly prohibited ... '*Walls have Ears*' the Government posters proclaimed, and the Ministry of Defence repeatedly warned everyone that Hitler's spies could be anywhere. Never-the-less the Thames 'Tom Tom' had already brought rumours that a big Liberty Ship laden with thousands of tons of high explosives had gone aground at the Medway Channel entrance and the skippers of sister Patrol Boats returning to the Cliffe Fort base had confirmed it was indeed the SS *Richard Montgomery*.

Tidal flow to a large extent influenced the order and details of the day's patrol and all vessels were expected to conserve fuel where circumstances allowed. Today Buckie took advantage of the ebb tide to take them eastward down-stream to the Defence Boom, allocating their duties en-route with regards to the North Bank. Then to use the flood tide to help lift them westward bound back up the Thames again while attending to their South Bank duties. The sight at the West end of the Nore Swatchway[113] that greeted the crew was sobering. The huge USS *Richard Montgomery* was clearly stranded. Alongside her were tugs and lighters and close alongside was the SS *Empire Nutfield* an old steamer of 1,561 tons. Steam hoses had been laid across from the SS *Empire Nutfield* by way of providing steam pressure for the latter's winches and derricks. Frantic efforts were in progress to unload the cargo of thousands of tons of bombs and munitions. There was of course nothing that HMY *Sheemaun* could provide in way of material assistance, so stemming the tide, Buckie kept HMY *Sheemaun* standing-off half a cable's length[114] away, her crew ready for any emergency such as a man

---

113. Swatchway - The local term for a navigable channel that runs between two elongated sandbanks.

114. Cable – a marine measurement of 1/10th of a nautical mile or 185 metres.

falling into the water or if the need arose to take personnel ashore. They had a ring-side view of the disaster unfolding before them. Taff ran up the flags –

Foxtrot Oscar - I am standing by

Stanley who was standing by the bow cast the lead over the side and called out -

'By the mark four… and hard sand…'

He looked at Buckie who scowled back

'Whae tha's only twenty five feet[115]… she's well stuck…'

It wasn't long however before one of the Medway Royal Navy Auxiliary Patrol Service Boats arrived on the scene and closing up to HMY *Sheemaun*, her skipper shouted across that having taken some exhausted personnel ashore he had now returned on-station with fresh hands. He thanked Buckie for having filled-in. His orders were to stand by and so HMY *Sheemaun* would be free to continue her patrol.

As subsequent patrol duties allowed, and as and when HMY *Sheemaun* passed by the SS *Richard Montgomery*, Skipper Buckie and his crew had a 'Grand-Stand' view of the unfolding drama. It was evident that the surrounding mini-flotilla had managed to off-load some of her deadly cargo, but the huge ship's back had broken. The once proud hull that heavily laden, had crossed the Atlantic Ocean and withstood a major storm, was now shattered and lying in two halves with the remaining holds submerged underwater. The hectic salvage efforts had been halted on 4th September as no further off-loading could be done. Inevitably further patrol duties of HMY *Sheemaun* took her almost weekly

---

115. 7.6 metres

to the vicinity of the wreck of the SS *Richard Montgomery*. The crew all agreed that it sent shivers down their spines. Stanley looking aft at the masts and derricks standing up out of the swirling waters gritted his teeth…

'It's one thing to be diving over magnetic mines… we're in a wooden boat and that's proved to be pretty safe… well… so far… but that wreck with… they say several thousand tons of unstable explosives that could go bang anytime… I don't like it… not one bit…'

The rusting masts of the wreck of the SS *Richard Montgomery* protruding at Low Water, beneath which still lie thousands of tons of high explosives. Photo by RP taken from *Sheemaun May* 2007

Andy interjected –

'It's true then, what Murphy and Sod have said.'

Buckie scowled –

'Whae d'yer mean? Murphy an tha' fella, I'll nae say t' other name it's noo a decent Christian name.'

Andy laughed –

'Well they described laws so it's claimed. Murphy's Law decrees that whatever can go wrong will go wrong, and Sod's Law decrees that when it does go wrong, it does so with the worst possible outcome.'

Buckie snorted –

'Tha's about jes right then... makes yu think!'

1944

An illegal Stow-Away

'We Didn't Mean to Go to Sea'

Arthur Ransome 1937

Prime Minister Winston Churchill had coined the phrase 'Battle of The Atlantic' in 1941 when Hitler's 'pocket battleships', armed raiders, bombers and U-Boats were sinking many hundreds of merchant ships, ships that had been bringing essential supplies to Britain, many of their brave crews being killed in the process. Back then it had seemed that Hitler by cutting off vital supplies for armaments and vital food would indeed succeed in starving Britain into surrender. However international politics and technology had intervened. The United States of America declared war on Germany in December 1941 after which, air cover was greatly improved for transatlantic convoys and Hitler's U-Boats were being hunted and sunk in ever increasing numbers. The result was that more and more convoys with their huge cargoes of precious supplies were getting through to Britain and this was very evident to those in the Thames Estuary.

In the lead up to the 6th June Operation Overlord or D-Day as it came to be known, there had been a build-up of shipping with literally hundreds of vessels in the Thames Estuary, both merchant transports and warships. Not that those performing their routine patrol duties in the Thames Estuary would have been aware of the implications until the last moment when vessels departed through the Defence Boom 'gates' by the hundred, bound for the Normandy landings. Hitler's war-exhausted forces in Europe were now 'on the run' and by the end of August most of northern France had been liberated. Back home in Blighty the feelings were a mixture of relief and anxiety, for Londoners and people living in the South and South-East of England were still under attack. Hitler's V1 flying bombs were crackling and buzzing their way over the Thames and the East and South Coasts one after another, as many as one every five minutes. It was as if they were on an invisible rail-line. Daily they were killing scores of people and destroying hundreds of buildings. The even newer German V2 rockets were still plummeting down out of the skies but conventional heavy bomber air raids were lessening dramatically, and hope was growing that the end of the war was in sight.

It was Sunday morning and HMY *Sheemaun* lay secured at her Cliffe Forte berth while the crew checked the guns and cleaned and oiled their equipment. Mechanic Stanley Dodd RNVR, had been off duty for a week, enjoying the break to catch-up on precious time with his wife 'Girl', his little boy Michael and their new baby Barrie. Michael was now just four months short of his fourth birthday.

Stanley wanted to show HMY *Sheemaun* to his little boy. They had taken the Steam Train from Upminster to Liverpool Street Station, from where they had crossed to London Bridge Station for the connection to Gravesend Station. Then walked over the bridge to the platform bound for the historic 'Hundred of Hoo' rail-line where they boarded the little three coach train which ran on the Cliffe Fort branch-line. It had been a lengthy but interesting journey. On the way, among the many fascinating activities of that time, they had seen a Hospital Ship discharging wounded servicemen. By the time they arrived at the Cliffe Fort security little Michael was quite tired. At the control barrier the Duty Sentry waved them through with an exaggerated salute much to Michael's delight who returned the salute. Grinning after them the sentry called out after Stanley -

'No cats today then!'

Of all the Auxiliary Thames Patrol Boats, HMY *Sheemaun* was Stanley's favourite. Not only was she solid, seaworthy and comfortable, but while serving on her Stanley enjoyed good companionship and there had been many exciting experiences. He lifted Michael aboard and the crew all made a fuss of the little fellow. Michael was shown around the deck and allowed to touch the Hotchkiss machine guns. He was put in the Carley float and given some ropes to play with, then into the wheel-house where small fingers pulled and pushed at the wheel. Having been lifted down the steep companion way, Michael was shown the rifle rack and then put to sit down at the table with some biscuits and orange juice, by which time he was ready for a sleep. Buckie with his thumb between his fingers pretended to steal the little fellow's nose -

'Hey Stan wha's tha 'bout cats tha' sentry was on aboot?'

Stanley ginned -

'...oh that was last year when we...'

But Stanley's words were lost as the jetty telephone rang. Skipper Buckie leapt up and raced to answer it -

'Yes... Yes... on our way Sar!'

Casting off the mooring lines as he leaped aboard, HMY *Sheemaun* was already being carried away from the jetty by the making tide. The engines which had been ticking over were now 'gunned'. Buckie gave a few orders, warps were coiled, the gun area cleared, and an ammunition box put beside it. The crew put on their webbing belts and holstered their Webley .455 six shot revolvers. HMY *Sheemaun* cleared swiftly away from the jetty and made for the mainstream.

Meanwhile down in the saloon Stanley who had been amusing a tired little boy, suddenly found himself alarmed by the change in engine tone and the movements of a ship coming alive. He knew well what was happening but this time he would have to keep out of the way, he also had to keep Michael quiet! Now he was a supernumerary and with responsibility for a stowaway in the form of his little boy! In the event little Michael was good as gold. Sensing the atmosphere of urgency and being well used at home to be scrambling into the air-raid shelter at the first howling of the air-raid sirens, then waiting baited-breath for the bombs to fall, Michael knew when to keep quiet and obey his mummy and daddy. Buckie peered down the companionway into the saloon and caught Stanley's eye –

'Jesuus… man… I clean forgot ye had yer wee bairn aboard…
Ah well it's just a routine an' it's a lovely day for a sail!'

HMY *Sheemaun* punched against the incoming tide off Lower Hope Point and then headed East into the Yantlet Channel. The gun crew scanning ahead reported that at about a mile distant was a vessel low in the water and lumbering slowly towards them, black smoke curling away from her funnel in the light south-westerly wind. Apparently, because of all the fuss and commotion carrying on around the sunken USS *Richard Montgomery* this small tanker had not been intercepted and examined. That she was a known 'Regular' made no difference so far, as security was concerned, a concealed enemy agent could cause mayhem at the Hole Haven fuel dump. As the distance between them closed it was evident the tanker had not been examined as she was not flying the pass-code flags for the day.
HMY *Sheemaun* ran up her now well-worn flags –

Foxtrot Delta Quebec –'Heave-too – I will board'

For a few minutes nothing seemed to happen with the tanker... but no... she was losing way... and then the tanker hoisted the reply flags

Tango Foxtrot – 'I agree – will comply'

Ten minutes later coir fenders were being put out as HMY *Sheemaun* swung around to come up on the tanker's lee side which made of course good sea-sense but took no account of what the tanker was carrying. As they came alongside the waft of oil fumes carried a'lee by the wind was quite over-whelming.

Andy and Taff scramble up the boarding ladder, pistols in their holsters. Buckie at the wheel eased HMY *Sheemaun* to stand away and Mick stood by the Hotchkiss. It all looked quite menacing and even though they had met the tanker skipper at a previous examination search, this was war and security was paramount. The papers were in order and a quick search of the crew quarters and engine room and stores confirmed the crew list. That there was no way anyone could remain for long stowed-away in or between the fume ridden tanks and survive, made the examination of this ship much easier than if she had been a dry cargo carrier! The tanker skipper was given the flag code for the day and bade safe voyaging. Half an hour later HMY *Sheemaun* docked back at Cliffe Fort Naval Jetty and discharged her own supernumerary crew and one small stow-away. Stanley had been very relieved that they had not been detailed to do an examination in proximity to the SS *Richard Montgomery* now lying there awash in the sands, broken in two halves and laden with thousands of tons of explosives. The day's log and report when handed it in later made no mention of a small stow-away!

It would come about that some seventy years later Michael Dodd recalled this incident to me -

'… I remember trotting down a long jetty and Dad stopping by a boat and talking, and then I was lifted onto it… I remember the guns and playing with the Carley float although I wouldn't have known what it was. I remember pulling the wheel and being taken down into the saloon where there were rifles on a rack… I remember the engines but don't remember going anywhere. I do remember we stopped by a big black ship and two of the crew went up a ladder to it. They were dressed in black, had pistols and were wearing gas-masks… I don't remember going back home afterwards…'

Mike reflected that with hindsight the 'big black boat' he remembered was a small coastal oil tanker and the examination crew would have had their gasmasks in case they had to inspect areas permeated by toxic oil fumes.

71 years later - Michael Dodd once again in *Sheemaun's* Saloon - photo RP

1944

Hitler's 'V' Bomb Terror Menace

'And a ton came down on a coloured road,
And a ton came down on a gaol,
And a ton came down on a freckled girl,
And a ton came down on the black canal.
And a ton came down on a hospital,
And a ton on a manuscript,
And a ton shot up through the dome of a church,
And a ton roared into the crypt.'

From the Rhyme of the Flying Bomb - by Mervyn Peake.

As aforesaid, Hitler believed that by subjecting the British people to unbearable terror and random mass killings he could force the United Kingdom to surrender. Accordingly, his scientists at the secret weapons research centre at Peenemunde developed the Vergetlungswaffe or Vengeance Weapon. First launched in June 1944 from coastal sites in Northern France and Holland this was an early form of 'cruise missile'. It had a simple cylindrical fuselage tapered at the front and rear and carried on two short wings. Measuring only 27. 3 feet (8.32m) long and with a wingspan of 17.6 feet (5.37 m). At the rear was a basic tail-plane and stacked on the rudder stock was a tube almost a 'stove-pipe' – the pulse-jet engine. The only moving part being a shutter valve at the front of the pipe.

The V-bomb was catapulted from a ramp. Its forward movement would force air in through the shutter valve, to be spray-mixed with petrol and then spark ignited. The explosion would slam the shutter valve closed and the hot, expanding gases would exhaust out backwards from the jet nozzle providing a forward thrust. As soon as the pressure in the jet pipe fell, the shutter valve would re-open and the forward movement of the missile would force another charge of air into the combustion chamber of the jet pipe. A spark ignited the fuel charge and the process would repeat about 40 times a second for as long as there was a supply of fuel and air. It made a sound like a very loud motorcycle. In addition to fuel, the fuselage carried almost two thousand pounds of Amatol high explosive and simple mechanisms for controlling the altitude. The flight speed was about 350 mph (563 kph) and height controlled at about 3,000 feet (914 m). At a pre-determined time, the elevator would be locked down, the fuel shut off and the missile would spiral randomly down to explode on whatever was below.

The Flying V Bomb or 'Buzz Bomb' raids started in 1944 on June 13th a week after the D-Day landings. Unlike raids by piloted bombers, these raids occurred day and night and in any weather. The 'Kill Zone' was indiscriminate. Initially around a hundred V1 bombs fell on the London area every hour! In about three months more than six thousand civilians were killed, seventeen thousand injured and more than a million homes destroyed by the V1 bombs. It is estimated that more than nine thousand V1 bombs were launched against London of which nearly half were shot down by British Fighter planes or by ant-aircraft fire. Some bombs became tangled in the wires of the Air Raid Prevention Balloons; some were shot down by armed vessels in the Thames. But such a small and fast weapon presented a very difficult target to defend against. These hideous devices blasted off from launching ramps in Northern France to hurtle across the South Coast and from Holland to fly across the Thames Estuary all aimed at London and guided by a radio beam system. V bombs were launched as frequently as one every five minutes or so day and night. It was an extremely dangerous situation and very difficult to defend against.

The defence barrage balloons played a significant role, with at any one time some seventeen hundred balloons being deployed aloft directly in the path of these 'Flying Bombs'. On the Thames a civilian crew would manage the Balloon vessel and a small crew of airmen managed the balloon. A powered winch usually in the hold or a low part of the barge would be used to 'fly' the balloon.

Unlike the land-based balloon units, those at sea could not secure the balloon down to earth if the wind was too strong, it had to be flying all the time, so servicing and re-inflation with the highly inflammable hydrogen had to be performed as best could be managed. During stormy weather, even winched as low as practical, a balloon, with its large surface area and negative weight could become very difficult to handle and dangerous. In the Thames estuary numbers of fishing vessels, and moored barges were adapted to fly these anti-aircraft balloons. The Royal Navy Thames Auxiliary Patrol Service played an important role in keeping these vessels supplied, assisting with crew changes and communications.

Those simple balloons it is said, accounted for two hundred or so flying bombs which tangled with their steel wires. About a thousand V1 bombs were shot down by fast flying Hawker Tempest fighters, American P-51 Mustangs, Supermarine Spitfires, fast Mosquito fighter-bombers and much later, the new British twin jet fighter, the Gloster Meteor. The shore-based anti-aircraft (Ack Ack) Bofors guns and fast-firing 'Pom Poms' also downed many V1 bombs.

The Thames Auxiliary Patrol Service vessels including HMY *Sheemaun* also took every opportunity shoot at a V1 bomb, but the target was small, fast, at the limit of machine gun range and the gun crew had to be very quick off the mark! There is no record as to what success the Auxiliary Patrol Vessels had in this respect, but the crews did their best and 'having a go' with a machine gun gave much more satisfaction than shaking fists into the air!

Gunner Taff Davies on HMY *Sheemaun* advised –

'Look boyo they go dead straight… so imagine that line, track the sight about fifteen degrees in front of the bloody thing, aim about ten degrees above and give it a good squirt…'

The Thames estuary area was a boiling pot of fighting activity. At night carbon-arc searchlights probed the night sky. Observation posts were constantly telephoning information to command posts. On the north and south banks shore based anti-aircraft batteries pounded the skies with explosive fragmentation shells. All along the Thames armed vessels did likewise. Almost every moment somewhere up and down the Thames guns would be firing and in daylight fast fighters would be hunting down the evil pilotless V bombs. Fragments of shrapnel and pieces of airframes rained down often causing damage to property and person. Day and night the stench of cordite drifted on the winds.

All in all, it is believed that nearly eighty percent of the V1 flying bombs were prevented from hitting their indiscriminate target – the civilian Greater London area. Never-the-less, the two thousand or so that did get through wreaked terrible damage, death and injury.

German V1 Flying Bomb - Exhibit at Manston RAF Memorial Museum. Photo R.P.

1945

The End of the Second World War in Europe and the 'World's End'
8ᵗʰ May

'If you win, you need not have to explain … if you lose,
you should not be there to explain!'[116]

Adolph Hitler

This year at last saw the final collapse of Hitler's Axis forces across Europe. The organisation and structure of his Deutches Reich or Third Reich was imploding around him, supplies of food, weapons, fuel and essentials were exhausted. Most of the German population was close to starvation and like a massive chain of stacked dominoes falling across the map of Europe, German troops were surrendering everywhere. Over three quarters of a million Axis troops surrendered on the Eastern Front, over a hundred thousand had surrendered in Italy and naturally news of this was filtering North across the Channel. Throughout Blighty generally and in London and amongst those whose duties were on the Thames Estuary, men's spirits were mounting. By April over one and a half million Axis troops had surrendered or had been captured by the Allies; so very many that it was a major problem to contain them and to feed them. At home in Blighty the ongoing severe limitations of fuel, food and vital supplies, meant that Britain had no reserves left with which to provide accommodation and food for even a small portion of the many thousands of dis-armed German troops and war-prisoners. More than a million former Axis troops were being confined in encampments up and down the

116. Goodreads.com/quotes/tag/war

Rhine Valley in Rheinwiesenlagers, which were little more than hastily thrown up barbed wire enclosures with minimal or no accommodation. Facilities and food had to be severely rationed. Thousands of Hitler's former Axis troops trapped and homeless, were fading and dying from exposure, malnutrition and disease in these camps. Sadly, but perhaps understandably men serving with the Allied forces, now war-hardened and embittered by the deprivations, by the sacrifices and killings they had been forced to endure at the hands of their erstwhile enemy, showed little sympathy or mercy.

For some months the Thames Estuary had been largely spared from the accustomed intrusions of the Luftwaffe and the fast, heavily armed and bravely commanded Schnellboots. No longer did huge German bomber formations with their engines droning and throbbing bring menace to the night sky. It had been some time now since any fast hedge-hopping enemy day fighter had zoomed overhead machine-gunning anything that looked a likely target and significantly the threat for those dreadful pilotless V1 bombs had ceased since the Allies had over-run and neutralised the launching sites in Northern France and Holland.

Towards the end of April news was also filtering through of the unimaginable and horrific findings at the Bergen-Belsen concentration camp; findings that would soon become known as Hitler' Holocaust of the Jews. On the 29th April the Nazi forces in Italy surrendered. The next day Hitler committed suicide. On 2nd May the Berlin Defence Forces surrendered. On 4th May this was followed by surrender of the German Forces in North West German, in Denmark and in the Netherlands. On the 5th May Admiral Doenitz ordered all the German U-Boats to cease hostilities and return to their bases. The next day he unconditionally surrendered all the German military and naval forces to the Allies and at 10.00 on 8th May the German occupying forces on the Channel Islands surrendered. On that historic day at 3 O'clock in the afternoon Prime Minister Winston Spencer Churchill made his momentous BBC radio announcement that -

'Hostilities will officially end at one minute after midnight tonight, but in the interests of saving lives the 'Cease Fire' began yesterday to be sounded all along the front, and our dear Channel Islands are also to be freed today'

King George VI broadcast his famous speech by radio from Buckingham Palace, and everywhere in Britain there was a huge sense of relief, but no family had been spared from the loss of loved ones and with so many sailors, soldier and airmen still far away from home there was little room in people's hearts for care-free rejoicing. Civil discipline and governmental authority had to be maintained while there were still such enduring hardships. Restriction of Thames shipping movements after dark was still mandatory for although no more bombs and mines had been dropped, there was an ever-present risk from the many hundreds that were as-yet un-detected and lying 'dormant' and unexploded! At last merchant shipping movements in the Thames began to increase and warship movements were now mostly concerned with relocations. But it was not yet Peace-Time for although the European War was over, a fierce war was still being waged in the Far East against the almost demoniacal Japanese forces who had allied themselves with Hitler.

Aboard HMY *Sheemaun* on 8th May it was patrol duties as usual, but everyone aboard now believed the War would soon end and hopefully life would resume as normal – whatever that might now mean. The Thames Auxiliary Patrol Service boats were not fitted with radio. For them communications between vessels were by voice – often bawled through megaphones, flashed by Aldis lamp signal or by hoisting flags and of course by the usual couriered written orders.

Buckie was heading HMY *Sheemaun* up-river with the flood tide, when astern of them with a huge white 'Bone in its Teeth' came a tug tooting its whistle, clouds of steam and black smoke swirling after it, the crew were waving frantically and one man on the bow was waving what looked like a towel. Buckie eased the throttles back and cursed the 'Maniac' who was skippering the tug. He prepared to turn HMY *Sheemaun* into the tug's surging wake so as to 'ride' the heavy wash that would hit them as the tug passed.

On the tug foredeck, a waving crewman, megaphone to his mouth, shouted across the momentous news that Prime Minister Winston Churchill had just announced the end of hostilities in Europe. A great shout of jubilation went up in HMY *Sheemaun*'s wheelhouse, the crew shaking hands and clapping each other on the back. Buckie pushed his thumb on the horn button as if his life depended on it. No hands were on the wheel when the wash from the tug came broadside on and HMY *Sheemaun* did such a Victory Roll that the crew were sent sprawling and Taff fell halfway down the companion way! But what would they do now? There was no precedence and they had no orders that covered such circumstances. Buckie who had by now grabbed the wheel and brought them back on course was grinning from ear to ear –

'Occhh… that's it lads we'll head for the old Tilbury Fort it's jes o'er there tae star'bd… there's a wee jetty for tying to… and the World's End Pub[117]… whae a watering hole!'

Another ten minutes saw HMY *Sheemaun* berthed against a little jetty, just across the Thames from where on the southern bank at the Northfleet wharves, the concrete Maunsell forts

117. An old English Pub (Bar/Diner) dating from the 17th Century and said to be Haunted by the ghost of the renowned Highwayman and Robber 'Swift Nick' who was hanged in the year 1684.

had been built only a few years earlier. This time the mood was very different. HMY *Sheemaun* had never been left un-attended but this time she was secured to the quayside and locked while the crew walked the fifty or so yards along Fort Road to the World's End Pub. Celebrations were already in swing - bugger the restrictions on opening hours! The Public Bar was crowded with men and women crying for joy, dancing and hugging each other. Despite all the celebrations and carry-on Stanley Dodd found himself fascinated by a relic from the old days of whaling – a sinister looking whaling harpoon usually mounted on the wall[118] behind the bar. The harpoon had been taken down by one of the watermen who was parading around waving it in the air and shouting -

'Up yours Adolph!'

Then using the harpoon as a giant baton, he led the happy gathering as they sang Vera Lynn's already famous D-Day Song –

'I give you a toast ladies and Gentlemen
I give you a toast Ladies and Gentlemen
May this fair land we love so well
In Dignity and freedom dwell
While world may change and go awry
There'll always be an England
Where there's a country lane
Wherever there's a cottage small
Beside a field of grain.
While there's a busy street
Wherever there's a turning wheel
A million marching feet

---

118. Mike Dodd told me of his father's reminiscences about *Sheemaun* and those heady celebrations at the World's End Inn and the story about the harpoon above the bar.

Red, white and blue
What does it mean to you?
Surely you're proud?
Shout it aloud
Britons awake!
The Empire too
We can depend on you
Freedom remains
These are the chains
Nothing can break
There'll always be an England
And England shall be free
If England means as much to you
As England means to me.'

Many were the smiles and tears of joy in that smoke laden bar.
Smiles and tears which in that emotionally charged and jubilant throng were high-lighted tragically by the contrasting tears
and anguish of the many amongst them whose loved ones had
made the final sacrifice. A jubilant RNVR Crew returned HMY
Sheemaun to her berth at Cliff Fort. When later the skipper came
to write up the official log book for the day, some discretion
seemed in order!

There would be more celebrations to follow at the base, but
modified routines and duties would have to be followed for a
few more months, after which it was hoped that no-one would
have to subsequently helm or navigate an Auxiliary Patrol Boat.
For Stanley Dodd those pints at the World's End pub had probably been of the sweetest brew he could remember. There was
however still much uncertainty about the immediate months
ahead and a very uncertain future lay ahead for the crew, for
their families, for the World and for HMY *Sheemaun*. But the
Nation needed a boost to morale and despite all the hardships

and strict rationing of food and essential supplies, countrywide arrangements were being made apace for Victory Celebrations.

Soon afterwards King George VI ordered that a special personal message be sent to all the schools in Britain -

8th June, 1946

TO-DAY, AS WE CELEBRATE VICTORY, I send this personal message to you and all other boys and girls at school. For you have shared in the hardships and dangers of a total war and you have shared no less in the triumph of the Allied Nations.

I know you will always feel proud to belong to a country which was capable of such supreme effort; proud, too, of parents and elder brothers and sisters who by their courage, endurance and enterprise brought victory. May these qualities be yours as you grow up and join in the common effort to establish among the nations of the world unity and peace.

George R.I

However, a fierce war was still being waged in the Far East. Russia had also declared war on Japan and the Japanese, refusing to accept the reality of their position, were fighting desperately, now defending their very homeland. Then for the first time in world war history on 6th August an atomic bomb was dropped. The target was the City of Hiroshima and on 9th August a second atomic bomb was dropped on the City of Nagasake. Finally, on August 14th, the stubborn Emperor Michinomiya Hirohito accepted the conditions drawn up at the Potsdam Meeting by the Allies and the Nationalist Government of China, and Japan surrendered unconditionally. The Second World War was at last over. An estimated fifty-five million people had been killed, but to what avail? A question that may never be fully answered. History will be the judge.

Sheemaun salutes Stanley Dodd RNVR and her War-time Crews

Time-Line –

- In the British General Election of 5th July 1945 Winston Churchill's Conservative Party was defeated by the Labour Party's Clement Attlee. Britain had a new Prime Minister.

- HMY *Sheemaun* was decommissioned and transferred to the Department of Naval Sea Transport with which she served until finally laid up on 6th November 1945 and sold out of Naval service in 1947. The Certificate of British Registry C344 - 'Blue Book' confirms this second registration in 1947.[119]

- Clothing material was severely rationed. The following year French engineer Louis designed the Bikini which had to be small enough to pass through a wedding ring!

---

119. Sadly, for posterity and the interests of historians, the Small Vessel log books were destroyed by the Navy Records Department in 1950.

PART THREE
The Post-war Years
1947

Operation Blackcurrant and
Sheemaun is for Sale

'The more it snows – tiddeley pom,
The more it goes – tiddeley pom,
The more it goes on snowing
and nobody knows - tiddeley pom,
How cold my toes – tiddeley pom,
How cold my toes are growing – tiddeley pom'

A A Milne – The House at Pooh Corner

After braving Hitler's Nazi onslaught and still reeling from the savagery of War, Britannia was dealt another cruel blow this time by the elements.

'Operation Blackcurrant'

The Second World War had left Britain and Europe financially and materially ruined. Britain was in deep recession. Fathers, mothers, brothers, cousins and children had been killed in their thousands, families dispersed, and businesses decimated. Many foods, most fuels, soap, clothing, and most commodities were still rationed or in very short supply. The summer of 1946 had been the wettest for years, the wheat harvest lay in ruins and bread rationing had been re-introduced. As if that wasn't hardship enough the winter of 1946 - 47 then produced the coldest winter freeze for a hundred years. Snow storms swept the country. On January 28th temperatures plummeted to minus 20° C

(68° F) and were to remain well below 0° C for several weeks. Thousands of tons of stored potatoes and other root vegetables were frozen solid and ruined, hundreds of thousands of sheep and cattle froze or starved to death and transport by road or rail became virtually impossible. Clement Atlee was Prime Minister and Emanuel Shinwell his Minister of Fuel and Power received death threats from some of those citizens who had 'Had Enough'!

From Whitstable on the Kent Coast, the view looking north across the Thames Estuary was that of a blur of dark grey skies with almost blizzard conditions. The sea appeared to be whipped into white foam, except that the white capping on the sea was not foam and spray, it was sea-ice! The river Medway was frozen; the sea-water at Chatham and Sheerness docks was frozen. *Sheemaun* with her decks covered deep in snow lay ice-bound at her Chatham berth. The docks were at a standstill, there was no form of transport able to function and everything was frozen solid. The exception being the few dozen or so coal or oil-fired vessels that with their boilers still fired and steaming were just warm enough for some ice to melt and they had steam hoses available to blast some ice away – just so long as they had fuel remaining. All ferry services were disrupted and many unable to operate. The stockpiles of 'King Coal' were frozen solid and what little coal it had been possible to dig out from them, could not be transported very far. The whole of the UK was at a frozen standstill.

Aged eleven years, I was one among the intake of new-boys at Cheltenham College Junior School. The school had been built two years after the death of Queen Victoria and its architecture very much reflected the Victorian ethos of fresh air and discipline. The Senior School proud of its reputation for being a military and classical college that had sent many Old Cheltonians on to military and political careers. I had never been away from home before and now found myself boarded in a long dormitory on the second floor. There were fifteen beds ranged down each side, separated by wooden divisions into 'horse boxes' with a curtain across the open end. Each 'horse box' had its own sliding sash window and there were three sash windows at the far end of the dormitory. *'Fresh air is good for you'* was the mantra, double glazing and roof insulation had yet to be invented. At that time, as he would later discover, it was fashionable to treat tuberculosis patients by exposure to fresh cold air and cold salt bathing at hospitals such as the Royal Sea-Bathing Hospital at Margate. And so, at post-war Cheltenham College – with its tough military ethos - the expectation was that every window had to be open at night. The result being that the bitterly cold winter winds whistled through thirty-three open windows in a long narrow dormitory!

While *Sheemaun* lay frozen to her berth at Chatham Docks in Kent, together with my fellow pupils I was similarly affected in Cheltenham. We awoke to snow on our bedside chairs and ice on our pillows from frozen breath. The padded cotton coverlet, the two thick (army pattern) blankets and the coarse bed sheet sometimes froze into a cardboard like tunnel. We adapted by wearing two pairs of pyjamas under our dressing gowns, and socks and gloves when going to bed. In the morning some boys would have to wriggle out from their beds leaving the frozen blankets and coverings standing like a little igloo! Fortunately, all pipes were frozen so the de-riguer cold showers (toshings) had been abandoned and rules were then relaxed to allow dormitory windows to be kept closed.

One hundred-thousand or so emergency worker consisting of British and Polish troops, German and Italian Prisoners of War, Canadian troops and many hundreds of volunteers toiled to clear roads and railway lines and assist with distributing food. Electricity supply was reduced to nineteen hours a day and in addition there were frequent 'Blackouts'. At times the Houses of

Parliament and even Buckingham Palace had to resort to using candles and oil lamps. Under the 'Emergency Measures' Act the Government together with the Royal Navy and the Army organised 'Operation Blackcurrant'. In 'Operation Blackcurrant' the Royal Navy dispersed submarines and other vessels with powerful electrical generators to coastal towns and dockyards and engineers from both the Army and the Navy managed to link the generators of these vessels to the National Electricity Grid.

March at last saw the mercury climbing above zero but a deep depression then blew in from the Atlantic and brought with it the wettest March for three hundred years and even worse it was accompanied by severe gales. But Planet Earth, carried by unstoppable Newtonian forces on its orbit around the sun, at last began to receive warming rays to its northern hemisphere. The big thaw that followed resulted in massive country-wide flooding. Gloucester and Tewkesbury, just two amongst the scores of other similarly affected towns, villages and hamlets, were underwater and emergency food was being distributed by Australian and Canadian voluntary aid-workers. It was a tough time for everyone, tough for parents, tough for workers, tough for schools and very tough for young college boarders, an experience never to be forgotten by those who endured it.

With the ice and snow finally gone and floods largely drained away. The month of May saw the sun shining. Fields and hedgerows were green, and memories of the hard winter were fading. Meanwhile, at Chatham Docks *Sheemaun* was back at work engaged in harbour duties and ferrying personnel etc., but the little ship was beginning to look tired, her paint and varnish in need of work and her engines in need of an overhaul. Water dripped into her saloon and cabins through deck seams which had been forced open by the expanding ice during the Big Freeze.

Spring sunshine also bathed the West Country and with

temperatures a week or so ahead of those felt in the County of Kent the fertile red earthed fields in Devonshire County were already turning green. At about that time the pupils at Cheltenham College were, to their amazement, issued with packs of usually forbidden chewing gum. We were told it would prevent us from suffering colds and illnesses. The chewing gum was laced with penicillin and we were, in fact, part of an experiment to see if penicillin could reduce the infection rate in institutional populations! No one could then foresee that microbial resistance to anti-biotics would one day become a global problem.

As the warming sun shone across the River Dart Estuary fourteen-year-old Officer Cadet John Julian Robertson Oswald stepped proudly out from the Royal Naval College Dartmouth to commence his career with the Royal Navy. John Oswald, who preferred to be known as Julian, was to about to embark on an as yet untrod pathway that would take him towards a glittering naval career in the years ahead. One day the paths of Admiral of the Fleet Sir Julian Oswald GCB[120] and *Sheemaun* would briefly coincide!

Meanwhile after the most severe winter in living memory, the temperature was at last rising and it was again possible to move vessels around. Vast amounts of once essential war equipment and materials no longer required by the Ministry of Defence would have to be disposed of at auction, especially equipment that was costly to maintain. Amongst the many smaller vessels no longer needed was *Sheemaun* and she had been taken west to Littlehampton to be included with a motley collection of small craft, harbour tugs, a couple of naval pinnaces, some sailing gigs, and some tired looking motor yachts all listed 'For Sale as Seen'.

---

120. Grand Cross of the Order of Bath – An Honour Created in the year 1725 by King George 1st reflecting the medieval ceremony in which Knights of the realm were bathed as a symbol of Purification.

Perhaps not surprisingly *Sheemaun* stood out as being a pretty and still sea-worthy looking little ship although clearly in need of some restorative work. Amongst the throngs of onlookers and potential buyers was Mrs J O M Scott of Fitzwilliam Square, Dublin.

Mrs Scott was looking for a comfortable motor yacht and hoping for a good bargain. She had stepped aboard and examined some of the motor yachts on display and had particularly liked the looks of the one named *Sheemaun*. She had given the *Sheemaun*'s wheel a turn or two and it had felt good. Her bid had been successful and now she found herself the proud but apprehensive owner of a pretty 1930s Gentleman's Motor Yacht. But a motor yacht that from stem to stern was showing the wear accumulated from her years of War Service as an armed Thames Patrol Boat and the wear and tear of a further two years in service with the Department of Sea Transport. Her engines were just about on their last legs and would need to be replaced and the vessel needed a full and thorough re-fit. When Mrs Scott was appraised of the likely cost of this and the likely time-scale, she understandably had second thoughts and so the broker was instructed to once again advertise *Sheemaun* for sale.

Time-Line –

- Leap Year 1948. In Britain National Service Conscription was regularised. All men aged 18-26 had to serve for 18 moths full time in the armed forces.

- Clothes Rationing ended.

- Royal Astronomer Fred Hoyle introduced the term 'Big Bang'.

- Playwright and historian Julian Fellowes was born.

- George Orwell published his book 'Nineteen Eighty-Four'.

- The Berlin Blockade was lifted.

- 20th November Princess Elizabeth was married to Philip Mountbatten the Duke of Edinburgh at Westminster Abbey.

- There was an epidemic in Britain of poliomyelitis which killed many hundreds of children and left thousands paralysed.

- India gained Independence from British rule.

- Soap was still used for washing clothes and washing one's hair. Detergents were yet to come on the market. There was no such thing as Hair Conditioner. Toothpaste came in squeezable lead – yes, lead tubes. Boxes and containers were made of wood or cardboard, bags were made of paper, sacks were made of jute or other fibre. There were no plastic bags, no cling-film, no polystyrene, no polythene products.

- The following year – 1948, on 5th July Health Secretary Aneurin Bevan would introduce the National Health Service, paid for by taxation and entirely free at point of access for all British people.

- The HMT *Empire Windrush* arrived in the UK with 492 Jamaican immigrants.

1949

London Heathrow Airport
October 19th

'Fly me to the moon
Let me play among the stars
Let me see what spring is like
On a-Jupiter and Mars.'

Frank Sinatra

Lt. Cmdr. Roy Calvert-Link RNVR[121] together with his wife Margaret climbed up a spiral staircase and into the spacious luxury of the upper floor on the massive four-engined Boeing Stratocruiser N1028V. They settled into a pair of comfortable-seats holding hands as they gazed down at the scurrying personnel below on the tarmac, bustling to load the last of the luggage and cargo into the cavernous hold beneath them. The Second World War with its fears, its tragedies and all that hard work on de-gaussing ships in the Thames Estuary and of finding ways to defeat the feared Nazi magnetic mines, was at last behind them. Roy's time in the Royal Navy had been stressful but it had been interesting work. He might not have been exposed to the rigours of 'Front Line' fighting but he had known what it was to be bombed and shot at and he had seen at first hand the horrors of mutilating injuries and death. He also had come to realise the importance of the work he had been doing. Any shortfall or miscalculation when the magnetism in the huge hull of a steel ship was being neutralised could easily have cost many lives. He had served his country and he was now happily

---

121. Roy Hanson Calvert-Link b.11.6.1904 – d.21.3.1967. Lies buried in plot G696 Glendale National Cemetery, Richmond USA.

married. But the war experience and more recently his exposure to American culture and technology had left him feeling restless. His application for United States Citizenship had been accepted.

Ahead of them a new and exciting life was beckoning, a life in the United States Navy. Roy now a war-hardened expert in naval magnetics, de-Guassing and mine detection was excitedly looking forward to a new life in America, to a new post waiting for him in the United States Navy. Margaret, still a little apprehensive and worried at leaving her relatives and family at home in Britain, was at the same time thrilled and excited at the prospect of their home-to-be. A new home, a home that would provide them with luxuries such as an electric washing machine, an electric vacuum cleaner, coffee grinder, a wonderful electric refrigerator, air conditioning and many other luxuries as yet almost unimaginable back in war-torn and exhausted England.

The stewardess was telling them to extinguish any cigarettes and pipes, to fasten their seat belts and listen to safety instructions. Then the four mighty Pratt and Whitney radial engines one at a time coughed, wheezed, sputtered and jerked as they roared into vibrating thundering energy, momentarily belching out great smoky clouds of unburned fuel. After a few minutes the engine tone settled to a pulsing, throbbing growl. The engineer, seated at the control desk before an array of glowing dials and switches, minutely studied a flickering green oscilloscope screen as he switched between modalities to variously display engine temperatures, induction pressures, spark plug performances, exhaust temperatures, oil pressures, fuel line pressures etc. The readings showed all were normal and a nod was given to the Captain. The next moment they were bumping and swaying as the Stratocruiser taxied out to the end of the runway where it came to a halt.

Each radial engine with its twenty-eight cylinders, was capable of developed a staggering three and a half thousand horsepower, turning a massive four-bladed propeller sixteen-feet[122] in diameter. The huge airliner pulsating and vibrating with energy was now held back only by its brakes as the Captain eased the throttles forward. Suddenly as the brakes were released they felt themselves being pushed back into their seats. The Stratocruiser lifting its nose began to heave itself down the runway then as it gained speed the Captain fully opened the throttles and now they really were being pressed back into their seats. After a few moments the vibrations and the pounding eased, the engine note became less urgent and the pressure eased. They were airborne.

Margaret swallowed and sucked hard on the boiled sweet as advised and issued by the stewardess, but her ears still popped as she had been warned, although not uncomfortable it was a little disconcerting. Roy squeezed gently on her hand. They were flying West to a new life, to a new home at 624 Boulevard East, Weehawken, on the Hudson River, New Jersey just five or six miles North of New York ... Far below them the English Coast faded into the haze.

Putting his hand into his breast pocket Roy withdrew his wallet, within it was his new US Citizens Passport and as he took that out for another re-assuring glance, a photograph slipped out and fell between their seats. Margaret with her slim hand, reached down and retrieved what was a photograph of a graceful motor-yacht, the *Sheemaun*. She knew how much he had loved that boat.

The speakers crackled and the steward announced that they were now flying at three hundred and forty miles an hour at an altitude of twenty-five thousand feet. Passengers could smoke, and the cocktail bar and observation lounge were open. Margaret lay her head on Roy's shoulder and closed her eyes. As the massive Stratocruiser continued to thunder its way across the Atlantic a stewardess was pushing a trolley towards them

122. 4.9 metres

laden with plates and tasty looking dishes… and a wine list…
a delicious aroma of coffee wafted through the cabin. Dinner
was being served. This was so very different from the life of post-
war rationing and austerity that was fast disappearing over the
horizon behind them.

1950

Sheemaun and Major Harry Emory Chubb
CBE, M. I. Mech.E.Director of Chubb & Sons Lock & Safe Company

Sheemaun lay for some further weeks moored at her Littlehampton berth. The little ship was clearly in need of an extensive re-fit and there was concern as to the reliability of her aging engines. But Major Emory Chubb evidently knew a classic when he saw one and Mrs Scott, was happy to accept his offer.

Emory Chubb's story is that of a global business success. His great-grandfather Charles Chubb in 1804 worked as a ship's iron-monger and later together with his brother Jeremiah had set up a locksmith business in Wolverhampton. As the Chubb brothers cleverly devised and ingeniously crafted ever more sophisticated and effective locks and security devices, their successful business correspondingly expanded. In 1823 King George IV awarded the company a special license and the Chubb Company thereafter supplied the locks for His Majesty's Prison Service and to the General Post Office. In 1851 the Chubb Company provided security for the Koh-i-Noor diamond when it was exhibited at the Great Exhibition. The Chubb & Sons Lock & Safe Company went on to become a world-wide establishment providing security for governments and Royal families alike. Charles Chubb's grandson George Hayter Chubb was knighted in 1885, created a Baronet in 1900 and in 1927 was raised to the peerage as Baron Hayter of Chislehurst.

An article in the 1909 June 12th edition of the journal *'Flight'* on p344 reports on the 'Aero Club of the United Kingdom'. The article records Mr H Emory Chubb among the newly elected members. The members of the elite Aero Club of the United

Kingdom enjoyed a close association with the equally select Motor Yacht Club and together the clubs yearly organised a widely attended

'Sailor-Aeronaut Race'

Emory Chubb had an expert eye for tradition and quality in general and a fondness for Rolls Royce and Bentley cars. Through his association with the Motor Yacht Club he acquired an acquaintance with motor yachts. During the First World War he had served with the Royal Army Service Corps, the predecessor of the modern Royal Logistic Corps, while being at the same time the managing director of the Chubb & Sons Lock & Safe Company. Emory was to generously offer his administrative skills during the Second World War when at the age of sixty-two years he was appointed Deputy Superintendent to the Special Constabulary, Hertfordshire – a role with full responsibilities but voluntary and unpaid. He was also Honorary Advisor to the War Department Sea Transport Fleet in which *Sheemaun* had served for two years.

Lloyds Register of Yachts for 1950 records Mr H E Chubb as the owner of *Sheemaun* – Registered Home Port – Littlehampton, and so my wife Maura contacted the late Emory Chubb's cousin, the current Lord Hayter, in the hope that he might have some recollections or access to records in relation to the boat that Emory had owned, albeit briefly.

Lord Hayter – 'Call me Bill', charmingly received the enquiry with warmth and enthusiasm but was not aware of any family history relating to *Sheemaun*. This was hardly surprising for Emory had owned *Sheemaun* for less than a year and at a time when the boat needed a substantial re-fit before any benefits could be enjoyed. As does everyone who steps into *Sheemaun*'s wheelhouse, Emory Chubb would have put his hands to her mahogany wheel, but it was a different type of wheel that Emory favoured as Bill amusingly described –

> 'He had a rather splendid Bentley saloon and used to take my father shooting in Scotland… He was coming back from Scotland with my grandfather, Archie Chubb, who was driving. But Archie was a terrible driver and finally Emory insisted on taking over. Shortly after, a tractor pulled out from a field right in front of them. Emory, cool as a cucumber, put the Bentley into a four-wheel drift and managed to shoot through the gate into the field behind the tractor. Now stuck in the field, my grandfather's only comment was – "you should have let me drive!"

> Incidentally the Bentley still survives – my brother found Emory's log book for the car and took it along to a Bentley Club gathering and there was the car. So he handed over the log book to a most appreciative owner.

> I attach a couple of photos of Emory.

> Regards!

> Bill Hayter (Lord Hayter)'

Of course, when Emory Chubb came to own *Sheemaun,* as Mrs Scott had discovered, he found the little ship was much in need of a major re-fit. Having taken appropriate professional advice as to the extensive work needed and the time it might take, Emory evidently decided against further expenditure and *Sheemaun* was once again advertised for sale. I cannot help reflecting that was perhaps in some ways a missed opportunity for as well as the pleasure of comfortable cruising, *Sheemaun* could have provided Emory with quite lively and at times breath-taking experiences. While not able to perform 'four-wheel slides' through farm gates, given adverse winds and currents *Sheemaun* can move her twenty-five tons quite alarmingly and in all three axes as she has demonstrated on a number of occasions – for Farm Gate and tractor, substitute Lock Gate and a fast cross-tide!

But it was not to be and Emory Chubb, a Bentley Car enthusiast, quite understandably preferred a beautifully crafted and leathered Bentley steering wheel to a beautifully crafted mahogany one with spokes, and at the age of seventy years and suffering from rheumatism he probably felt that helming a twenty-five-ton vessel in rough seas was not perhaps such a good idea! After a few brief months of ownership, he sold her in July 1950 to Mr Thomas Vernon Haydon for £4,750.00

Major H. Emory Chubb.
Managing Director.

Harry Emory Chubb as a young officer. He died in 1960 aged 80 yrs. This photo kindly provided by Lord Hayter

1950

A new owner for *Sheemaun*
The Branksome Tower Hotel
The 1953 Coronation
Spithead Fleet Review and
Clandestine Voyages to Jersey

'We'll mak our maut, and we'll brew our drink,
We'll laugh, sing, and rejoice man;
And mony braw thanks to the meiklr black deil,
That danc'd awa wi' the Exciseman.'

Robert Burns 1792

The Branksome Tower Hotel was one of the few large hotels in the South of the country that had escaped both being requisitioned during the War by the Government for defence or emergency civilian purposes[123] and being bombed in Goering's fateful Fokke Wulf attack on Bournemouth. The pre-war fantasies and evil intentions of one of the Hotel's former guests, Generalfieldmarschall Werner Blomberg, and his maniacal Fuhrer had not played out according to plan. Hitler's Unternehmen Seelowe or Operation Sealion was never enacted, but dreadful atrocities had been inflicted on the world, fierce battles had been waged, millions killed and millions more rendered homeless. Eventually Hitler's megalomanic plans failed, he committed suicide, and Great Britain and her Allied forces emerged the exhausted victors from a War which had inevitably

---

123. Judge Haydon's granddaughter Mrs Shirley Critchley, who was a child at the time, told me that she recalls seeing convalescent wounded Servicemen at the Hotel and walking in the grounds.

come to impose very difficult and austere times on a long-suffering population. During those times when there was strict rationing of almost every commodity, especially food and petrol, the continuing existence of the Hotel depended solely on its ability to still function as a hotel.

Branksome Tower Hotel operated under the governance of a Limited Company that had been established through the advocacy and guidance of lawyer Thomas E Haydon KC[124], later Judge Haydon KC and who of course was not in a position personally to manage a commercial enterprise. In due course the management appointed Judge Haydon's eldest son Thomas Henry Vernon Haydon to take responsibility as the Resident Director.

After the War had ended and as Great Britain slowly recovered economically, the fortunes of the Branksome Tower Hotel improved. Thomas Haydon, who preferred to be known as Vernon, set out to enact his grand vision for the Hotel. Once again there was a Head Butler in charge. The waiters were immaculately attired, the page-boys and lift-boys all wore buttoned uniforms and 'pill-box' caps. A lady Housekeeper supervised the domestic staff of cooks, cleaners and chamber-maids. A Head Groundsman supervised the gardeners and a Head Chauffeur supervised the fleet of chauffeured Rolls-Royce and Bentley limousines which were always available for use by the guests, and to provide a taxi service to collect them from and deliver them to the station. The Hotel could provide garaging for up to fifty cars. Most of the suites had open fire-places but in addition there was a furnace room, from which via a system of hot-air conduits and vents, modelled after the Roman Villa hypocaust system, the whole building could be maintained at a comfortable temperature even in the coldest of winters.

Guests were expected to abide by a dress code. Informal smart

---

124. King's Counsel - A senior British Barrister at Law

wear was to be worn in the morning if one was not otherwise in sporting attire. Gentlemen could wear sports jackets and flannels, ladies could wear jumpers and skirts or slacks. Then for the afternoon ladies would be expected to wear dresses except of course for sportswear as worn on the tennis and squash courts or appropriate beach-wear when on the beach. Formal wear was required in the evening and an orchestra played in the lounge or ballroom. For the guests' dress-wear the Hotel offered a cleaning and pressing service and garment repair. A choice of fine wines and the best spirits were always available.

Activities and sports were enthusiastically supported by Judge Haydon KC who was himself a keen tennis player and a founding member of the All British Tennis Club based at Wimbledon. His daughter Dorothy was a Hampshire County player and his granddaughter Shirley was also a keen and talented tennis player who in her turn would gain an international reputation. The tennis courts at Branksome Tower Hotel were second to none. The private south-east facing beach, from which in 1937 Hitler's Generalfieldmarschall Werner Blomberg had so carefully studied the local terrain and coastline, now offered the tranquillity of formal gardens and pathways. There was a row of a dozen furnished chalet/beach-bungalows arranged along the promenade which was set with sunshades and loungers, laid out just a few yards back from the delightful sandy beach. The beach facilities included a rowing boat and a sailing dinghy, and these were kept in the Hotel's beach boat-store. Professional coach tuition was available for tennis, for golf, for swimming and sailing.

This then was the 'Downton Abbey' Hotel of its time offering a tempting almost regal grandiosity for those whose aspirations could afford it.

The Hotel was described in an advertisement placed in the 1949-50 Poole Guide[125] as –

'The Cap Martin of England

Not even the French Riviera can excel in beauty and charm the magnificent and commanding position of this most famous of all British Hotels outside London. Branksome Tower stands upon its own thickly wooded cliffs overlooking the sea, and the private beach and sea promenade are reached by winding walks through lovely grounds without crossing any road. The cuisine, the cellar and the service are equalled by few hotels in the British Isles and are widely known and appreciated by knowledgeable travellers from all over the world. Four first-class Hard Tennis Courts with Professional in attendance. Squash Court. Private sea-promenade. Resident swimming Instructor and Masseur. Twelve acres of grounds. Garage for sixty cars. Fully licensed. Five excellent golf courses within easy reach. Two hours only by train from London. Write for further information and photographic brochure to T H V Haydon, Resident Director.'

Vernon Haydon enjoyed his life next-the-sea and he had some sailing experience. Brought up and groomed in the style of the 1920s and 1930s Vernon had a natural taste for classic quality in the grand British tradition as well as having what his niece Shirley Critchley described to me as a rather profligate fondness in general for the finer luxuries in life, especially such luxuries as could be provided aplenty through the auspices of the Hotel! He had an eye for a fine motor car and would sometimes drive around in one or other of the Hotel's Rolls Royce or Bentley

---

125. Per Iris Morris *"Looking Back at Branksome Park"* Old Thyme Publishing 2005

limousines, always kept so shining and immaculate by their liveried chauffeurs.

Vernon Haydon (Lt) with his father Judge Haydon (centre) and brother Gerald Haydon. From a photograph kindly supplied by Judge Haydon's Granddaughter Shirley Critchely

Despite all this stylish flamboyance Vernon had a mischievous side to his nature. I understand from Shirley Critchley that on one occasion when his father the Judge was due to be away sitting at a County Court session, Vernon opened his father's robing bag and substituted the silken robes and horsehair wig with a cheeky waitress outfit of frilly cap, apron, black dress, suspender belt and stockings! The mind boggles at what must have gone on in the judges robing room! No doubt in the long tradition of British Law, pranks like this have happened and contingency measures prescribed by solemn be-whiskered members of the Bar would no doubt have been available to spare the embarrassment and anger of any brother member of the judiciary!

Managing the very substantial and splendidly conservative establishment of the Branksome Tower Hotel impinged upon Vernon's creative imagination. He began to feel that something was missing from this luxurious and scenic way of life, a something he couldn't quite put his finger on it, a something that niggled at the back of his mind. Then one day in May 1950 while reading the Times he found an advertisement that caught his eye, a 1935 gentleman's motor-yacht was for sale.

Yes, by jingo! That was just what was needed and yes, a decent motor-yacht could also be used to take hotel guests out on short day-trips, on tours of Studland Bay and around Poole harbour or even further afield. It would add a certain unique ambience to the image of the Hotel. Vernon arranged to meet the vendor Mr Emory Chubb, at Littlehampton and to view the boat, which when he saw it, immediately appealed to him although it did need quite a lot of restoration. A deal was done, and hands shaken on a figure of £4,750.00. That was a good sum of money which allowing for inflation and updated to the year 2017 would have been equivalent to £154,236.00 ($ 206,750.)! Emory Chubb must have been well pleased with the deal, but Vernon Haydon knew a fine little classic vessel when he saw one not-withstanding that much re-fitting work had to be done. Shipwrights and marine engineers at Messrs Camper & Nicholsons of Gosport were consulted and their advices and estimates were carefully considered. It does appear that at an early stage even the 'profligate' Vernon was having second thoughts for a year later, perhaps hedging his bets, he placed an advertisement in The Times -

M.Y. "SHEEMAUN." 45-foot OCEAN CRUISER; G. L. Watson designed, new Thornycroft engines; complete in every detail; beautifully fitted out below deck; any survey or trial; fitting out in May; lying south coast; price, £4,900.—Write Box E.484, The Times. E.C.4.

However, no sale took place and Vernon was to keep *Sheemaun* and complete what had become a substantial re-fit. Where the war service years had left their marks, some planks were replaced, loose stanchion bases re-fitted, leaking pine decks were re-caulked with pitch and a new deck canvas was laid and painted to make it water-tight. The boat could then be dried out internally. A new foremast was set up and rigged. Worn and damp upholstery was thrown out, the fo'csle heads was taken out and the obsolete though still functional Rippingille® Cooking Stove was removed. The space occupied by the focs'le heads was converted into a wardrobe. The galley was re-organised and above where the Rippingille® stove had stood on the starboard side, a tiled worktop was built in with drawers and cupboards under. To the port side a matching tiled worktop was fitted with a sink and cupboards underneath and just to midships of this a new 'Colette' Calor Gas® stove with oven was fitted.

The Colette Stove in 2010 - Photo RP

and above which on the portside of the bulkhead a Calor Gas® Ascot Water Heater was installed.

The gas water heater as at 2010 - photo – RP

This new equipment of course needed a gas supply and so a gas bottle was housed in a deck locker built just forward of the wheelhouse, a copper supply pipe being run between the two; an installation which continued to give sterling service for another four decades.

Vernon kept *Sheemaun* on a mooring just East of Brownsea Island with access via a motor tender called *Sea Creature* which was berthed at his private jetty at the bottom of his garden on Sandbanks[126]. Local boatman Tom Godden looked after *Sheemaun* and *Sea Creature*. Tom came from a well-known and respected sea-going local family who had long been associated with the Royal National Lifeboat Institution, they also provided a wide range of boating services at Poole. Tom would take *Sheemaun* across to the quay at Poole where Branksome Tower Hotel guests could have easy access to her and parties

---

126. Sandbanks Beach is a small peninsula of sandy beach by Studland Bay and the entrance to Poole Harbour. It constitutes one of the most expensive fragments of real-estate in Britain and has the fourth highest land-value in the World.

would be taken for sight-seeing trips around the harbour and around Studland Bay. Weather-permitting *Sheemaun* could be anchored just off the beach in Studland Bay, where her unique profile, white hull and teak wheelhouse with its four wind cowls would have been a splendid and familiar sight. At anchor in sheltered water there was comfortable room on the after deck for six seated in deck-chairs and likewise four on the foredeck but for optimal day-cruising comfort six guests in addition to a skipper and paid hand would have been appropriate.

1953 The Spithead Coronation Fleet Review Picture from the Official Fleet Review Souvenir Booklet held on *Sheemaun*. Published by Pitkins, 9 Northington St. London WC1

June 1953 was a momentous month; the Coronation of the young Queen Elizabeth was to happen on the 2nd and in the previous days and weeks a massive build-up of British and Commonwealth War-Ships in the Solent was orchestrated in preparation for the Queen Elizabeth's Coronation Spithead Fleet review. Joining with these were other ships from many Nations around the World until line after orderly line of massive grey warships lying at anchor could be seen stretching almost from horizon to horizon.

On Monday June 15th the Nation and the World witnessed the awe-inspiring sight of the 1953 Coronation Spithead Fleet Review. In all there were at anchor more than three hundred vessels; amongst them the huge battleship HMS *Vanguard*, the aircraft carrier HMS *Eagle*, dozens of cruisers, destroyers, frigates, mine-sweepers and mine-layers, fast patrol boats, submarines and supply ships. Present also was a Russian cruiser *Sverdlov* and the magnificent Italian Tall-Ship the *Amerigo Vespucci*. Many hundreds of celebrating private yachts were assembled at the designated areas.

1953 The Queen's Coronation Naval Review Picture from the Official Fleet Review Souvenir Booklet held on *Sheemaun*. Published by Pitkins, 9 Northington St. London WC1

Meanwhile at Sandbanks *Sheemaun* was made ready, a hamper and bottles of chilled Champagne were put aboard in an ice-chest, and colourful bunting prepared. The Branksome Tower Hotel house flag hoisted at the mainmast and a new red ensign flew at the stern. With Tom Godden at the helm Vernon Haydon, with his niece Daphne Crouch and her mother Betty cruised the few miles East to join with the throng of private yachts gathered in the Solent waters where *Sheemaun* then lay at anchor just a few cables short of the Western end of the massive and powerful assembled fleet while her privileged crew settled comfortably to celebrate and witness the historic Royal Fleet Review.

Picture from the Official Fleet Review Souvenir Booklet held on *Sheemaun*. Published by Pitkins, 9 Northington St. London WC1

Athough given the poor resolution of the above illustration *Sheemaun* cannot be identified, on the original booklet *Sheemaun* is identifiable as the third vessel seen at 40 degrees upward and left from the bottom of the white line which marks the division between left and right pages.

Far away at the Eastern end of the Fleet the Acting Royal Yacht[127] HMS *Surprise* flying the Royal Pennants was approaching the huge anchored fleet. Aboard were Her Majesty Queen Elizabeth, Prince Philip, the Queen Mother and Princess Margaret and other members of the Royal Family along with an entourage of Admiralty and other Government dignitaries. At 15.00 hrs on a signal from the Acting Royal Yacht *Surprise* a twenty-one-gun salute erupted from the anchored Fleet, the crashing booms echoing back from the Isle of Wight as clouds of cordite smoke drifted on the breeze. From *Sheemaun* also came rousing cries of *'Long live the Queen'* and enthusiastic popping of Champagne corks, her contribution to the twenty-one-gun salute! Then at 15.30 hrs the Acting Royal Yacht *Surprise* commenced the Royal Review of the Fleet sailing imperiously up and down the lines of assembled vessels, their crews waving their caps and shouting *'Hip Hip Hooray'* as ensigns dipped in undulating rows with *Sheemaun*'s doing likewise. At 5.35 pm the air was rent with a thunderous pulsating roar as Sikorsky Dragonfly helicopters zooming in low passed from East to West over the anchored Fleet. Minutes later the sky was filled as more than three hundred fighter planes and bombers, propeller driven, and jet propelled flew over in droves. There was then a period of relative quiet while yacht crews celebrated and socialised as tenders plied between the anchored yachts. As the afternoon drew into evening at 10.30 pm the assembled Fleet illuminated the Solent as more than a million lights were turned on and as if that was not awe inspiring enough at 10.40 pm one of the biggest of firework displays was set off. As the last of the

---

127. The Royal Yacht *Britannia* had been launched in February 1953 but was not commissioned until 1954

star-shells faded, the darkness that enfolded on the area was almost palpable. It was time to turn in!

One of the largest ships in that huge assembly of vessels was the cruiser HMS *Glasgow* flying Lord Mountbatten's flag. 'Peter' Gray was the 1st Officer and was accompanied on board by his young son Nicholas. Both would one day hold *Sheemaun's* wheel..

Later, Vernon Haydon feeling that *Sheemaun* was a little underpowered and following advice from Messrs Camper & Nicholson's engineer, he had the Thorneycroft diesels replaced by a pair of new David Brown 6 cylinder 90 hp engines that had just been developed for marine use. Posters were prepared and proudly displayed at the 1957 First Olympia Boat Show.

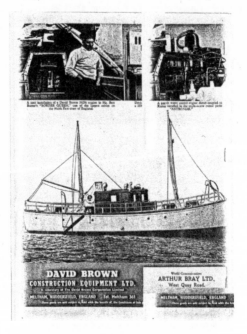

'Two David Brown MD6 engines drive the
twin screw motor boat *Sheemaun*'

Vernon's nephew Christopher Crouch recalled to me[128] that when he and Vernon sailed *Sheemaun* back from Gosport to Brownsea Island, one of the new gear boxes blew up catastrophically due to a failure to have filled it with oil!

'It was very difficult to handle her with just on engine… the outside wheel was very stiff [129]… we had to use the bigger wheel in the wheelhouse… Camper & Nicholsons quickly replaced the gearbox at their expense of course…'

The reader might understand that here I raise an eyebrow! *Sheemaun* after all, had been originally designed to cruise at her optimum hull-speed of seven knots powered by two twenty-seven horse-power engines. More powerful engines would indeed let her punch harder into heavy seas but would only make her slightly faster. However, by having to work much less hard, they would be more reliable. Was there an ulterior motive in Vernon's mind?

When he could get away from his duties of managing the Hotel, Vernon liked to spend time on *Sheemaun* and on special occasions he would cruise her to the Channel Islands. He was a competent seaman in his own right, although his nephew Christopher Crouch[130] told me that -

---

128. In conversation with Major Donald Christopher Crouch DFC then aged 87 yrs in October 2017

129. In fact, it wasn't stiff; the wheel was too small in diameter to apply the leverage necessary to turn the big rudder. Replaced later by a larger wheel made from the salvaged mahogany hand rails of the SS Canberra, steering *Sheemaun* from her bridge deck is now easy.

130. Major Donald Christopher Crouch DFC - Distinguished Flying Cross. Served with the Royal Army Air Corps as a pilot of fixed wing aircraft and helicopters. Christopher Crouch was a very experienced navigator and pilot. *'I preferred helicopters … if it was a hot day and one spotted an Ice-cream Van… well one just landed, bought an ice-cream and took off again….!'* Christopher was shot at and wounded while flying a reconnaissance plane in the Yemen

'He was hopeless at navigation!'

In fact, Vernon in earlier years had obtained his pilot's licence, so he must have acquired a sound working knowledge of navigation and it seems that he could manage well enough when he had to.

Having failed the 1939 conscription medical examination because of a First World War wound that affected his eyesight, Vernon spent his Second World War Years as Lance Corporal Haydon serving in Group 2 of the Dorset Home Guard on Brownsea Island and where of course he had access to weapons. Rumour has it that he kept an ex-Army revolver handy on *Sheemaun* 'For Security'! Shirley Critchley told me that he used to cruise *Sheemaun* to Jersey and back, and associated with those voyages there are fascinating rumours -

'… rumours of scandal and intrigue…'

In those difficult post-war years quantities of cash and gold sovereigns were taken in payments at the hotel office[131], so much so that Vernon always kept a couple of ex- military revolvers in one of his desk drawers. Quite how much of that cash and gold found its way into a British bank at the time is questionable for according to Shirley –

'*Sheemaun*'s holds were filled with boxes and boxes of gold sovereigns and spirited away to an undisclosed location in Jersey.'

But the World and Times were moving on. People were no longer so allured by the sentiments and habits of the 1930's

131. Britain had the highest rate of taxation in the World. With the Income Tax higher rate at 90%, Death Duties up to 80% and Purchase Tax up to 100%. It is hardly surprising that there was a huge 'Black Market' with those who were able to and preferred to pay in cash or in kind.

and now the Mediterranean beaches with their guaranteed warmth and sunshine were beckoning to the masses. The 1954 Amendments to the Convention on Civil Aviation, paved the way for a surge in mass tourism as cheap charter flights became available. Vernon, who had no formal training in management, found he was fighting a losing battle as the fortunes of the Hotel faded, staff drained away, the formal grounds were costing a small fortune to maintain, labour costs were escalating and there were new issues arising as to specifications and insurance. With little income available for repairs and replacements, the fabric of the once grand Hotel was deteriorating, and assets had to be sold off. The expenses of maintaining *Sheemaun*, which had been funded through the coffers of the Hotel [132], could no longer be sustained let alone justified.

In 1959 Vernon sold *Sheeman* to Ingram Ord Capper, Master Mariner and Stock-Broker. 1965 saw the Branksome Towers Hotel put on the market and not long after it was demolished to make way for a modern development of housing and flats. Vernon who had no children to succeed him; wrote a touching article in a local paper on 26th March 1965 finishing with the following lines –

'… Still working here to the very end are five old members of staff who, between them, have totalled 154 years of continuous service. Such a record is probably unique. To them as to the surviving members of the family concerned, the final parting is as sad one. It is inevitable as there is none to come after. The page finally turned at the end of the chapter of those better off times between the wars that have gone, the like of which will never be seen again.'

Sheemaun too had put in her little bit of service (and some

---

132. Conversations with Mrs Shirley Critchley August 2017

very clandestine voyages when she was used to smuggle gold off-shore to Jersey) while she was part of the historic Branksome Tower Hotel scenario.

In May 1974 Vernon Haydon returned to Jersey allegedly to retrieve the stash of gold sovereigns but the anxiety and tension must have been overwhelming for he suffered a heart attack in the plane on his return flight and died. He was seventy-five years old and now lies buried at Branksome. 'As for the gold sovereigns… they disappeared without trace! Perhaps somewhere between H M Customs and Vernon's chambermaid… we will never know!'[133]

Shirley Critchley – Winner of Open Veteran's Clay Court Championships 2012. Former crew on *Sheemaun*. Niece of the late Vernon Haydon

Sheemaun salutes Vernon Haydon, Christopher Crouch DFC and Shirley Critchley

---

133. Whispered to me by Shirley Critchley

Some Observations –

The Great Depression of the 1930s and the Second World War left Britain broke and hugely in debt. The Great British Public in the Post- War years was subjected to the highest level of taxes in the World. Tax on investment income was 98%![134] Purchase Tax was a tax levied on everything that was purchased with money. The amount of tax being determined by the notional 'luxuriousness' of the item and could be as much as 100%. As late as the 1950s & 60s the higher top rate of income tax was 90% which in 1979 Prime Minister Margaret Thatcher reduced to 60% and lowered the basic rate from 33% to 30%.

But, the Island of Jersey which had its own independent Government and Jurisdiction, levied an income tax at a mere 5%. There was no Death Duty Tax in Jersey and it was easy to open a bank account with few questions asked. All that was needed was the money to pay in and cash was very acceptable. The British Government and the Inland Revenue had no access to the banks in Jersey nor any right to make enquiries about the account holders.

A Gold Sovereign was a small, thin coin only 22.05 mm (0.86 Inches) in diameter and 1.52 mm (0.06 inches) thick. It weighed 8 grams and in 1950 had a value of £10. A thousand Gold Sovereigns would weigh 8 kilograms (say seventeen pounds) and would be worth then, £10,000 - allowing for inflation, in the year 2018 that would be around £180,000. I understand that *'boxes and boxes of Sovereigns'* were sailed across to Jersey in *Sheemaun*!

---

134. In 1966 Beatle George Harrison wrote the song entitled *Taxman* 'That's one for you, nineteen for me … should five percent appear too small, be thankful I don't take it all.'

Time-Line –

- Modern detergents were becoming available.
- 1952 – A National Health Service Prescription charge was levied in June. One shilling (0.5p) per prescription, and a charge of £1 for dental treatment.
- 1953 – April, Drs Watson and Crick discovered the structure of DNA.
- 1954 - Sir Richard Doll revealed the link between smoking and lung cancer.
- 1955 – Aged 18 I took part in the Acton Scientific Expedition to the summit of Mt Blanc 4808 m (15,774 feet) testing for sub-glacial Heavy Water deposits and taking cosmic ray readings.
- 1957 – The Treaty of Rome established the European Economic Community - the EEC.
- 1959 – A vaccination program was commenced to protect against polio-myelitis and diphtheria.
- The USSR amazed the World by putting 'Sputnik' the first artificial satellite into orbit.

1959

A New Captain takes *Sheemaun*'s Wheel

'The day you hear someone call me Captain
Will be the day I buy a boat.'

Guy Lafleur

Ingram Ord Capper's nautical career commenced when at the age of fourteen he entered Pangbourne Nautical College where from 1921-1924 he was in training as an Officer Cadet. From Pangbourne Nautical College he went on to serve with the British India Steam Ship Company. He left the BISC in 1928 and at the age of twenty-one became a broker at the Stock Exchange, eventually becoming a Council Member. However, in 1937 with world events bringing a 2nd World War ever closer, and in anticipation of war service to come, Ingram Capper after studying at the Little Ship Club in London, gained his Yacht Master Certificate.

On 6th October 1939 - just days after Great Britain was declared to be at War with Germany, Capper then aged 32, volunteered his services and was enlisted as a 'Temporary Lieutenant' to the Royal Naval Voluntary Reserve London Division. Only three days later on 9th October, he was appointed Commanding Officer of HMS *Cutty Sark* a submarine escort vessel. He must have been very proud to have been accorded command of such a splendid vessel.

The *Cutty Sark* had been built for the very wealthy Major Henry Keswick, a director of the international company Messrs Jardine Matheson Ltd. based in Hong Kong. Her builders, Messrs Yarrow and Co. Ltd. of Scotstoun in Glasgow, had cleverly used the plates originally made for a never-built First World

War destroyer. Looking every inch like a fast warship of that period, the *Cutty Sark* was launched in 1920 and fitted out as a luxury private yacht. At 263 feet (80m) in length and weighing 883 tons she was a substantial vessel. With four steam turbines of 5,000 hp she could easily reach a speed of 24 knots (28 mph) and her oil fuel bunkers gave her a range of some 3,400 nautical miles (6,296 km). As private yachts went at the time she was certainly unusual and eye-catching as well as luxurious. Major Keswick took her on an eight-month world cruise while he visited and inspected the various world-wide holdings of Messrs Jardine Matheson.

Acquired in 1926 by the Duke of Westminster the *Cutty Sark* sailed under Commander Richard Mack RN (Retired). She was a regular sight at Cowes, around the Mediterranean, at Biarritz and around the West Coast of Scotland. Her guests included the Churchills, Mrs Wallis Simpson and His Royal Highness the Prince of Wales, Coco Chanel and many other personages of fame.

The *Cutty Sark* was featured in Noel Coward's play 'Private Lives' in which two divorced couples now honeymooning with their new spouses find themselves staying at the same hotel on the Riviera! In the Balcony Scene Amanda asks –

'Whose Yacht is that?'

Elyot, played by Noel Coward, replies –

'The Duke of Westminster's I expect… it always is'

At the outbreak of WW2, and not surprisingly, the *Cutty Sark* was requisitioned by the Lords of the Admiralty. Her luxurious internal fittings were removed and put in storage. She was then converted to a heavily armed warship. This was a relatively straight forward operation as her basic structure was that of a destroyer. After some strategic areas had been strengthened she was armed with a substantial 4-inch naval gun, 2 pounder ant-aircraft guns. 0.5-inch ant-aircraft guns, heavy machine guns, and depth charges. She was also equipped as a submarine tender able to rendezvous with Allied submarines at sea and to provide them with spare parts, with ammunition including torpedoes, fuel, food and medical supplies etc.

In October 1942 a twin-engine RAF Whitley anti-submarine patrol plane Z9217 had the misfortune to suffer total engine failure and had crashed into the Atlantic south west of the Scilly Isles. Fortunately, the position of the crash or 'ditching' had been noted accurately by the navigator of an American Hudson bomber also on anti-U-Boat patrol. The Hudson was able to transmit a radio message back to its UK base with the details.

Prior to February 1941, when the Directorate of Air Sea Rescue was formed, Britain had no effectively organised air-sea-rescue capacity because of which a high proportion of airmen 'Downed' into the sea perished by drowning. Air Vice Marshal Sir Keith Park merely advising controllers

'Not to vector aircraft over the sea as too many (air crew) were getting drowned.'

In sharp contrast the German aircraft were equipped with inflatable rubber rafts and their crews advised that when over the sea, rather than bail out by parachute, they should make every effort instead to ditch their aircraft into the water and make use of the inflatable raft. The Germans also had well organised rescue services involving float planes, fast launches and moored shelter platforms.

The Whitley was one amongst those few British aircraft that had been provided with inflatable rubber life-rafts. Nicknamed the 'Flying Coffin' because of its shape, it had no wing flaps and instead its wings were set at a large 'angle of attack' which meant that although it flew relatively slowly it could take off and land at very low speed. After the crippled aircraft had been ditched into the Atlantic at the best angle its pilot Flight Sergeant McCubbin could manage, the crew of seven were able to deploy the life-raft and get themselves into it before the Whitley sank into the depths. However, one of them, second pilot Sgt. G. Mackenzie, had suffered a severe compound leg fracture and that combined with shock and hypothermia sadly led to his death after the first two days of exposure in the cold, wet and cramped life-raft. His comrades had no choice other than to solemnly commit his body to the cold Atlantic waters and then to set about preserving their own lives as best they could and pray and hope. There were no Allied vessels in that area of ocean at the time.

HMS *Cutty Sark* at the Royal Navy Base in Holy Lock, Scotland, was taking on stores when a message came through that the crew of a ditched Whitley bomber were in the Atlantic South West of the Scillies. As she was the only available fast vessel her commanding officer was ordered to take her with all haste and to search for the ditched crew.

Temporary Lieutenant Ingram Capper RNVR immediately saw to it that HMS *Cutty Sark* was quickly fuelled and watered while her boilers were fired and brought up to full steam pressure. He then took the ship out and with turbines whining and 20,000 horse power spinning into the propeller shafts she ploughed southwards leaving a surging wake behind her. Some very surprised fishermen and lobster-men had to scramble out of the way as quite unexpectedly some unusually large waves crashed onto the sands of Kilchattan Bay and likewise across the waters at Deadman's bay on the Isle of Bute. With a foaming white 'Bone in her Teeth' HMS *Cutty Sark* raced on down through the Firth of Clyde and South through the Irish Sea.

Heading his ship out from the southern end of the St George's Channel, Acting Lieutenant Commander Ingram Capper RNVR continued to drive her hard, further southwards into the grey Atlantic swell.

Out there in the grim and cold Western Atlantic Approaches any number of patrolling German U-Boats could be lying in wait seeking vulnerable targets. This was no place for a ship to be shining searchlights and firing flares. But HMS *Cutty Sark* was by no means invulnerable, she had special equipment for finding and identifying submarines, she had ASDIC she had radar, she had guns to be reckoned with and depth charges and she could out-run any U-Boat. Her officers and watchmen were specially trained in the science of searching for low-lying grey submarine hulls.

By means of received hyperbolic navigational radio signals, superb 'paper and pencil' navigation and skilled use of 'Dead Reckoning', a sextant and depth-under-vessel soundings, Ingram Capper brought HMS *Cutty Sark* to the precise position on the chart that had been reported by the navigator of the Hudson bomber. Allowance was factored in for tidal and current drift and a best guess made as to effect of wind and swell on the likely position of a wallowing rubber life-raft three days after it had been deposited into the seas.

Now it was down to intuition and eye-ball searching. Half a dozen of the ship's 'keenest eyes' peered through their Royal Naval Barr & Stroud Binoculars. The ship's ASDIC operator searched the depths for echoes while the radar swept the horizon and any nearby 'sea-clutter' echoes were carefully studied. No enemy presence was detected. Then at last a flare was seen and within minutes torch flashes were exchanged. The downed Whitley crew had been located. Capper ordered HMS *Cutty Sark* to be hove-to upwind of the life-raft while a ship's boat was quickly got away. Another ten minutes saw the exhausted survivors – Flt. Sergeant McCubbin and his remaining crew sergeants B. J. Sherry, K. Dagnall, A. Smith and C. Stewart carefully lifted into the ship's boat and a further five minutes saw the ship's boat lashed back securely in its cradle and minutes later the six cold and exhausted men were being warmed up and attended to in the *Cutty Sark*'s well-equipped medical station.

It was thanks to the brilliant pin-point navigation of the Hudson bomber navigator and the skill of the Commanding Officer of HMS *Cutty Sark*[135], Temporary Lieutenant Ingram Capper RNVR, that those five surviving brave airmen were soon on their way at 24 knots back to Plymouth Harbour and good old Blighty. They had been through the awful experience of having to ditch their stricken aircraft into the Atlantic, the trauma of having to commit their dead comrade to the deep Atlantic and they had been exposed in a tiny, cold, wet life-raft for 84 hours with no realistic hope of rescue.

Under the war time emergency 'Lease-Lend' agreement between the USA and Great Britain, a new heavily armed corvette was launched in the USA in June 1943. The ship was to be named HMS *Kilchrenen*. The British Admiralty duly despatched Acting Lt. Cmdr. Capper RNVR to collect the ship from the Chicago shipyard. On arrival in Chicago, he found that the ship had to be paid for before he could take over command! Much taken aback by this unexpected situation, and after some urgent communications with the Admiralty, it was decreed that the purchase would be by means of a personal cheque written by Acting Lt. Cmdr. Ingram Capper, which in turn would be guaranteed by His Majesty's Government. And so, in 1943 it came about that a Royal Navy Warship had been bought in full by its Commanding Officer! Such a transaction must surely be unique in modern warfare history! In the event the cheque didn't bounce, and Ingram Capper's account balance was made good

---

135. HMS *Cutty Sark* was scrapped in 1948.

by the Admiralty. He found himself in command of a British warship, of which it could be said that he personally owned!

Ingram Capper then drove HMS *Kilchrenen* down the St Lawrence River and East across the Atlantic to take her place with the Royal Navy at her appointed base in Gibraltar. Equipped as a U-Boat hunter her area of patrol was off the East African coast. But by that period of the war Hitler's Axis forces were succumbing to the Allied defences on most fronts across Europe and so many U-Boats had been sunk or destroyed that the U-Boat danger in the Atlantic Ocean was greatly diminished. I could find no record of HMS *Kilchrenan* making any U-Boat kills. However, there was still a considerable amount of essential convoy traffic and HMS *Kilchrenan*'s duties were extended to include escorting convoys between the Mediterranean and Great Britain. Unfortunately on 14th November 1944 she was in collision with a merchant ship. Although severely damaged, Ingram Capper was able to procure sufficient damage limitation to enable his ship to be limped into the Port of Dakar for repairs where she remained until the summer. In July 1945 she returned to the UK to be laid up at Sheerness[136]. She was later returned to the USA in December 1946.

In 1952 July – Captain Capper, a keen sportsman and crack shot with rifle and shotgun, was chosen to represent Britain in the United Kingdom Target Shooting team at the Helsinki Olympic Games. He competed in the British Team in the pistol and the hundred metres 'Running Deer' rifle events at Malmi.

Time marched inevitably on, and in 1959 when Ingram Capper was looking for a seaworthy motor yacht, he found an advert that caught his eye. A very pretty 1935 Gentleman's Motor Yacht was for sale moored at Poole Harbour. So, Ingram Capper arranged to meet with Mr Vernon Haydon at Sandbanks

---

136. Sheerness Port and the Medway Estuary were the areas in which *Sheemaun* was operating and very likely her crew would have seen HMS *Kilchrenan*.

and was taken out to *Sheemaun* at her mooring off Brownsea Island. Ingram Capper knew what he wanted and had already looked at several possible boats. When he saw *Sheemaun* he immediately appreciated her lines and strength. Anyone would be proud to own such a splendid little ship. He put his hands to her wheel.

It felt solid and secure, it felt good.

The virtually new David Brown engines started easily and ran smoothly and *Sheemaun* handled well. This was a little ship which over the decades had evidently appealed to previous owners and seemed to carry with her a certain lucky charm. The deal was done. Vernon Haydon was naturally very sad to part with a little ship with which he had shared such adventures, and which had brought great pleasure to the family, but the hotel business had changed and now he had other challenges to face.

Ingram Capper saw to it that *Sheemaun* was fuelled and victualled. Then with a couple of friends crewing he sailed *Sheemaun* from Dorset to over-night at Ramsgate, then Northwards across her old stamping grounds - the Thames Estuary, to head up the East Coast for Harwich from where she taken inland into the Orwell Estuary. Ingram Capper lived at the historic and picturesque Polstead Mill on the river Box - little more than a brook now.

The river Box flows through the beautiful Dedham Vale to join with the river Stour. The waters passing by Flatford Mill, made famous by the painter Constable. The waters then widen gracefully out into the Stour estuary with its gently shelving banks framed within beautiful wooded countryside, and then in turn the Stour opens into the wide Orwell estuary. The two wide rivers combining to offer a magnificent inland water-way setting for cruising sailors. His proud new possession - *Sheemaun* was taken to be moored at Ipswich Dock where looking every bit the classic yacht she would have been afloat at all states of the tide. Access by car from Polstead to Ipswich Dock would have been convenient and at Ipswich there could be found close-by at Fox's Boat Yard excellent shipwright and marine facilities.

Ingram Capper toyed with the idea of a possible commercial use for *Sheemaun* and in 1962 the 'Sheemaun Yacht Company Ltd.' was registered. 1964 saw Captain Capper listed as a member of the historic Little Ship Club in London and *Sheemaun* was listed as one of the Club's vessels. In the event, however the Sheemaun Yacht Company Ltd., never actively traded and no trading figures were recorded. An announcement by The Companies Registration Office at 55 -71 City Road London EC1, was duly placed in the London Gazette 14th September 1965 to the effect that the Sheemaun Yacht Company Ltd., was among the list of companies that would be dissolved unless due cause could be shown to the contrary.

Having enjoyed cruising the East Coast Rivers and harbours in *Sheemaun*, for Ingram Capper the time had come to move on and that same year *Sheemaun* was advertised for sale. She was purchased by former Lancaster Bomber Captain, Mr T W H Burton of Hunstanton, Norfolk.

Ingram Ord Capper Master Mariner, Member of the Little Ship Club, Member of the Worshipful Company of Goldsmiths and Member of the Worshipful Company of Gunsmiths 'Slipped his cable'[137] on 12th July 1986 aged 79 yrs.

Sheemaun salutes Ingram Capper.

---

137. An old nautical term denoting the death of a sailor.

Time-Line –

- The M1 - Britain's first major Motorway opened on 2nd November 1959. There was no speed limit. I was one the first motorists to use the just-opened road that very same day when returning to London after a weekend camping and climbing in Snowdonia. It was a terrifying experience with cars hurtling at high speed in fog. There were numbers of fatal tail-end pile-ups with the flames from burning piles of vehicles giving an ominous flickering orange glow to the all- enveloping fog.
- Singapore was granted self-governing status.
- Barclays Bank became the first bank to install a computer.
- The Antarctic Treaty was signed.
- The Mini Car appeared on British roads
- 1960 The first LASER was successfully operated.
- 1961 the British farthing coin was discontinued.

1960

The London Hospital

Twenty years after baby Michael Dodd had been born in the war-torn London Hospital, a medical student ascended those same wide, polished oak stairs that Stanley Dodd and his pregnant wife 'Girl' had climbed. He would put his hand to the same big brass door handle of Mary Northcliffe Ward and push open the same wide door. His feet would follow in the very same footsteps of the Dodd family. Entering the same room in which baby Michael had been delivered, those young medical hands would help another East London young mother to deliver her baby.

Those same hands, the now much older hands, are mine. Little did I know that forty-seven years later as owner of *Sheemaun*, I would also retrace the same footsteps across a wooden deck and come to hold the same mahogany ship's wheel as had the capable hands of Stanley Dodd RNVR when serving in *Sheemaun* in the Second World War and that the same wheel had been touched by the little hands of his 'Stow-away' son Mike!

Mike Dodd holding *Sheemaun*'s wheel in 2015. The wheel that in the 2nd World War his late father Stanley had held and that he had touched when aged 4 yrs. Photo RP

1965

Hands that had piloted a Lancaster Bomber now hold an Historic Mahogany Wheel

For most of those brave young bomber pilots and crews who survived the War, life would never be the same. Night after night, they had risked their lives and limbs while carrying out the task of obliterating the German factories and homes far below them. They all knew it was inevitable that innocent, hard-working people had been killed and wounded by the thousand. Co-lateral damage is the deceptively innocent sounding euphemism used today, but no words can erase the psychological burden that they would carry for the rest if their lives.

Thomas Burton had dreamed for some time of finding a life away from crowds and responsibilities. Having sold out his shares in the family business to his son Brian, he was now free to follow his dreams. Dreams that would lead him to search for a suitable boat. A solid sea-worthy vessel that would provide comfortable accommodation, be capable of extended cruising and be his soul-mate. His search ended when twenty years after the end of the war, at age 48 yrs. Thomas found *Sheemaun* advertised for sale lying at Ipswich on Britain's East Coast. He liked the look of the little ship, she was soundly built, in good order and powered by a pair of 90 hp six-cylinder David Brown diesels she could punch through heavy seas in almost any weather. She had a well laid out and comfortable wheelhouse and her wheel felt solid and secure. A cruise down the Orwell and back to test her pace and performance was entirely satisfactory. A deal was done with Ingram Capper and in February 1965 Thomas Burton became *Sheemaun*'s new owner. He cruised her from the Orwell River, around the East Coast to the Norfolk Broads and to her new berth at Reedham Dock, but the exploration of further and far-away warmer waters were in his mind.

In May 1965 Thomas Burton sailed *Sheemaun* from Reedham, East across the southern North Sea to Holland and cruised the peaceful and picturesque Dutch and German inland waters before heading West along the coast to Calais, through waters of course that *Sheemaun* knew well from old times. Then together with his son Brian, Thomas set off in fair weather homeward bound for Great Yarmouth. But the weather deteriorated, a strong easterly wind got up and by the time they were approaching Great Yarmouth the conditions had become severe.

'We were completely exhausted and vowed never to do that again!'[138]

As is generally the case and fortunately was the case in this instance, a sound vessel will look after its crew even if they are having a tough time. Despite being thrown around by the heavy seas, *Sheemaun*'s sturdy diesels had not missed a beat as she punched her way home through the boiling waters, her canoe stern brushing aside the angry following seas as she headed West into the foaming entrance of the river Yare[139].

Later that year Thomas took *Sheemaun* across the English Channel and then South, down through the French canals to the Mediterranean, then West to the Spanish Mediterranean Sea and to the harbour of Calp where *Sheemaun* was berthed to bask under blue skies and the warm Mediterranean sun. The

138. Told to me in August 2017 by Brian Burton

139. 'Further North there is no reliable refuge nearer than Lowestoft, or at a pinch, Yarmouth… they should not be considered in NE to E by SE winds of much over Force 4.' Dick Holness writing in East Coast Pilot - Imray 1st Edition 2005

picturesque harbour of Calp is located about 100 km (62 miles) East of Ibiza and 110 km (68.2 miles) South of Valencia. From this sunny location, cruising opportunities under clear blue skies abounded; the beautiful island of Ibiza being a day-sail away.

In 1967 after these wide-ranging cruising adventures, Thomas felt the need to head back to England. Accordingly, he cruised *Sheemaun* homeward-bound for Reedham Dock, re-tracing his outward-bound tracks.

With her Mediterranean odyssey behind her, *Sheemaun* was once more advertised for sale.

Sheemaun lying at Reedham Dock 1967 –
Photo by Rear Admiral Gray CB.DSC.

Having sold *Sheemaun* into the care of Admiral 'Peter' Gray, Thomas Burton moved from Norfolk and retired to a flat overlooking Dartmouth Harbour. His next boat was to be a converted Lifeboat that shared with *Sheemaun* in having also been designed by G L Watson & Co., and a little hint of the influence *Sheemaun* had on Thomas' sentiments would be found in the name he gave to his new boat, which he called the *Sheemaun Neumaro 2.*

Bidding farewell to the England he had sacrificed so much to defend and closing his apartment in Dartmouth, Thomas Burton travelled south to the warm, dry aromatic climate of Morocco where he would end his days.

Sheemaun salutes Flight Sergeant Thomas Burton RAF

Time-Line –

- Plastic bags and plastic containers were becoming cheaply and widely available. Few could foresee that accumulations of discarded plastic products would soon pose a major environmental problem on Planet Earth.

- Wines went on sale in the convenient 'Bag in a Box'.

1966

Major Donald Christopher Crouch DFC

Way back in 1938, eight-year-old Cristopher Crouch together with his little sister Shirley and their parents, stayed at the Branksome Tower Hotel where their uncle Vernon Haydon was the managing director. It had been little Christopher and Shirley who hiding in a laundry basket, had so unwittingly upset Adolph Hitler's spying envoy, Baron Werner Blomberg. The pair of practical jokers also caused upset to other guests, who having put down their shoes by the bedroom doors to be cleaned and polished ready for the following morning, then found that their shoes had been switched around by the mischievous children!

In the 1950s Christopher Crouch was serving as a young officer in the Royal Army Flying Corps. As duties allowed and when on leave he often returned to the Branksome Tower Hotel and enjoyed outings on *Sheemaun*. Generally crewing for his uncle Vernon and sometimes cruising her single-handed. Occasionally a cruise might take several days with some nights spent swinging to the anchor or tied up to a jetty.

On Tuesday, 19th July 1966 the 'London Gazette, second supplement published an announcement by the Ministry of Defence –

Distinguished Flying Cross
Major Donald Christopher Crouch (407795) Royal Tank Regiment Serving with Army Air Corps

'On the morning of 2nd February 1966. D Squadron, Special Air Service Regiment, who were operating South West of Al Milah reported a party of approximately twelve armed men moving away from their positions to the North. Since it was essential that this party be definitely identified as dissidents before fire could be opened, Major Crouch, whose flight of three aircraft was in direct support of D Squadron, was requested to carry out a reconnaissance of the area. He embarked additional Special Air Service men in the three helicopters, took off, and led them at low height, to the reported location. Upon rounding a bend in the Wadi, they sighted the armed party, who immediately scattered, and opened fire on the aircraft, hitting Major Crouch's machine. The fire was from rifles and a light machine gun. With this positive indication, the three helicopters, taking advantage of dead ground, deployed their Special Air Service lifts in cut-off positions very near, and to the North of the enemy, and additional troops were air-lifted from Habilayan to reinforce the position from 1st Battalion King's Own Yorkshire Light Infantry. A running fight then continued for the rest of the morning and the afternoon to eliminate the scattered dissidents. Throughout the whole of this period Major Crouch was almost continuously in the air over the battle area controlling his flight in the redeployment and reconnaissance necessary to track down the remnants of the gang. During this phase of the operation his aircraft was again holed. Later in the morning with complete disregard for his own safety he successfully evacuated a badly wounded Non-Commissioned Officer of D Squadron from a very exposed position under enemy fire and his aircraft was hit for a third time. The action ended at dusk and was an outstanding success. Four dissidents were killed including two important gang leaders, and at this date it is known that a further four were wounded. Major Crouch's handling of his flight throughout the operation was outstanding and could not have been achieved without his aircraft. The example set by his own personal courage and initiative was an inspiration to all both in the air and on the ground and in the highest traditions of the service.'

The following extract is from the book *'Likes of Leicester'* by Rose Mallock -

'Each flight had four aircraft. One, 8 Flight, was commanded by the remarkable Major Greville Edgecombe AAC, the other, 13 Flight by the equally inspiring but very different Maj. Chris Crouch RTR. Both had recently been decorated. Greville was awarded the AFC for a truly astonishing mountain casualty evacuation under recce flares. Chris had received the DFC for his part in a spirited up-country encounter between dissidents and the SAS.'

Chris Crouch came to retire from the Army on 23rd May 1973. Forty-four years later when aged 89 years of age, in conversation with me, Christopher laughed the matter off –

'We had been sent out to the Yemen to try to keep peace and hold back the dissidents who were hell-bent on causing mayhem and destruction. Well it was pretty tough at times although mostly we just sweltered in the heat. The difficulty was that while we were concerned with the dissidents, the Yemenis were fighting amongst themselves... been doing it for generations and still are so far as I can see. They were all armed and all looked much of a muchness. So, our job was to distinguish which among them were the dissidents. The best way was to fly close over them; the dissidents would fire their guns at us while the others didn't bother.

As well as helicopters, I flew in Austers, they were nice little aircraft... you could land and take-off almost anywhere and they could stay in the air longer than a helicopter. You could fly low down, zoom over a sand-dune and onto the Yemenis. If they fired, you got out quickly and made your report. Sometimes we were hit... I took a bullet in the thigh once. If we thought we had been hit, we used to land quickly out of sight behind a sand-dune and we always kept a supply of pencils. You see, those rubber-lined self-sealing petrol tanks didn't really seal after a bullet went through, so we used to stick pencils in the holes and then take off quickly and head for base...'

In 2017 Major Donald Christopher Crouch DFC told me of the pleasures he had cruising in *Sheemaun* in the 1950s. Chris Crouch is another member of the distinguished group of people who over the years have put their hands to *Sheemaun*'s wheel.

1967

Rear Admiral 'Peter' Gray CB. DSC. Takes a New Command

It can surely be said of Admiral 'Peter' Gray that he had the salt of the seas and the rum of the Royal Navy coursing in his veins. The son of a clergyman, he had progressed from humble Officer Cadet to Midshipman, then to Lieutenant and Lieutenant Commander, to Commanding Officer and finally to the high position of Rear Admiral. The course of his outstanding career having been pencilled across many an Admiralty World-Wide chart and he had been named in Despatches several times. As has been related in previous pages, 'Peter' Gray, as a serving Royal Navy Officer had years of fighting experience. Experiences at a very personal level in numerous furious sea battles; all of which, regardless of which side won, had time and again tested brave men to their limits and often to their deaths.

The year 1951 saw 'Peter' appointed as Naval Deputy to the Supreme Headquarters Allied Powers Europe following which he was to Command the 5th Frigate Squadron and took part in what proved to be the politically inept 1956 Suez Canal Operation. Subsequently he was appointed Captain of HMS *Osprey* the naval air anti-submarine school at Portland. His final appointment was as Rear Admiral at the Imperial Defence College but when faced with the prospect of –

'… a future life chained to a desk.'

'Peter' Gray is quoted as saying –

'I told the Admiralty that I did not wish to be considered for further employment'[140]

---

140. Obituary - the Daily Telegraph – 23rd June 1997

After years of serving in the tempestuous war-riven waters of the Atlantic Ocean, of the Pacific Ocean, of the Arctic seas, of the South China sea and the Mediterranean Sea and after chilling first hand experiences of torpedoes, guns and depth charges and attacking planes, Europe and the World in general was at last no longer at war. The inland waters of post-war European countryside had been largely restored, and so, what could be more romantically enjoyable than cruising quietly along those beautiful Dutch, German and French European canals? The ideal vessel surely would be a Dutch motor barge. And so together the Grays made enquiries and searched through the boating journals that advertised such vessels. Various boatyards were visited both in Britain and across the Channel. Eventually 'Peter' and Sonia Gray found one for sale at Topsham on the River Exe and which appeared to meet most of their needs. It was the fifty feet long (15.3 m) *St Michel.* A Lemmesteraak traditional Dutch sailing barge, which had been laid out internally to provide comfortable living accommodation. Hands were shaken, and the *St Michel* became a floating continental home to the Grays. The 'Visitor Book' which had accompanied 'Peter' Gray onto every vessel he had served in or sailed in since March 1942 was taken aboard the *St Michel.* On 1st June 1956 the first visitors to sign the book were Dudley Pope, the famous author of sea-faring adventures and his wife Kaye, at that time the Popes were living and cruising on their 21-ton cutter when not in residence at their New Bond Street address.

Nicholas Gray who had often sailed with his parents on the St *Michel* told me that his parents spent many seasons happily cruising the Dutch waters and the Baltic and sometimes over-wintering on their barge, but it was a heavy and awkward vessel to handle and the great oak lee-boards one hanging on each side of the barge, each weighing 'about a ton' added significantly to the difficulties.

'How my mother coped as the sole crew I do not know...
I sailed a lot on the barge and she was a monster to sail...
lowering and raising the 60-feet long[141] solid wooden mast
was a manoeuvre I will never forget.'

'Peter' and Sonia spent a decade pleasurably exploring the
Continental canals, during which time a further seventy-three
visitors penned their signatures into the 'Visitors Book'. But the
Grays were not getting any younger and they both felt that the
time had come to seek a lighter and more manoeuvrable vessel.
The *St Michel* was put up for sale in the late autumn of 1966.

Once again Admiral Gray and his wife Sonia made enquiries and searched the yachting magazine advertisements in their
renewed quest for a suitable and comfortable vessel. Eventually a
likely little ship called the *Sheemaun* was found lying for sale at
Reedham Dock in Norfolk. Un-beknown to the Grays, Thomas
Burton had cruised extensively in *Sheemaun* having taken her
across the Channel, south through the French canals and thence
to a berth at the port of Calp in Southern Spain. It was only in
the recent previous months that Thomas, retracing his tracks,
had motored *Sheemaun* East from Calp, then up through the
French canals and North across the Southern North Sea to Great
Yarmouth. From there he had cruised inland and up the river
Yare to Reedham. By any measure this had been a substantial
cruise which yet again, had demonstrated the seaworthiness and
boundless cruising capacity of *Sheemaun*.

The Grays drove up to Reedham to where *Sheemaun* was lying.
Despite finding the vessel in laid-up state ready for the coming
winter, with her masts down, the aft bridge deck steering wheel
removed, and her decks cluttered; Admiral Gray and his wife
Sonia liked what they saw. This was a proper 'Little Ship' the
wheel house would be snug and comfortable, she offered good

---

141. 18.28 meters

accommodation, she had twin screws and would manoeuvre well. Her wheel felt secure and seamanlike.

Rear Admiral Gray CB. DSC. Inspecting *Sheemaun* as she lay at Reedham in 1967. Picture kindly provided by Nicholas Gray

A price was agreed with her owner Thomas Burton, and hands shaken. Of course, there was some work to be done but that would be mostly a matter of tidying and cleaning. The masts would have to be set up and re-rigged. There were several deck leaks which were treated to a thick coat of Jeffreys' deck paint applied from a bucket using a broom! The deck leaks however were to present an ongoing problem.

But this was a sound little ship that could be warmed and dried throughout and was just begging to go off cruising. The boatyard fitters then spent some weeks setting up the masts and carrying out repairs. The engines were run up and the topsides given some fresh paint and varnish. With the interior dried out and with some fresh upholstery *Sheemaun* was soon made ready to welcome her new owners and to take on stores and those personal effects that make a boat special and unique to its new family and crew. Much prized among those many personal effects and treasures to be taken aboard was the well-travelled and now historic Visitor Book. The name 'SHEEMAUN' was duly entered at the top of the next blank page and the first visitor recorded -

1967

April 6th PB Lumdenner   *'Astral'* Reedham Norfolk

For *Sheemaun* a new period had commenced. Over the next fourteen years she would be widely cruised while providing a comfortable and safe home for the Grays, who lived aboard for some six months of most years. Once again Littlehampton would become her registered Home Port. Admiral Gray cruised her East up the Channel and across to her old cruising waters in Holland, from there she would be cruised further East to explore the Baltic Sea and then West again to the German canals and the Dutch, Belgian and French inland waterways, many of which she had cruised in her pre-war years with Harold Bell and post-war years with Thomas Burton. The Grays then sailed *Sheemaun* back across the Channel to enjoy the extensive cruising grounds of the United Kingdom East and South Coasts.

During the fourteen years that the Grays cruised in *Sheemaun* some seventy-three visitors signed the Visitors Book. Among the many signatures reflecting the Gray's voyages and adventures, are those of 'Peggy' Larken, Nicholas and Jo Gray, the signatures of Admiral Gray's son-in-law Lord Brougham and Vaux and Lord Brougham's daughter Henrietta. On 17th August 1972 while *Sheemaun* was moored in Calais, 'Peter' and Sonia Gray entertained 'Doc' 'Bob' Shiers FRCSE, of 'Operation Ironclad', and his wife Elizabeth and family who were cruising in their yacht

- the *Maid of Cuan*,[142] the Visitors Book being duly signed by the 'Doc' and his family.

In 1973 on 31st January the 'General Register and Record Office of Shipping and Seamen' of the Department of Trade and Industry allocated to the *'Sheemaun'* the Call Sign Mike Lima Oscar November and Official Number 125369.

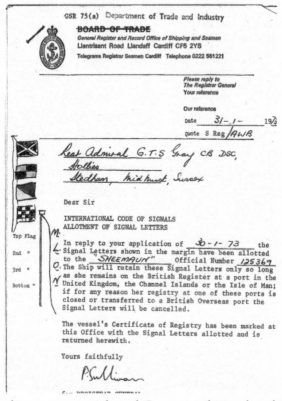

Later that same year, Admiral Gray was admitted to the Royal Yacht Squadron as a distinguished Naval Honorary Member. However, through archaic Squadron ruling, the yacht of an

---

142. '...on board of which all of my children were conceived.!' - 'Bob' Shiers in conversation with me years later!

honorary member was not allowed to fly the squadron's white ensign even though Royal Naval members were arguably better entitled to that honour than the non-naval members of the Squadron! On principal Admiral Gray insisted on flying a large 'Red Duster' which rumour has it so incensed some Squadron members that the rule was changed, and subsequently Royal Navy Honorary members could fly the Squadron's white ensign. *Sheemaun* was happy to comply!

After fourteen years of cruising in *Sheemaun* and having enjoyed 'Some of the happiest days in my life…' Admiral Gray's health was not improving and so the decision was taken to put the brave little ship once more on the market and perhaps to look for a smaller vessel. An advertisement was placed, and discreet enquiries made.

A fellow former Royal Naval Officer soon stepped forward in the person of Lt. Cmdr. Ian Pearson RN who as Principal Officer of Pangbourne Nautical College happened to be looking for a suitable 'Little Ship' that might serve as a cadet training ship.

'I had been taking boys to sea in various borrowed craft and stumbled on an advertisement for the sale of *Sheemaun* in a Portsmouth newspaper. After showing her to my son and realizing I could take her up the Thames to Pangbourne, it was a very easy decision to buy her there and then! Regular expeditions took place with an enthusiastic crew, the best of which was Pangbourne to Paris and back.'[143]

Like many before him, Ian Pearson when he saw *Sheemaun* liked the look of her. The mahogany wheel felt good and this was basically a sound and seaworthy little vessel.

---

143. Letter 12th January 2018 from Ian Pearson, typed by his wife Reggie as sadly, Ian, by now afflicted with Parkinson's Disease, was finding it difficult to write.

Time-Line –

- 1969 July 20th American Neil Armstrong became the first man to walk on the moon.

- 15th February 1971 - The historic British Imperial Currency, in which the £ was made up of twenty shillings, with each shilling was worth twelve pence; was abandoned and replaced by the Decimal currency. The new Decimal currency with 100 pence to the £ was so much simpler. No longer did we have threepenny pieces, Half Crowns worth 2 Shillings and sixpence, or the sixpenny piece worth 2.5 new decimal pence and the Guinea worth 21 old shillings or 1.05 new decimal Pounds!

- 1974 The Three-Day Week. Coal Miner's industrial action reduced the supply of electricity so much that Commercial and Industrial usage was limited to 3 days a week. Many pubs had to close, and TV broadcasting ceased at 10.30 pm.

The Nautical College Pangbourne
Cadet Training Ship *Sheemaun*

Lionel Stephens[144] writes that Pangbourne College can trace its proud and historic origins way back in the seventeenth century at a time when London City merchants were trading around the globe making, and sometimes losing, their fortunes. In 1836 Mr. Thomas Devitt and Mr. Joseph Moore set up their shipbroking firm in the City and by the eighteenth-century Devitt & Moore owned twenty-nine sailing ships and two steam ships. As time passed it became increasingly obvious to Thomas Devitt that ships were dependent on the men who sailed in them and that, aside from the traditional apprenticeship, there was no formal training in seamanship.

In his late years Thomas Devitt came to be known as 'The Grand Old Man' of the City. Then an influential and very wealthy man he was much involved with charitable work. In conjunction with Lord Brassey the two men established the 'Brassey Cadet Training Scheme'. Although steamships, with their cutting commercial edge were clearly superior to commercial sailing ships, Lord Brassey and Thomas Devitt with good reason believed that there was no better practical training for a seaman than could be provided by his serving on a square-rigged sailing ship, and of course that academic tuition was equally important. By the beginning of the twentieth century the Brassey Training Scheme owned five large sailing ships. One of these, the

---

144. Lionel taught at Pangbourne Nautical College from 1954 until his retirement in 1986 when he was Second Master. Lionel published his book on the Pangbourne Nautical College and its History in 1991. (Dovecote Press). His son was a cadet on *Sheemaun* training under Lt. Cmdr. Ian Pearson. Lionel has kindly permitted me to use material and pictures from his book.

engine-less iron clipper-ship the *Harbinger*, had masts towering up to two hundred and ten feet (64m). The *Harbinger* on her voyage from London to Melbourne and back once managed a day's run of three hundred and forty miles! As well as working the ship, keeping watches, doing deck work and handling sails aloft etc. the cadets daily attended instruction classes and underwent formal examinations.

The intervention of the First World War however inevitably and radically affected British shipping. Because of various mishaps, the requisition of vessels by the Government and the action of German U-Boats in sinking many fine sailing vessels, the facilities and funds available for cadet training suffered greatly. Thomas Devitt then in his late seventies searched for a suitable location to create a shore-based Training College, somewhere with close access to an estuary or river. The Clayesmore Estate or 'Tower Court' at Pangbourne looked very suitable and in September 1917 the Nautical College at Pangbourne was opened.

The College 'Brig'- late 1920s - berthed at the river frontage
Picture – by courtesy of Lionel Stephens

The College had acquired a naval cutter which was converted to a square-rigger by adding a bowsprit and stepping two masts, it was known as 'The Brigg'! Also in the 'fleet' were four 14 ft. [145] sailing boats, some rowing boats and a coal-fired river steamer.

Some 65 yrs later - Sheemaun at the same Pangbourne berth in 1984 - unknown photographer

Under the command of Executive Officer Lt. Cmdr. Ian Pearson, *Sheemaun* served the College well; she provided many scores of cadets with their first real hands-on experience of navigation, boat handling and seamanship. Crewed by up to six cadets at a time *Sheemaun*'s cruising area was extensive ranging from the Upper Thames, downstream through to the Tidal Thames and her familiar war-time patrol area of the Thames Estuary, South across to the Channel coasts of France and Belgium, South-West across to the Channel Islands and several voyages were made up the Seine to Paris. Each voyage would have had its special moments of elation, anxiety, frustration and achievement. The going at times would have been tough. Wet weather and heavy seas meant that her leaky decks would leave some cadets with wet sleeping bags! Memorable

145. 4.26 metres

and character-building experiences indeed some might say! To negotiate the Thames Bridges upstream from Tower Bridge it was necessary to take down the masts and secure them across the wheelhouse.

Sheemaun about to pass under Henley Bridge 1983 with cadets aboard. Photo courtesy Mrs Forward

Pangbourne College Parade 1982 - Photo courtesy Andrew Adams

There are numerous stories and adventures relating to *Sheemaun* while she was under the command of Ian Pearson and taking Pangbourne cadets on sail-training cruises. Tales such as that about a propeller shaft that uncoupled when in a French port. Fortunately, the C.O. of a Royal Naval vessel that happened to be nearby felt that *Sheemaun's* proudly worn CCF (Combined Cadet Force) defaced Blue Ensign could not be let down so a Naval diver and engineer were sent across and between them the propeller was pushed back into place and the coupling re-bolted. Another tale – and anonymously – from a former cadet who struck a deal with his CO; that instead of playing rugby, he would re-paint the heads in *Sheemaun*. This however expanded into the mammoth task of painstakingly scraping off layer upon layer of old lead paint as part of the preparation, a task that took many weeks. I am minded perhaps rather wryly, of the old nautical term 'Swinging the Lead'. Perhaps 'Scraping the Lead' might have been a contemporary Pangbournian version, Health & Safety must have been in its infancy!

There were other scrapes and near misses - such as a river grounding.

'… I remember feeling quite proud that we were possibly the largest boat on the upper reaches of the Thames – certainly in terms of draft! We once ran aground under Whitchurch Bridge on the outskirts of Pangbourne, less than a mile from our winter berth! We got our longest mooring warp out… rowed to the Victorian iron bridge, tied a bowline and winched ourselves back into deep water with the anchor capstan. We were slightly concerned about collapsing the bridge!'

With thanks to former *Sheemaun* Cadet - now Captain Richard Forward MN.

Other stories abound, of which some of the printable ones are mentioned. The sources of which remain anonymous…

'…the Seagull outboard wouldn't start…'

'…the autopilot was rarely used it was very touchy. You needed to hold a very straight course before engaging it…'

'… aft by the wheelhouse… we stored a huge bag of potatoes! Motoring through London… we enjoyed lobbing potatoes up onto the road bridges to confuse… or worse… the commuters. Not too bright with hindsight! Small spuds were also good ammunition against seagulls…'

It was not *Sheemaun* that broke down on 8th October in 1982 when she was cruising in the Solent with Pangbourne Cadets on board. For during the raising of the King Henry VIII's former Flagship, the *Mary Rose,* one of the huge lifting rig legs partly failed and *Sheemaun* stood by ready to assist if need be.

Pangbourne College - MFV *Sheemaun*
Some extracted examples from the Log Books

9-10 Oct 1982   Solent - Littlehampton

8 Oct   Went off on CCF trip on *Sheemaun* at Hamble. Hope to see the *Mary Rose*[146] being lifted from the sea bed off Portsmouth on Sunday.

10   Lifting rig leg broke so raising of 'Mary Rose' was postponed. Standing by aboard *Sheemaun*. Later that afternoon, we went to Littlehampton where we drove "Blue

---

146. The *Mary Rose* – Flagship of King Henry VIII, sank in 1545 with loss of all hands. *Sheemaun* stood-by as the wreck was being raised.

Peter III" an Atlantic 75 RNLI Lifeboat! The coxwain was father of a guy at school.

11   *Mary Rose* was lifted at lunchtime today. We were back at school.

<u>23-29 Oct   Littlehampton - Pangbourne</u>

23 Oct   Half term. Aboard *Sheemaun* from Littlehampton to Brighton.

24   Rang home from Ramsgate. Lost my watch overboard in Brighton Marina!

28   Mum & Emma (Sister) went to Henley and watched *Sheemaun* go under the bridge, driven by me. Spent the night alongside at Henley.

<u>11-14 April 1983   Pangbourne - Chatham</u>

11-14 Apr   CCF trip on *Sheemaun* to Chatham. [Fell in while provisioning!]

Stops overnight: Henley 11th, Staines 12th, HMS President 13th, Chatham14[th]. Then returned by road to Pangbourne

<u>20-21 May   Chatham - Southampton</u>

May 21-22   CCF trip to Chatham to Chatham on *Sheemaun*

<u>27-30 May   Southampton - France</u>

27-30   Half term. Taking *Sheemaun* from Chatham to Littlehampton.
30   Returned home. Good fun, rough seas yesterday.

<u>10-24 July 1983   France and Channel Islands</u>

10-21 CCF trip on *Sheemaun* to Channel Islands with Ian Pearson & John Spriggs (Royal Marine CCF commander) in charge (Southampton - Yarmouth - Alderney - Jersey – St Malo - Lezardrieux - Tréguier) We were split into A & B groups. One group would "Yomp" and camp ashore between ports while the other would be aboard. John Spriggs was admitted to and put in isolation hospital at St Helier with infective hepatitis.

20 By ferry from Jersey to Weymouth - force 6-8.

21 Returned home

17 Aug Family Jaunt in the Solent.

The Pearsons invited the Family for a day-sail on *Sheemaun* from Southampton Docks to Cowes, swam off Osborne Bay, Isle of Wight

21-24 Aug My sister & I, Ian & Reggie Pearson, David Carr & Ruck Nightingale went on a brief trip (non-CCF) aboard *Sheemaun*

22 My sister had to move into our boys' cabin because hers is leaking!

24 Returned home.

1984

22 July 21.30 Cadets Ward, Rowland, Erse, Mahoney leave by Brittany Ferry

24 July At St Malo

09.05 Cadets Morley, Stephens, Farquhar, Dawkins, Minter arrived by ferry. Met by JDRS Maintenances etc.

21.30   Cadets Gilnott & Doyne-Ditnos leave

25 July Voyage St Malo to Lezard Rieux

07.30   Call the hands
10.30   Slip & proceed to lock
11.15   Lock in – 11.30 Lock out
12.15   Left buoyed channel Co 290(m)
12.50   Off Le Vieux Banc
13.45   Off Cap Frehat
17.55   Passing through the Chenal de Ferlas
18.05   Enter Riviere de Pontrieux
18.45   Arrived at Lezard Rieux
19.15   Had supper
21.00   Went ashore to have a drink

Farquhar sick over stern all day. Reason - Chicken supper - no one unwrapped the giblets, under-cooked. Remains eaten next evening courtesy of Mr A

Paris to Conflans 26/6/86

07.45   Call The hands - sky overcast
Breakfast
Bach + L-M to get provisions Sunshine
09.30   Leave berth & dock fuelling bay
10.00   Jamieson still missing. Temp 70 deg ??
Leave fuel berth avec Jamieson
French lunch
Lock in at Sartre Ville
Saw *Seahawk* British Boat with opposite sex on board.
Arrived Conflans
Bangers + booze located & used
22.00   Engineers try and fix weed trap

Boulogne to Dieppe 19/7/86

07.30   Call the hands. Harbour master comes aboard. Change the impeller

10.00   Sail for Dieppe. Main compass 20 degrees out!

19.00   Arrive at Dieppe berth alongside ready to go through lock

21.05   Entrance into Port Duqesne

21.10   Alongside three smelly fishing boats – Cmdr Ps worst ever berth!*!

Voyage Hayling Island to Beaulieu 15 August

10.31   Slipped and proceed

11.40   Harry brought up!

11.15   Passed Chichester Bar

11.20   Harry brought up!

11.30   Went into wind over tide

11.40   Tea!!!!

11.50   Harry brought up

13.45   Arrived at Beaulieu

15.45   Doyne experiments with syfon

16.00   bale out the boat

16.30   Tea!!

18.30   Supper

19.00   Off to the boozer

21.00   Tea & bed

Lionel Stephens refers to *Sheemaun* in his book -
Pangbourne College
The Nautical College and its History
(Dovecote Press 1991) pp 164 -165

'The spirit of enterprise remained high. In 1985 the CCF[147]

---

147. CCF - Combined Cadet Force

celebrated its first ten years, with *Sheemaun* circumnavigating the UK via the Caledonian Canal...'

I feel it would not go amiss to add a little bit of hidden history, for *Sheemaun* has whispered to me that a young man named Gordon Thomas Seccombe Gray happened to have been a cadet at Pangbourne Nautical College from 1927 to 1929 after which he entered the Royal Navy as an Officer Cadet.

A Pangbourne Dormitory in 1920 - from Lionel Stephen's book

In the foreground one can see the Sea Chests in which the cadets stowed their belongings. On each side of the fireplace are wooden racks in which are stowed the hammocks and paillasses, above is a stout beam with hooks from which the hammocks were slung. It is quite evident that the fireplace had not emitted any warmth for many a year! Cadet 'Peter' Gray could have been boarded in this very dormitory or another one almost identical, and maybe also Cadet Ingram Orde Capper. In the years to come 'Peter' Gray would feature significantly in the story of *Sheemaun* for not only did he go on to have a most distinguished naval career with ultimately the rank of Rear Admiral, he would come in his retirement to own and cruise *Sheemaun* for some fourteen years and in 1981 would pass on custodianship of *Sheemaun* to the care of Lt. Cmdr. Ian Pearson, First Officer of Pangbourne Nautical College.

And so, as ordained by fate and a certain little thread picking its way in and out through the warps of the tapestry of time, *Sheemaun* came to be the Training Flagship at Pangboune Nautical College where both Admiral Gray and Ingram Orde Capper had been cadets.

The many events of those busy six years from 1981 – 1987 no doubt remain as treasured memories for those former cadets, now all men in their middle years. My wish is to share with the reader and those venerable Old Pangbournians and their famous College the story of *Sheemaun* from her launching in 1935, long before she became the Pangbourne Flagship. A story that has been slowly emerging from the mists of time, and to record her post-Pangbourne history which is also fascinating.

Sheemaun salutes Lt Cmdr., Ian Pearson and those many
Pangbourne Cadets who sailed in her

1975 - 1986

I discover the Tidal Thames and un-wittingly retrace some of *Sheemaun*'s old haunts

In 1973 I had been privileged to be appointed as a consultant surgeon to the City & East Landon Area Health Authority; however, the daily commute from my home in South London to North London via the Thames Blackwall Tunnel was too often frustrated by the heavy traffic. Even worse there were the inevitable 'break-downs' in the Tunnel or its approaches. It made sense to live just north of the Thames and close to the hospitals I served. In due course a riverside property came available which was one of five new Town Houses with a communal riverside terrace located on the site of the Crown Wharf overlooking the River Thames Blackwall Reach. The property provided quite breath-taking unobstructed views of the Thames across some three miles (5 kilometres) from Blackwall Point to Greenwich and was only sixty yards 54.8) metres) away from the Thames Division River Police Blackwall Station, the Blackwall 'Nick'[148]. There was also access over the sea wall via a ladder to a stretch of sandy beach that became exposed when the tide was out. My long association with the Thames had begun.

---

148. Nick – various meaning. One of which is a slang term for a criminal being caught 'nicked' by a police officer. Term for a Police Station.

From a painting of my London Docklands home at Crown Wharf. *Debrett* is seen at her mooring. The painting by the now internationally acclaimed artist Mackenzie Moulton – who was then a Thames River Division Police Officer, was made before the Canary Wharf development - note the open clear skyline!

Within a couple of years, I had been granted a permit by the Port of London Authority to lay a mooring just twenty-five yards (22.8 m) from my riverside terrace. This was done and a suitable boat in the shape of the *Debrett* a 27 ft (8.2m) 1970 fibre-glass Seamaster® cabin cruiser was found for sale at Tollesbury on the

371

River Blackwater. In due course *Debrett* was moved to her new mooring just off Crown Wharf on the Isle of Dogs and just ninety yards (100 m) downstream from the Blackwall Nick. At that time, I had limited knowledge of the Thames, but gradually as I adventured out in *Debrett* on those mysterious and historic waters, lessons were learned, and experience was gained - 'experiences' which included most of the possible boating-handling errors and catastrophes short of actually sinking!

Inevitably with my home only fifty yards from the Blackwall Division River Police Station[149] and my boat moored close by the Police Boat dolphin.[150] A close and very happy association with officers of the Blackwall Nick was to develop, indeed I sat for my VHF Radio Licence examination at the Wapping Police Station. However, the initial meeting with my police neighbours, was to say the least rather unusual.

On that occasion I was sitting one Sunday on my riverside balcony amusing myself by 'plinking' with a small air-pistol at flotsam such as bottles and bits of wood that swirled past on the tide. On answering a persistent door-bell ringing, I was confronted by a tall and muscular looking Police Officer who pointed out that it was forbidden to fire any weapon or projectile into or across the River Thames - Ooops. And so duly admonished and having apologised to the officer, I put away the little air-pistol and put the matter out of mind.

However, a couple of weeks later, again on a Sunday and while seated peacefully on the balcony enjoying the river view, I was shaken by a loud Boooom! Simultaneously a large black smoke-ring unfurled and rolled out across the river as pieces of smouldering wadding splashed sizzling into the water almost

---

149. Opened in 1894. In 1947 The entire central heating system was replaced at great cost. One of the officers said - 'I expect they'll close the place now'. He was right and a year later the station was closed and sold off!

150. A floating pontoon to which boats can be moored

half way across to the south bank. This was followed by the unmistakeable smell of black-powder wafting across the balcony. It appeared to have come from the Police Station riverside yard! Re-tracing some of Admiral, Lord Horatio Nelson's very footsteps made two centuries previously, I walked the sixty yards along the narrow and ancient Coldharbour lane to the Blackwall Police Station and peered through a gap in the big double yard-doors. There in the station yard was a group of Officers, including the tall one and who seemed to be in charge. They were clustered around a still smoking iron cannon which propped up on some timbers was pointed across the river!

A loud clearing of the throat '*Ahhemm*' quickly drew a rather embarrassed attention from the group of warrant-card holding pyro technicians. Suffice it to say, this little group of officers were also talented amateur historians whose Thames Patrols had allowed them to discover some of the scores of ancient abandoned cannons that can still be found on the muddy and overgrown banks of the Thames. One of these cannons had been dragged back to the station, cleaned up and had just been 'tested' with a small charge of black powder. No mention was made again with respect to the discharging of weapons towards the Thames, but I became closely educated in matters of historic muzzle loading weaponry! The officer concerned, Cornishman John Tremlin, became a good friend. Aside from being a dedicated police officer, John was very much involved with an historical group that commemorated and re-enacted past medieval and later historic English battles, but he was a modern man as well and a pilot of light aircraft. I was sad to learn of John's premature death[151].

There followed many years of close friendship and adventures involving the Thames River Police Division based at Blackwall

---

151. Sadly, John died some years ago. He was a well-respected police officer and amateur historian and a member of the Sealed Knot Charity that present dramatic re-enactments of medieval battles.

Station, who I found to a man, were dedicated to the policing of the Thames, while at the same time always empathetic and helpful to those whose living depended on those murky and often dangerous waters. Off-duty officers sometimes helped to crew on *Debrett* and sometimes I would be taken as 'Honorary Doctor' and occasional 'Honorary' extra crew-hand on Thames Patrols. Sometimes late in the evening, a bright light would flash through the bedroom window. Peering out I would see down below a Thames Division Police Patrol Boat and a call would come something like –

'Oh… sorry Doc… somehow our searchlight flashed in your window!… er… fancy a trip…?'

Of course, 'Doc' was delighted and pulling on his boat gear would hurry down three flights of stairs, across the terrace and down the terrace ladder to be received into the Patrol Boat - which just happened to be there. The night Thames patrols were fascinating and sometimes 'Doc' was useful, for as acting 'temporary helmsman' he could hold the boat on station stemming the tide, while all three crew officers went ashore or aboard a vessel to deal with an issue. Without the 'Honorary' helmsman, only two officers could deal with the incident because one officer would have to remain on-board in control of the boat.

I was in due course admitted as an Honorary Scarab, and that really was an accolade. The London Metropolitan River Police Division have a tradition that stems from 1798 and was the first ever policing body. It was set up by Scotsman and magistrate Patrick Colquhon and seaman John Harriott to police and make safe the dangerous and smuggling ridden London Docks. In the late 1970s I was an 'Honorary' crew on the old wooden *Patrick Colquhon,* a fast but then purely ceremonial launch, now replaced by modern 40 knot Targa patrol launches

- that's fast – 46 mph or 74 kph! Anyway, the traditional Thames Police Division emblem is the water-beetle or Scarab Beetle. The Thames Police Division burgee depicts the Scarab Beetle with a red (port) eye and a green (starboard) eye. *Sheemaun* as an honorary Scarab is proud to fly her Scarab Burgee with its red and green eyes.

I recall an occasion when I was invited to sit-in as 'Honorary' Doc on a winter's night patrol. The duty sergeant asked me if I would like to see a machine gun. Somewhat amazed, I naively expected a machine gun to be taken out from one of the lockers - but no. Instead the sergeant pushed open the throttle and switched on the searchlight. Leaving behind it a white boiling wake, the Police launch was then turned to cream across the river heading and directed towards a rusty Russian freighter moored just downriver from the Trinity House Wharf. As the searchlight picked out the hammer and sickle painted in yellow on the dirty red-banded funnel, the bridge door was flung open. A huge skipper in fur hat and wearing a heavy grey great-coat emerged and heaving a large machine gun over the bridge coaming, squared up behind it and levelled it at us. An experience I will never forget! Then with a flick the helm was put over and the patrol boat sped down past the length of the freighter tooting its horn. The huge Russian skipper held the machine gun up in the air with one massive hand and gave a cheery wave with the other hand while grinning widely. This was acknowledged by a few flashes from the blue light and hand-waves were returned. The sergeant laughed and explained that this was a game that both sides understood. One of the games, which at that time of very worrying international East-West or so called 'Cold War' tensions, facilitated ordinary seamen to express their natural underlying readiness for comradeship. Sergeant X, now long-since retired, and I have remained close friends ever since.

Another story relates to a waterside warehouse fire. It was late evening and dark, the flickering red and orange flames from the blazing warehouse lit up into the night sky. A senior Fire Officer had been ferried to the location so that proceedings might be better directed from the water-side from which vantage point a good view could be obtained. Standing solidly on the foredeck, this gentleman was indeed resplendent sight in his peaked cap with silver braid and his uniform with its silver epaulettes and many silver buttons. To set it all off he was wearing shiny leather thigh-boots. As the boat approached the wharf, the Fire Officer standing at the bow gestured to the helmsman to go in closer to the wharf... but ... the tide was falling away. The helmsman warned that it was getting very shallow.

'Nonsense'

Was the bellowed response.

'I'm in charge... you will follow my directions...'

The helmsman shrugged his shoulders –

'Yes Sir'

The resplendent Fire Officer pointing ahead, commanded –

'Now... go forward to that ladder...'

The helmsman, appreciating that to get the boat nose-on to the ladder would probably involve pushing the boat through some soft mud, obediently gunned the throttle, but the keel bit into firm mud and the resplendent Fire Officer who was on the bow leaning forward ready to grab the ladder, was propelled from the foredeck, taking three quick 'cycle-pedalling' paces as he flew through the air and sploshing firmly into the oozing mud. Of course, nobody laughed although there were a few silent smirks. The air was briefly rent with an explosive narrative that included words some might feel surprised at, given from whence they came!

But now there was need for an urgent 'Man Overboard' rescue exercise, and quickly as the tide was receding. A looped line was thrown to Sir in the mud with bawled instructions that he secured it under his arms and held tight. The now compliant Sir did what he was told. The helmsman went astern and with a flurry of mud and water the boat pulled away, towing after it one fuming Fire Officer. It was just a matter of recovering Sir back on-board. But oh, what a messy sight beheld the crew; without his splendid silver peaked cap, the red faced, angry and balding gentleman looked very different from the authoritarian figure that had boarded only half an hour ago, and worse, the loud sucking slurping noise that accompanied his delivery from the mud, it was revealed had been when his shiny thigh boots had been sucked off to become another relic of history kept by Old Father Thames. Sir, now muddy and shivering, sans cap, sans thigh boots and sans dignity was delivered safely and discretely ashore while his deputy and the shore fire-crews made a good job of containing the blaze. If there is a moral to this story, then it is that Old Father Thames is a great teacher and a leveller!

Time-Line –

- Since the end of the Second World War a state of intense military and political tension and stand-off had existed between the communist Eastern Bloc - the USSR and its satellite states and the Western Bloc – the USA and allies. Both sides had massive military capability and nuclear weapons. The Berlin Wall built in 1961 by the communist East German State was a focus for this tension and there was a real fear across the World that a Third World War could break out – with nuclear weapons. This threatening international situation was known as the 'Cold War'. At the time it was recognised that London Docklands were one of the 'Ground Zeros' at which USSR missiles were targeted.

- There was no Thames Barrier then and high tides regularly came within inches of the tops of embankments and sea-walls, with water slopping over onto pavements should a passing vessel send in a swell.

- I was once shown a store of emergency equipment reserved for a major catastrophe such as might occur should the Thames over-flow or a missile strike the London area. The 'Emergency Equipment' consisted simply of bales and bales of plastic Body Bags, waterproof labels, cordage and torches – a sad and very alarming sight!

- 1984 Saw the Miner's Strike as the coal industry became obsolete. The Country was in political turmoil and the strike resulted in the loss of 26 Million working days. Prime Minister Margaret Thatcher's Government took a firm stance and the destructive strike was ended.

- The Thames Barrier became operative in 1984.

- 1985 saw the UK's first 'Mobile Phones'. They were big and heavy, some as big as a brick. The car-phone was the size of a brief-case and usually installed in the boot of the car!

- The 'Cold War' as the critical East-West tensions were called, ceased to exist when the economy of the United States of Soviet Russia collapsed, the USSR was dissolved at the end of 1991 leaving the State of Russia and fourteen independent states. Now almost three decades later in 2018 one might well ask - What's changed?!

But time and tide wait for no man, events occur, and time brings change. The West India Docks and Canary Wharf became deserted after the invention of 'Containerisation'. Cargo ships' holds were no longer loaded and unloaded item by item by large teams of hard-working dockers. Instead, the new Container Ships went to specially equipped ports such as Felixstowe and much later Thames Gateway. No longer was I being almost blasted out of my bed at night by the huge steamers that would silently glide to within fifty meters of my bedroom window, then give one long then three short blasts on their sirens as they went astern prior to manoeuvring into the West India Lock Entrance only a hundred or so meters away. No longer were dock workers congregating in their many hundreds as they 'clocked' in and out of the big security gates in the high dock walls. No longer were there cargo bales to be heaved, craned and stowed. The shipping trade had been re-located to Felixstowe and Tilbury where facilities had been established for handling the now standardised shipping containers that could be lifted directly onto the waiting lorries.

No longer could I wander around the then silent docks picking blackberries and watching wildlife. Those almost seismic changes that had happened in a mere two years, had put an end to hundreds of years of traditional dockland manual cargo handling. Inevitably there were dynamic and rapid changes in the local businesses, in the population, and in the local hospital clinics and accident departments. About fifty percent of my acute work had previously consisted of managing dockworkers' sometimes horrific injuries. Outpatient and Physiotherapy clinics that had for decades been swarming with dockers suffering from lumbago, sciatica and multiple strain injuries would come to serve a very different population. One East London trait that seemed to hang on for another decade or so was the good old Cockney accent and humorous banter, but even that was to be washed away by the tidal inrush of widely differing ethnic cultures and languages.

Set up in 1981, The London Docklands Development Commission brought rumours of new developments which many felt were utterly fanciful, such as plans for a docklands airport! However, could an airport really be built in the middle of the derelict Royal Docks? That was a ridiculous idea, just as was the notion of building great skyscrapers on the derelict Canary Wharves! As for the idea of driver-less trains running around the area on raised rails, well, local people knew full-well that a Docklands Light Railway would never be possible and for what purpose?

Of course, the passage of time, the inspiration and determination of the Canadian Reichmann brothers and money ... lots and lots of money, and brilliant civil engineering, would see all this come about and much, much more.

Crown Wharf forty years later photographed from *Sheemaun*.
The immense Canary Wharf development now fills the skyline.
My Town House was the second from right of the block of white
buildings. Note how at High Tide the ground floors are well below
the water level! The bow-fronted house on the right is, according
to local tradition, where Lord Horatio Nelson used to meet with
Lady Hamilton. Photo – RP

It was from Crown Wharf that I came to explore the tidal
Thames from Tower Bridge to the outer Thames Estuary as
duties, time and tides allowed. In my faithful little Seamaster®
cruiser *Debrett* I would cast off and take the tide seaward, exploring and gradually getting to know the Thames and its creeks,
its sandbanks and back-currents and to marvel at the wildlife.
One of the pleasures was to venture into the Medway estuary
and anchor overnight in Stangate Creek alone among poppling
Kentish mud flats, the crying seabirds and plump seals. The
contrast with life in East London could not have been greater.
Meanwhile in the fashionable New Docklands, huge blocks

of flats and tenements were springing up, ever more densely crammed in alongside massive commercial skyscraper developments, dust and debris swirled everywhere. This was perhaps not the most inviting environment in which to be bringing up a young family, it was time for a change!

Taking a big risk, I resigned from my appointment and a life in the now increasingly impersonal and congested London Docklands area was exchanged for a life in the fresh green Kent countryside. *Debrett* was sailed from Blackwall in East London to Faversham Creek off the Swale in North Kent. An historic and wild creek, where sailor and adventurer Alan Reekie had bought the recently closed railway branch-line and sidings at Faversham Wharf and the old Cattle Market, and from it had established the Iron Wharf Boatyard.

Alan together with partner Peter Dodds created a secluded little boating world. A surreal world, where people while maintaining and building their boats, could relate with fellow dreamers and exchange tools and wisdom. It was a place where on a hot summer's day, one could lie on one's back in the long marsh grasses absorbing the dreamy pastural aromas as flittering grass-hoppers rasped, butterflies floated, and bees busied themselves amongst the wild-flowers and brambles. Watching as they soared high above, the Marsh Harriers circled lazily like eagles. It was a place where, one minute one might be changing engine oil and filters, then the next moment someone might light-up a barbecue and a dozen or so of like-minded souls would assemble. Jacket potatoes, sausages, steaks, bacon, baguettes and bottles of wine would materialise, and someone would strum a guitar. Engine oil and filters, time and responsibilities would all be forgotten as glowing embers and heaven-ward swirling sparks took over from the setting sun.

This was being alive, it was living and experiencing. A life that was so far removed physically and spiritually from the competitive commercial life that had overtaken London's fast re-developing Docklands. A Docklands no more other than by name, its thousands of new residents neatly filed away in their filing-cabinet towering blocks of apartments. In contrast at the Iron Wharf Boatyard there was a loosely linked trusting community where a person's station in life was irrelevant, butcher, fisherman, farm-worker, bohemian, and surgeon: it made no difference, all shared an understanding of the tides, the appreciation of fresh air, the seasons and the need to be on a boat and feel free.

It was through the auspices of the Iron Wharf Boatyard that in a new mind-set I would begin to explore the expansive Medway estuary and the tidal and outer Thames Estuary. It was from there I would come to experience the tides and currents and the varying moods of waters that could vary from tranquil to dangerous. Unaware at the time, that I was becoming familiar with those same waters that three and a half decades previously and in very different circumstances, the patrolling HMY *Sheemaun* with her RNVR crew and armed with machine guns and rifles, had pulled exhausted airmen from the waters, had been strafed by German planes, had stopped and inspected coasters and barges, had dealt with the extremely dangerous mines, had returned fire at Hitler's strafing fighters and at his pilotless flying-bombs.

1987

Sheemaun has a new owner and works her magic on his life too

'As soon as I get on my boat, something inside me changes, then I really feel what living is. A boat is an amazing place to learn about yourself.'

Laura Dekker[152]

As if on a giant car wind-screen in a giant car-wash, sheets of foaming salt-water blasted across the mud flats to then spume across the Emsworth Channel. Given it was July, these were very unseasonal gale force winds with lashing rain sweeping from West to East across southern Britain, bringing with them damage and floods. Straining at their moorings the scattered yachts lay head to wind. On some, where the sails had not been securely stowed and lashed, wildly flapping canvas tried to tear itself to shreds. The tide however was ebbing, and *Sheemaun* lying at her tidal mud berth on Hayling Island's east shore had settled into the mud, no longer chafing at her mooring lines. Commander Ian Pearson had decided not to take *Sheemaun* back to her fresh-water berth at Pangbourne Nautical College on the upper Thames. The time had come for the proud old boat to seek out a new owner. Hopefully, she would find a caring custodian prepared to undertake the necessary substantial re-fit and the on-going care. It was with some apprehension that Ian Pearson instructed broker Peter Gregson of Wooden Ships Ltd. based in Devon to put her on his books.

---

152. In 2010 Laura Dekker at age 16yrs set off from Gibraltar and sailed around the world solo in her 38 ft (11.6m) yacht *Guppy*. The youngest person ever to complete a solo circumnavigation.

In common with so many others who are instinctively drawn to the sea and boats, like so many previous owners of *Sheemaun*, I was in the habit of dreamily browsing through various boating and yachting magazines. Then, coming across the Wooden Ships' advertisement in the *Practical Boat Owner*, I was at once attracted to the photograph of a boat called *Sheemaun*.

Quite beyond any sense or reason, something indefinable spoke to me. On a purely pragmatic basis, this appeared to be an old but substantial vessel that would almost certainly need a prolonged and expensive re-fit. However, she was of a size that could be easily handled, while offering comfortable accommodation, excluding her saloon, in three separate cabins. Furthermore, she had two engines and an auxiliary rig, which suggested a good margin of safety and were desirable features ... but there was also an indefinable 'je ne sais quoi' air about her that was special, a something that appealed to the heart. And so, a telephone call was made to Peter Gregson of Wooden Ships requesting that further details to be posted. In due course I arranged to meet with the vendor Ian Pearson aboard *Sheemaun* at her mud-berth on Hayling Island.

August 1986. Ian Pearson seated, little Suzie Pell aged 8yrs peers into *Sheemaun*'s wheelhouse. Photo RP

It was love at first sight. Ian empathised and could not have been more helpful. He accepted that *Sheemaun* would need much more than a tidy-up. Her decks were leaking in several places to the extent that naval ingenuity had in critical areas below, fitted internal plastic gutters draining into plastic bottles! Her port engine had a 12v alternator, while her starboard engine had a 12v dynamo and consistent with this anomalous arrangement, her electrical system, revealing its various layers of add-on evolution, was in dire need of a total overhaul. Her hull needed attention by way of burning off the many layers of tired paint, followed by a good look at her timbers and then a proper re-paint. Her smoky David Brown 6D diesels could do with a re-build or even replacing.

Surveyor Alan Olford carried out a General Condition survey and reported in early December. Yes, there was a lot of work to be done and much more than had initially been anticipated. Estimates were mulled over and on 6th January 1987 a deal was done at £10,000.[153]

Ian and his wife Reggie were happy to know that *Sheemaun* would be cared for. After all. no-one likes to see a proud old boat neglected and left to deteriorate. Reggie Pearson put a little bouquet of sea holly[154] in the wheel-house for 'Good Luck' and Ian wrote this charming letter -

---

153. Allowing for inflation, in 2018 that would equate to £20,487.17.

154. The bouquet of sea holly has ever since been kept where Reggie placed it above the wheel house windscreen.

HARBINGER,
PANGBOURNE COLLEGE,
PANGBOURNE,
BERKS. RG8 8LA.

7th Jan 1987

Dear Dr Pell,

I am so glad that "Sheemaun" is now in your loving care, and I do hope that, once you have done that is needed to her, you will have a very happy and successful time.

We have had five very good and active years, but now I can concentrate on trying to be a good Housemaster!

I enclose all the various papers and documents that I think that you ought to have, including a detailed (if out of date) turnover that I received from the previous owner, Admiral Gray.

I do hope that you will soon be able to rescue all the mattresses & covers from the ravages of winter.

I will arrange for the liferaft, which belongs to the R.N., to be

On the recommendation of surveyor Alan Olford, Ian kindly delivered *Sheemaun* to Coombe's Boatyard at Bosham to await a re-fit, which weather and season allowing, would end up taking the best part of two years.

Sheemaun lying at Coombes' Yard pre-restoration in 1987.Photo - RP

During the re-fit the insurers requested a valuation be undertaken by Messsrs Castlemain Marine Ltd. Their Director John Ridgeway reported on 1st November 1988 –

'... The yacht has been the subject of a very extensive overhaul by Messrs Coombes and some of this work is still going on. The appearance is very pleasing, being of classic design and when the fitting out is complete there is no doubt that she will be fit to take her place with the pick of surviving 1930s 'Gentleman's Yachts.'... if asked to sell 'Sheemaun' when fully fitted out, I would advise asking in the region of £120.000[155] ...'

I must confess to being somewhat 'gobsmacked' by that letter! So, it seems; sometimes it pays to follow one's gut feelings and intuition. Appreciating that I now owned a 'Classic 1930s Gentleman's Yacht' I found some consolation for the expenses

155. In 2018 that would equate to £214,383.60

of the re-fit, but more importantly, I found myself entering on a quite unexpected pathway. For a seed had been sown, a seed that would germinate into a thirty-year quest to uncover *Sheemaun*'s story.

In June 1989 after months of restoration work at Coombes' Boatyard Bosham, the proprietor Mr Bob Greenshield, declared *Sheemaun* to be sea-worthy and ready for departure. The final bills were settled tide-tables and diaries consulted and a departure date set for 22nd July. The Yard had put *Sheemaun* on to a mooring where she would be afloat at all states of the tide. I had arranged that my friend and colleague 'Doc' Shiers FRCS and my nephew Maxwell Wallace-Jones would crew for the voyage to Ramsgate. On the previous day, a smiling and optimistic trio were delivered by taxi from Bosham Station to Coombes Yard with our kit bags and charts and we were ferried out in a small work-boat to the waiting *Sheemaun*. Newly painted and varnished, the boat smelled and looked good.

As gear was being stowed the 'Doc' enquired where the dinghy outboard engine was located, the yard-hand just shrugged his shoulders, a Parisian waiter would have been impressed! A search of the ship soon ascertained that there was no outboard to be found, clearly *Sheemaun*'s little Suzuki outboard motor was still somewhere at Coombes' Yard now a third of a mile away, but 'Time and Tide wait for No Man'. There was a tide to catch and the yard-hand was in the process of casting off for his return to the yard. Leaning over the rail the 'Doc' called down to the yard-hand-

'Our outboard's been left at the yard…'

The yard-hand just shrugged. In response the 'Doc' pointing to the yard-boat outboard shouted –

'We'll take that one, you can have ours…'

The yard-hand now looked worried, as he clearly did not relish the task of having to explain to the manager why he had had to row back to the yard sans outboard. He remained immobile sitting on the thwart. Leaning further over the guard-rail the 'Doc'[156] almost exploded –

'That's an order'

Then with perfect timing he roared –

'MOVE'

The yard-hand jumped as if electrified and undoing the clamps, meekly handed the small outboard motor across. The next few hours were spent inspecting the ship and settling in. The wheel felt secure and one a half turns each way gave full rudder. The ship seemed generally in good order, so we launched the dinghy and enjoyed an exploration of the Bosham mud-saltings and wild-life. Later a decent evening meal of steak and kidney pie was washed down with a bottle or two of 'Doc's favourite claret. We listened spell-bound as 'Doc' Shiers reminisced on some of his past adventures, then he stopped and leaned forwards across the saloon table almost confidentially –

'You know… something's been niggling in my mind and now I know what it is… I've been on this little ship before… years ago… somewhere in France… probably Calais, then she was owned by an Admiral… can't recall his name just now.'

---

156. 'Doc' had been the Surgeon Commander on the Cruiser HMS Dauntless in the 1942 'Operation Ironclad' when the Island of Madagascar was brought under Allied control. It was a serious operation in which 770 were killed and 780 wounded.

The 'Doc' was quite right, for many years later when Nicholas Gray kindly passed his late father's Visitor Book into my care, therein I found were the signatures of 'Doc' and his family.

17.8.72 Kate Shiers, Sarah Shiers, Doc. LGP Shiers, Harry Shiers and Elizabeth Shiers. All crew of the *Maid of Cuan*. Address then at 9 Weymouth St. London W1

I will never forget that first night of my first voyage in *Sheemaun*, snug and comfortable in my cot-berth as the ebb tide gurgled past gently rocking the old boat and wondering about admirals and past owners. The following morning, after breakfast and coffee, we stowed things away and ticked off the skipper's check-list. At 08.30 the engines were started and warmed up and at 09.00 we cast-off and headed for the notorious Chichester Bar, hoping that the yacht ahead was skippered by a local who knew the bar and that his yacht drew more than our four feet-ten inches (1.3 meters). Half an hour later we were out at sea and heading East for Ramsgate and *Sheemaun*'s new home port.

Finding myself ever busier in my professional and family life, I found little time to cruise in *Sheemaun*, however day-sailings were enjoyed and occasional escapades at week-ends, but it became clear that the elderly David Brown diesel engines, despite having been re-built at Coombes yard, would now have to be replaced. Of course, the heart of a motor-yacht is its power unit and a reliable power unit contributes hugely to the safety of the vessel. Advice was sought, and the differing views considered. After the expensive but disappointing experience of replacing them with old but re-conditioned engines. Listening to my ever-sensible wife Maura, I bit the bullet as they say, and ship-wright Steve Parish installed a pair of brand-new state-of-art modern Beta Marine diesel engines.

2009 - *Sheemaun's* engine room with the new Beta Marine Diesels

When installing the new engines, it was evident that one or two soft planks would also need replacing, which task was skilfully carried out by Steve. *Sheemaun* has never looked back since. While it is true to say that a wooden hull needs constant attention, the practicality is, that provided a good coat of protective paint is maintained and rain-water is not allowed to soak into the timbers, a well-built boat will last for a hundred years or much more.

Not so long after *Sheemaun* had taken her berth at the Royal Harbour Ramsgate, an unknown photographer took her picture. Some years later I received a package from an acquaintance living in the Midlands. This gentleman had bought a jigsaw puzzle and having assembled all the pieces, realised it was a picture of *Sheemaun*! He kindly posted it to me. The jigsaw having been made at Heemstede in Holland by Fame Puzzles

This jigsaw is now assembled, framed and proudly displayed on the bulkhead in *Sheemaun*'s saloon. It sometimes sparks a conversation when an eagle-eyed visitor spots that the picture is reversed left with right. Ramsgate is the wrong way around and what appears to be *Sheemaun*'s starboard side, is in fact her port side!

PART FOUR
The 21st Century
2003

Sheemaun is Recognised as Meriting Inclusion on the National Register of Historic Ships

'Look down the years! Behold in pageant there
The ships of England! These have played their part
In history. Have sailed and kept your seas,
From Dover's cliffs unto the westward Start.'

Isabella Kiernander

There had been in the years following the Second World War, a growing concern expressed amongst historians, that Britain's heritage of historically significant vessels was being lost. Over time, spanning decades or even a century or more, vessels that have been regarded as no longer functional or not worth maintaining, were generally allowed to deteriorate, or converted to house-boats, broken up or sunk. Furthermore, there was no formal authority or coordinated system in Britain for recognising and recording historic ships and vessels of National significance.

Eventually, in 1992 the National Historic Ships Committee was established. Later, Lord Lewin, Chairman of the Trustees of the National Maritime Museum at Greenwich, would set up the Advisory Committee on National Historic Ships as a non-departmental Government body. This Advisory Committee had responsibility to report to the Department of Culture, Media and Sport and remit to advise the Secretary of State as to matters of historic ship preservation and funding priorities. A National Register of Historic Vessels was established, and vessels were sought that

- Were at least 50 years old.
- Were demonstrably and significantly associated
- with the UK.
- Were more than 33 feet (10.07 metres) long.
- Were substantially intact.
- Had a pre-eminent National or Regional significance.
- Spanned a spectrum of UK Maritime History.
- Illustrated changes in construction or technology.
- Merited priority for long-term preservation.

Quite unaware of the existence of such an Advisory Committee, I had been making my own efforts to unearth the past story of *Sheemaun*. One of my lines of enquiry had led to the Department of Maritime Studies at St Andrews University, that resulted in details of *Sheemaun*, being passed on to the newly established and Government supported National Register of Historic Ships. After which one might say that 'Things moved quickly'! I was contacted and *Sheemaun* was listed to be visited and inspected. She was immediately recognised to be an excellent example of a G L Watson designed 1930s Gentleman's Motor Yacht and with a significant and special history, having been an armed Royal Navy Auxiliary Patrol Boat in the Second World War and later a Cadet Training Ship. Accordingly, she was entered at No. 1939 on the register of the United Kingdom National Fleet of Historic Ships.

On 21st March 2003 I received a letter from Paula Austin,

coordinator of the National Register of Historic Vessels confirming that *Sheemaun* had been identified as a vessel meriting inclusion in the National Register of Historic Vessels and enclosing a document signed by Admiral of the Fleet Sir Julian Oswald GCB. *Sheemaun* is indeed honoured to have received Sir Julian's attention. She is now one of the few notable British historic vessels to have been recognised and certified as such by a First Sea Lord!

The Certificate which bears Sir Julian's[157] signature will long be a treasured part of this little ship's provenance.

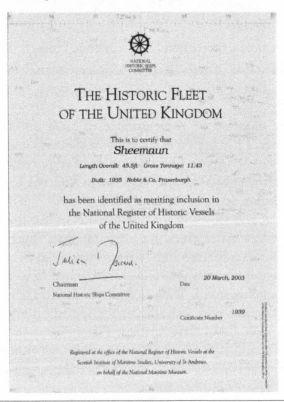

NATIONAL
HISTORIC SHIPS
COMMITTEE

THE HISTORIC FLEET
OF THE UNITED KINGDOM

This is to certify that
Sheemaun

Length Overall: 45.5ft Gross Tonnage: 11.43

Built: 1935 Noble & Co, Fraserburgh

has been identified as meriting inclusion in
the National Register of Historic Vessels
of the United Kingdom

Chairman
National Historic Ships Committee

Date   20 March, 2003

Certificate Number   1939

Registered at the office of the National Register of Historic Vessels at the
Scottish Institute of Maritime Studies, University of St Andrews,
on behalf of the National Maritime Museum.

---

157. After a brilliant navel career, Admiral of the Fleet Sir Julian Oswald GCB, 'slipped his cable' on the 19th July 2011. He was 77.

And so, I became accustomed to answering the emails and correspondence that ensued, and *Sheemaun* learned to take her place among her fellow historic ships at the various Maritime Festivals and exhibitions to which she was invited. Now that she was in the public eye, questions arose and stories about her history began to accrue.

2005

A Close Brush with Death
July, Thursday 7th

'And all the winds go sighing, for sweet things dying'

Christina Rossetti

It was a warm and sunny morning, the few fluffy cotton-wool clouds that drifted lazily across the skies, serving only as if to emphasise the blueness of the heavens above. The world seemed to be at peace as *Sheemaun* lay quietly at her Ramsgate berth. I was busy in the wheel-house, the doors and roof-hatch were set wide open to best catch any cooling breeze. Up a'top of the coach-house roof a technician from Grundon Marine Ltd. was checking over the GPS antenna and the Raymarine® chart-plotter system, poking here and there with his multi-meter test-probes.

Meanwhile in London, my daughter, Suzie now aged 24 years and a *Sheemaun* family crew-member, had an important day ahead, for Suzie was due to commence in her new position with a marine insurance underwriting company at the prestigious Lloyds Building. Smartly dressed in her city suit and wearing her mother's treasured pashmina scarf, she mingled with the early-morning commuters in the jostling crowds at Edgeware Underground Tube Station. Suzie would be taking the next east-going train from platform Four on her way to Monument Station, which was only a few minutes' walk from the dramatic fourteen storey Richard Rogers designed Lloyds Building where she would be starting in her new post.

At 08.42 the next Circle Line east-bound train thundered into the station and squealed to a halt, the doors slid open and as on myriad previous occasions, hundreds of busy commuters disgorged themselves onto the platform. Suzie, standing at the head end of the platform wanted to be near the front of the train, but the jostling crowds had already filled the two front coaches, so she boarded into the third coach and considered herself lucky to find a seat. The doors swished shut and the train jerked off into the tunnel.

No one on that train, on that fateful day, would get to their destinations as they had anticipated. At 08.50, six innocent people, would be dead together with their evilly intentioned suicidal assassin, and many more would be injured, for sitting in the second coach, on the left side just in front of the rear doorway as one would look towards the front of the train, was the brain-washed suicide-bomber and terrorist, Mohamed Sidique Khan.

At 08.50 Khan detonated his rucksack bomb.

Suzie describes the experience of a blinding orange flash and explosion. The inter-carriage doors were blasted down the corridor just missing her but injuring the gentleman sitting near her, she was hurled sideways. The carriage was filled with foul smoke and dust. People were screaming, the lights flickered and dimmed, the train screeched to a stop.

Trapped in the carriage with debris and broken glass everywhere, Suzie found herself choking in the smoke. It was a scene of carnage and confusion. As Suzie and her fellow survivors tried to make sense of their situation, it soon dawned on them that this had been a bomb explosion and for all they knew there might be more than one bomb. Many of the injured were crying and moaning.

'I remember a train on the other line stopping alongside. Its lights were on and I could see the people inside. Only the glass windows and an air-gap separated us, but our lights had gone out, they had no idea that we were there next to them and we couldn't make them hear us…'

As the smoke and dust gradually settled, Suzie realised that the explosion had happened very close-by at the rear end of the carriage just in front of the one she was in. The lights flickered on and she could see bodies, pieces of clothing and mangled metal, there were fragments of glass everywhere.

'I knew at once I had to help as much as I was able.'

Through the clouds of choking dust and smoke she made her way forward into that carriage.

'It was terrible, there were people crying out… one man had a smashed leg, it looked broken and with a huge wound that was pouring blood. I knew I had to stop the bleeding, so I raised his leg and wrapped my scarf tightly around it… he was so frightened. I did my best to reassure him that help was coming, and he would be alright…'

Suzie described how those that could walk were then guided forward by the train driver and told to climb down from the front cab and to make their way along the tracks back to the station which was about two hundred metres away.

'There was what looked like a huge hole in the carriage floor with a man's torso and head sticking up… it looked as if the lower part of his body was missing…'

She found herself next to a big and strong looking man, his ears were bleeding. He was dazed and appeared to have been deafened and he had lost his sense of balance, she helped him get down from the train cab. Suzie recalled how she did her best to comfort and physically support other injured victims. There were scores of people, many crying and many injured. Gradually the dazed survivors and walking injured carefully made their way in the pungent smoke, along the tracks back towards the hazy glow of the station lighting from which direction, and mercifully, the emergency services personnel began to arrive.

Across on the other side of the world at the office of the international company Solcorp Inc. in Taipei City, Taiwan, it was just after 5 pm local time and the staff were preparing to finish for the day and close-down. But… a blinking electronic news-flash on one of the office's flickering screens caught the eye of Suzie's brother, expert data-analyst and programmer Rodney Pell Jr.

The initial reports coming across indicated that four serious explosions had taken place in London within the last hour or so. There had been significant loss of life and multiple injuries. One of the bombs had been exploded at the Edgeware Underground Tube Station. Rodney was aware that back in London his sister Suzie would have been using that station quite possibly at the very time of the terrorist attack. His repeated attempts to reach his sister by mobile phone proved worryingly futile, so he 'phoned me and his brother Geoffrey. Although very concerned at the news now coming from Taiwan, I tried to re-assure myself and my sons that it was very unlikely that their sister would have been involved.

Oh, how wrong can one be!

Now, alerted by his brother via the wonderful world-wide information technology system, Geoffrey Pell who was close-by in London, made his way to the Edgware Road Tube Station to search for his sister. There he joined with the confused and milling crowds. There were rumours of an electrical current surge having cause an explosion on the rail-lines, or possibly, of a bomb having gone off in a train. The tube-train systems and public transport systems had been closed. Being jostled amongst the hundreds of confused and agitated people now crowding around the tube station entrance, it seemed there was little that Geoffrey could do. Yet, suddenly amongst all the confusion he was able to identify his barely recognisable sister as she staggered from the station. Her hair was tangled with dust and debris, her once smart suit was tattered and stained, and her face was bleeding from a myriad of glass abrasions. Geoffrey helped her get to Paddington Hospital where she was assessed and received treatment for dust inhalation and superficial contusions and abrasions that would in time heal, hopefully with little trace.

Seventy-five miles from London, busying myself on *Sheemaun* at her berth in Ramsgate Marina, I had been increasingly worried by the mobile-phone messages coming from Taiwan and London and with up-dates on the situation, but by mid-morning it was apparent that Suzie had indeed been involved, and had escaped death and serious injury literally by a whisker.

It would later be revealed that there had been coordinated terrorist suicide bombings across London. Three suicide bombers had blown themselves to pieces almost simultaneously on underground trains and another on a London bus. Fifty-two people had been killed and more than seven hundred injured. London Transport systems were shut-down for that day and services significantly disrupted for weeks. The World was horrified.

It would take Suzie many months to move on from that terrible experience and it would be several years before she could face travelling again on a London Tube Train. Hundreds of families had been affected by that act of pointless and wanton terrorism and killing. Suzie although so perilously close to the explosion, was lucky to escape with minor injury. The amazing communicative power of the internet was dramatically demonstrated, for although thousands of miles apart, Suzie's brothers were able to coordinate their actions and offer support, while also appraising me of the situation some hours before news broke on the media. On that terrible day, when so many loved-ones were killed and so many injured, Suzie was found to be selfless, thoughtful and brave. *Sheemaun* salutes another courageous and memorable crew-member.

Suzie on *Sheemaun* four years later – Photo RP

2009

Sheemaun is invited to attend at the Mayor's Festival of the Thames

From *Sheemaun's* cruise journal

THE SKIPPER AND CREW OF
'SHEEMAUN'
WERE PROUD TO TAKE PART
IN
THE ANNUAL MAYOR'S FESTIVAL OF THE THAMES

HELD ON 11th – 13th SEPTEMBER 2009
FOR THE FIRST TIME.

ASSEMBLING AT LONDON'S St KATHERINE'S YACHT HAVEN, A UNIQUE COLLECTION OF HISTORIC AND CLASSICAL VESSELS ALL WITH CONNECTIONS TO THE RIVER THAMES AND LONDON'S PAST

(Supported by *Classic Boat***)**

The necessary voyaging up and down the Thames was also eventful and interesting and worth recording

THE CREW

Skipper Rodney Pell

1ˢᵗ Mate Maura Pell

Hon. Sail Master
Tim Hunt

Master
Shipwright Steve
Parish

1ˢᵗ Midshipman
Charlie Hunt

2ⁿᵈ Midshipman
Chris Downing

Wednesday 9th September p.m. The crew duly mustered on *Sheemaun* at Ramsgate outer marina. Sadly, Maura Pell and Steve Parish were unable to join ship at this point. Personal belongings and gear were stowed, and safety checks and equipment and vessel familiarisation routines were then satisfied. The passage plan had been finalised for a casting off on Thursday 10th at 06.30, three hours before L.W. Ramsgate we would be at the Red Sands when the tide turned and then get an eight-hour tidal push up the Thames to Tower Bridge for the intended arrival at about 17.30 hrs. We had aimed to be in London a day ahead of the Friday 17.00 deadline for locking in to St. Katherine's Haven.

Berthed adjacent to us at the Ramsgate pontoon had been a 15-meter Bavaria sloop the *Good Vibrations*, with a German crew of ten. Their skipper announced they would be casting off at 05.30 hrs and were also bound for St. Katherine's Yacht Haven. But they would be taking the Prince's Channel which was deeper but adding some 6 miles to the voyage as compared to the Gore channel for which we had opted.

Thursday 10th September. Hon. Executive Officer Tim Hunt called the hands at 06.00 and saw to tea and breakfast while the two midshipmen our 'snotties' cleared decks and cast off the sail covers and ties as there was a promising if gusty N.E. wind. In warm early morning sunshine, we cast off at 06.35 and motored out of Ramsgate into a lumpy sea, rounded the Elbow Buoy and North Foreland promontory and set course West aiming for the 'Four Fathom Channel' which would take us North of the Isle of Sheppey and into the Thames Estuary. Our Imray Chart showed how the waters of this area just off the North Kent coast are a worrying maze of dangerous sand-banks and shallows.

Making a good 6 knots over ground against the last of the ebb we set all sail after rounding the Foreland and with a stiff N.E. breeze in our favour *Sheemaun* settled onto starboard tack heading West along the Gore Channel. Watching the soundings carefully as we approached the Hook Spit and East Last buoys which mark the narrow and shallow channel leading from the Gore Channel to the Horse Channel which in turn would lead us through to the Four Fathom Channel and so on to the mouth of the Thames Estuary.

To our North of our starboard side the stiff breeze was sending waves crashing over the exposed Margate Hook sands, we felt relatively safe in the lee of the sands where our water was calm, but it would have been very different at high tide!

As we closed the Hook Spit buoy from eastwards, the echo-sounder showed 0.5 meter, then 0.25 meter and then zero!!! We had been motor-sailing to keep up our schedule but immediately both engines were put into neutral for we could not afford any propeller generated suction to pull down the stern. Trinity House has since reported that silting is taking place with risk of grounding at L.W. at this location. As we sailed carefully through the narrow gap at about 4 knots and literally bumping across the hard sands, the Dover Coastguard crackled over the VHF…

'Mayday… Mayday… Mayday[158]… yacht - *Good Vibrations*… *Good Vibrations*… how many persons have you aboard…'

We were momentarily mesmerised but could neither see the yacht sending the Mayday nor receive its transmissions, we could only receive the Coastguard transmission. We knew that sea conditions in the Prince's Channel would be uncomfortable even for a large yacht, but we were ourselves in a tight predicament and there was no way we could head across the barely covered sands for the Prince's Channel to offer help as to do so would certainly put us aground. It was with much relief that we heard the Mayday had been stood down and replaced by a Pan-Pan[159] call and that the disabled yacht was to be towed into Ramsgate by the Lifeboat.

Hon. Midshipman Charlie Hunt went aloft as look-out - Photo RP

---

158. Mayday Mayday – The international maritime distress call for a life-threatening disaster at sea.

159. Pan Pan – The international maritime distress call for an urgent but non-life-threatening situation at sea.

Blogg 17.11.09 from Segel- Club eV Tespe Germany: (translated from German)

'...Wednesday 9 September. ...wind and waves have increased significantly. During the crossing the wind rises up to six Beaufort with stronger gusts, so that our '*Good Vibrations*' we plough on with 9 to 10 knots... we pass through a giant anchorage – probably about 30 cargo ships at anchor here...'

'Thursday 10 September – Bad Vibrations. On this day we will sail for London. The wind is still blowing strong. We have made loud noises like a cracking noise, then Mike... the rudder will not move... from one moment we are in irons. The sea is heavy, we are in a shallow in the Thames Estuary, sand bars not far away. Jaco throws in the anchor... to keep us safe... Micah broadcasts MAYDAY to all stations... everything goes at lightning speed but runs with great composure... In several radio contacts Micah coordinates the salvage operation with the distress control centre... The Coast Guard takes us astern... the emergency tiller turns out to be quite useless...'

(*Good Vibrations* was towed into Ramsgate Harbour by the Lifeboat, not the Coast Guard as blogged)

'Friday 11th September... Jaco, Mike, Matthew and Berni remain with our ship. We the remaining crew members make us by bus and train on the way to London... There in the harbour is also the *Sheemaun*, a historic sailboat that was with us in Ramsgate on about the same time as we had set out for London in the morning! In the heart of the port, many historic ships arrived, because this weekend the Thames Festival, a major maritime festival, taking place... We are warmly welcomed by the owner and invited to a tour of the boat (*Sheemaun*). In the heart of the port many historic ships have arrived...'

Johannes Bettany, 1 Vorsitzender, Segal-Club – Tespe eV. Feldberg 17a. 21379 Scharnebeck.

Leaving the Horse Channel and coming away from the lee of the sands, the waves and swell became much heavier, but this did not last long and after an hour we were over the Kentish Flats at dead low water in calm seas but a check on the depth showed only 0.8 meter under our keel, so we reduced to making a few knots for the next mile until we had cleared the shallows off Red Sands.

After passing the Yantlet Flats navigation became pilotage and an easy matter of buoy-hopping and eye-balling. When we arrived at Woolwich Reach we had to 'dodge' the ferries, keep an eye open for river traffic and then call in by VHF Ch 14 to Port of London VTS Barrier Control. This was unaccountably difficult. We did not seem to be getting through and only received their transmissions intermittently. A resort was made to the hand-held VHF radio but its battery quickly faded. A sea-bound tug seemingly charged at us on a collision course and kept on the collision course despite our skipper making a definitive turn to starboard. The tug came close and someone yelled from its bridge, but we could not make out what was said. I made some derogatory remarks about London river-tugs and London river-craft in general, but attention was then diverted by the Harbour Master's Launch coming up fast on the port beam. The ensuing shouted conversation revealed that our radio was not functioning, so my mobile phone number was requested. This was no easy matter for I not only didn't know my own mobile number, I couldn't read it without my specs and even then, had to take it into the shade to read the display! That meant leaving the helm, stumbling about down below and then coming back on deck to bawl the information across to the PLA Harbour Master. In the event all was sorted out via mobile phone and we passed through the Thames Barrier!

Approaching the Thames Barrier - Photo RP

Approaching Tower Bridge - this was before the Shard was built
Photo RP

Evidently the Barrier Control Officer thought he had a right Pratt on his hands for his parting words were that I should remember to pass other vessels port-to-port and keep on the starboard side of the river! Threequarters of an hour later we were approaching Tower Bridge and preparing to lock into the historic St. Katherine Docks, again all communications by mobile phone as our VHF mysteriously was inoperative!

Sheemaun at night in St. Katherine's Haven. Photo RP

By Friday evening *Sheemaun* was ready to take her part amongst the auspicious gathering of historic vessels and be open to the admiring crowds over the Mayor's Thames' Festival Week-End... but first the champagne reception on the floating Marquee and Participant's Dinner.

From the left – Suzie Pell, Charlie Hunt, The Skipper, Maura Pell, Steve Parish, Tim Hunt & Karen Parish – Glasses were raised to all past Masters & Skippers of *Sheemaun* in recognition of voyages and adventures since 1935! Photo Roy Bolton

Saturday 12th September proved to be hectic. Seemingly thousands of sightseers had gathered, and a continuous flow of festival celebrants drifted by on the pedestrian causeways variously engaging in conversation with who-so-ever might be on *Sheemaun*'s deck at the time, many came aboard and were shown the ship. Most were fascinated to learn that *Sheemaun* had been armed with machine guns and had served as HMY *Sheemaun* in the Second World War, and many took photographs of each other holding *Sheemaun*'s historic wheel.

From L to R – Sophie Hunt, Charlie Hunt, Mme. Bernadette - Baronne de Colas de Francs, Tim Hunt, Jackie Hunt, Lorna Woods, Maura Pell, Dr Brian Apthorp. Photo RP

Sheemaun hosted an international party. Lorna had travelled via the Philippines, Dr Brian Apthorp had travelled from Hong Kong. Bernadette, Barrone Colas de Francs, had flown in from Nice and Tim and Jackie Hunt had come up from Surrey.

Our attention was suddenly taken by a group of men on the side-walk who were waving and shouting '*Sheemaun... Sheemaun...*' It transpired that they were the crew of Dutch Yacht *Good Vibrations* whose frantic Mayday transmissions we had received off the Margate Hook Sands. Their yacht *Good*

Vibrations which they had hired in Holland, had apparently lost its rudder. Without ability to control the vessel either by sail or by engine they had indeed been in a very dangerous situation in those seas and among the dangerous sand-banks. They had been towed back to Ramsgate and had travelled on to London by train. We wished them bon voyage.

Sadly, the Festival had to end, and so family and friends had to depart to the busy world of 'here and now'. Steve and Karen Parish had to return to Kent … where Steve discovered he had eaten the 'unlucky' oyster and which laid him low for several days.

Skipper and 1ˢᵗ Mate had scheduled to take *Sheemaun* on the early Monday high tide from Tower Bridge to Ramsgate … er well weather permitting. The weather did NOT permit, and heavy North Easterly winds prevailed in the Thames Estuary. It was a 'no brainer' and so we left *Sheemaun* at her berth to wait until the first window of opportunity presented, on the following weekend. On returning to *Sheemaun*, we were concerned to find that there were – functioning lights, no radar, no VHF, no chart plotter, no echo sounder, no navigation lights etc., panic was followed by putting brain in gear and careful investigation revealed that a switch on the Sterling Battery Charger system had mysteriously become switched off! Switching this on immediately restored power and charging and explained why the VHF had so mysteriously failed on the in-bound passage.

1ˢᵗ Mate Maura casts off as we lock out of St. Katherine Docks. Photo RP

We set off at 11.00 two hours before H.W. Tower Bridge and punching the last of the flood set course seaward and passing the many historic London River landmarks. The Skipper who had spent some 30 years living and working in Docklands and on the Thames has been drawn to reminisce ...

The famous and historic Pub, The Prospect of Whitby - Photo RP

The 'Prospect of Whitby' it is said, took its name from the Trading Schooner *Whitby* which brought its cargoes up London River. It would anchor off the Captain's favourite pub, and the Captain would then be rowed across to 'his prospect' to enjoy good food and ale! Two hundred years later I also used to tie up my *Debrett* to the pub balcony and following in the footsteps of the Captain of the *Whitby* knock back a steak pie and a down an ale!

The historic riverside 'Gun' Pub backing onto Coldharbour. - Photo RP.

Nowdays the Gun Pub is overwhelmed by the massive Canary Wharf development behind it. Local legend holds that more than two centuries earlier Admiral Lord Nelson would order that he be rowed across to the Gun Pub from Greenwich. He would go through the pub, exit into Coldharbour and turning right would walk a short distance up to what is now known as 'Nelson House' where he used to tryst with Lady Emma Hamilton.

Long before Canary Wharf was dreamed of, I used to meet up in The Gun with my East End docker patients and learn about things that 'dropped' out of crane slings and 'off the backs of lorries'! In those days of the early 1970s the pub could be a dangerous place for strangers and outsiders. One of my first visits to the pub was when I returned home from the hospital still wearing a suit. The pub was full of tough East End dockers in their work clothes. The bar room which was full of smoke and Cockney banter went suddenly silent as grim faces scrutinised this unwelcome outsider. Then a man who I had seen earlier in my clinic shouted out 'Hello Doc…what's your drink?' Immediately the hostile atmosphere softened, and I was admitted as a member of that very select gathering. Not only was I plied with drinks, but I found myself doing another and very different clinic as sleeves and trousers were rolled up to display various old and not so old injuries and my advices sought!

Photo - RP

415

The new white river-front buildings now standing on Crown Wharf date from 1968 but original Crown Wharf dates from the early sixteenth century and was used for the importing of tar and pitch. Even now slabs of hardened pitch can be found on the foreshore at low tide. The 2nd from right of the white houses had been my home for some 27 yrs. The Shacklady family had lived in the house on the far left for generations. I had enjoyed conversations with old Mrs Shacklady about past happenings on the Thames. The Shacklady men had been by tradition London Watermen, Thames River pilots and in the early 20th century Thames tanker drivers. The dark house immediately to the right of the white houses was where old Fred Gunn had lived. Fred was the last of four generations of Gunns who lived in that house, they used to build barges on the foreshore. I had replaced Fred's worn out hips for him. The assessing social worker was horrified to find that Fred's toilet was a privy hut at the end of the yard which discharged into the river. Fred would not hear of having a toilet installed indoors.

'...that's dirty y'know... unhygeinic... toilets indoors... that was never meant to be...'

Fred was a great character, a man of iron will, iron principles and a gentle, thoughtful neighbour. The residents of Coldharbour were sad when he eventually slipped his cable.

I used to climb down the ladder and comb the foreshore at low tide, collecting historic clay pipe-stems and bowls and oyster shells and other jetsam thrown into the Thames in past centuries. My motor cruiser *Debrett* was kept on a mooring just 20 yards off the sea wall and sometimes if the tide was right I would nip across the Thames for a sandwich at The Trafalgar Pub at Greenwich.

From my balcony I had watched the demise of the old docks,

the building of the Millenium Dome, now the O2 Dome, the building of Canary Wharf sky-scrapers and the coming of modern City Docklands.

Just seaward of Crown Wharf is the Trinity House[160] Wharf with London's only lighthouse. Now it is one of the locations from which the *Longplayer Variations* have been broadcast. *Longplayer* is a self-progressing computer program which creates variations based on a 20 minute and 20 seconds theme composed by musician Jem Finer, the music includes sounds made by Tibetan singing bowls and gongs. I understand that the *Longplayer Variations* are expected to play for a thousand years without repetition which will happen in 2999 when it will re-start! Given the benefit of a long series of very dedicated custodians *Sheemaun* could possibly still be around then!

Trinity Wharf at high tide with its unique lighthouse, where the locals used to say bad buoys were made into good buoys! - Photo RP

160. The Corporation of Trinity House dates from 1514 and is responsible for the setting and maintaining the light-houses, buoys and navigation marks for England, Wales, the Channel Islands and Gibraltar.

We passed a motor cruiser stranded. Thousands of vessels have likewise stranded over past scores of centuries on the unforgiving Thames mud-flats - Photo RP

Cliffe Fort – Isle of Grain where HMY *Sheemaun* armed with her twin Hotchkiss heavy machine guns was based in the 2nd World War. Photo RP

Then in failing light we found the Medway Channel marker buoys and kept the rusting and dangerous wreck of the S.S. Richard Montgomery well to starboard! Sailing on to Queenborough harbour, we picked up a mooring and went ashore to the Queenborough Yacht Club to be welcomed by the Commodore herself, Margaret Douse, who is also a chef and she cooked us a jolly good meal!

2010

National Historic Ships UK appoint
Sheemaun as Flagship

I was honoured and delighted to receive - on behalf of *Sheemaun*, a letter dated 20th April from Martyn Heighton, the Director of National Historic Ships, the following letter -

National
Historic
Ships

Park Row, Greenwich,
London SE10 9NF
Tel 020 8312 8558
Fax 020 8312 6632

20th April 2010

Dr Rodney Pell

Dear Rodney,

Re: National Historic Ships Flagship Award 2010

I am writing to thank you for your submission for the National Historic Ships Flagship Award 2010. This year we had 10 strong applications.

I'm very pleased to announce that *Sheemaun* has been selected as the winner of the National Historic Ships Flagship Award 2010. The decision to offer the award to the *Sheemaun* was based on your extensive sailing and visiting programme for 2010 promoting your vessel to a wide range of audiences.

I'd like take this opportunity to offer my congratulations on winning this award. As winner, *Sheemaun* will be awarded a £1,000 Flagship grant to assist in the costs of appearing at major national or international events. A grant fund claim form is attached with this letter. I'd be grateful if you could please indicate on this form what you anticipate to spend the grant award on. Once completed, please return the form to: *Paula Palmer, Office Manager, National Historic Ships, Park Row, Greenwich, London, SE10 9NF.* A broad pennant to fly on the *Sheemaun* marking her flagship status of the year will be presented to you shortly.

Yours ever,

Martyn Heighton
Director
National Historic Ships

This was hugely exciting as it was only in the previous year, 2009, that the National Historic Ships Committee had created the prestigious award and made funds available. The first award had been bestowed on the historic steam ship the SS *Shieldhall*, a substantial vessel of one thousand seven hundred and ninety-two tons, launched in 1955.

By comparison *Sheemaun* at her now twenty-six tons is a tiny fraction of that size, but twenty years older and with her amazing and chequered history, *Sheemaun* has over the decades punched well above her weight! It was a great honour and accolade that from amongst some two thousand officially registered British Historic Vessels, *Sheemaun* had become the second ever to receive the award.

National Historic Ships UK duly issued the Press Releases and the 'publicity clockwork' sprang into action! A grand occasion was held at the Royal Temple Yacht Club at which I was honoured to receive on behalf of *Sheemaun*, from Martyn Heighton, Director of National Historic Ships UK. the unique and special NHS Flagship Pennant. It was an occasion at which many guests attended, including the Commodore John Barrett, Nicholas and Jo Gray, shipwright Steve Parish, fellow yachtsmen, members of the press, members of the Royal Lifeboat Institution etc.

Martyn Heighton, Director of National Historic Ships of the United Kingdom, presents the prestigious flagship certificate.
Photo Royal Temple Yacht Club

'SHEEMAUN'
75th Year

75 year old yacht becomes national Flagship:
Ramsgate vessel *Sheemaun* is awarded new status as 2010 Flagship for the UK's Historic Ships

Sheemaun was built as a gentleman's pleasure yacht and requisitioned for naval duties during as an armed Thames estuary patrol boat throughout the 2nd World War. Now privately owned, she is enjoyed by the general public on both sides of the Channel. Included on the National Register of Historic Vessels, she has been awarded the accolade of Flagship of the Year 2010 by National Historic Ships in recognition of her wide-ranging public summer cruising programme. In this role, *Sheemaun* will be promoting the 1,200 other vessels on the National Register of Historic Vessels at events which include the Calais Fete de la Mer, the Swallows & Amazons Rally and the Mayor's Thames Classic Boat Festival.

Norfolk wherry *Albion*, valued member of the National Historic Fleet, has been named runner-up 2010. This honour has been created for the first time, due to the high level and quality of applications received. *Albion* carried 1,400 passengers in 2009, hosting public open days on the Broads. She has been given the sum of £250 in recognition of her runner-up status, with £1,000 awarded to *Sheemaun* as Flagship. Both amounts are to be spent supporting the vessels and promoting the Flagship of the Year project.

National Historic Ships, which is sponsored by the Department of Culture Media and Sport, is the official voice for historic vessels in the UK. We offer advice on ship preservation, promote historic vessels throughout the UK, and run a Strategic Grants scheme for the benefit of historic vessels on the National Register.

Members of the Press are cordially invited to join us on the following occasions:

■ 18 May 2010, on board *Sheemaun*, Ramsgate Harbour

Representatives from National Historic Ships will be hoisting the broad pennant marking Sheemaun's new flagship status

■ 15 May 2010, on board *Albion*, Ludham

National Historic Ships will be awarding the runners-up certificate

Opportunities for interviews & photographs on request

RSVP: National Historic Ships, Park Row, Greenwich, London SE10 9NF, Tel: 0208 312 8558

Email: info@nationalhistoricships.org.uk

www.nationalhistoricships.org.uk

Issued: 29 April 2010

The generous One Thousand Pounds Award was a much appreciated and valuable contribution towards the on-going maintenance of *Sheemaun*. Although ceremonial bunting is not usually flown when a vessel is under way, at the Boulogne 2009 Festival we were asked to fly as many flags as we could muster and to make a best colourful display.

Numerous yachting journals based in countries as far apart on the Globe as America and Japan gave space to the announcement! Below is page 6 from World Ship Review Issue No 60.

GENTLEMAN'S MOTOR YACHT *SHEEMAUN*

Sheemaun
Built in 1935 by Noble & Co of Fraserburgh, *Sheemaun* is a gentleman's pleasure yacht. Her hull is carvel built of oak frames with pitch pine and larch planking. She is ketch rigged and currently has two Beta Marine Diesel engines. In 1939, *Sheemaun* was registered to Lieutenant-Commander R H Calvert-Link of Hinton Buildings, Southampton, but in the same year she was requisitioned by the Royal Navy. HM Naval Base Portsmouth have confirmed that *Sheemaun* was assigned to the Thames Auxiliary Pool at Cliffe (North Kent) where it is almost certain that she would have been engaged in what have been described as clandestine duties.

Sheemaun was laid up on 6th November 1945 and then passed to the Department of Sea Transport (Merchant Navy), being sold out of service in 1947. From Portsmouth the Royal Naval History Unit has confirmed that the vessel was armed with two Hotchkiss Heavy Machine guns, they were pretty nasty things with a range of 4,500 yards and said to have been capable of taking out a light tank or even an E-boat.

From 1965 to 1972, *Sheemaun* was registered to T W H Burton Esq. She was then owned by Rear-Admiral Gordon Gray CB, DSC from 1972 to 1981. With his son, Nick Gray, he cruised *Sheemaun* extensively on the south and east coasts of Britain, the north coast of France, and the waters of Belgium, The Netherlands, Germany, Denmark and in the Baltic.

In 1981, Lieutenant-Commander Ian Pearson of Pangbourne Nautical College purchased *Sheemaun* cruising in here extensively from the Upper Thames to the south coast thence to Normandy and the Seine to Paris, to St Malo and the Channel Islands taking over the years many scores of cadets, six at a time, for valuable seagoing experience for a week or more and changing crews wherever there were connecting train, ferry, or bus services.

She was acquired by her present owner in 1987. The vessel had a major refit between 2001 and 2004 but more than 80% of the original vessel was sound and therefore retained. She is based in Ramsgate Royal Harbour and took part in the Portsmouth International Fleet Review in 2005 and was invited to the 2008 Brest International Festival of Classic Vessels.

National Historic Ships recognition
Sheemaun (45.50 feet loa; 11.43 gt; depth 6.00 ft; beam: 12.50 ft) was built as a gentleman's pleasure yacht, was requisitioned for naval duties during the Second World War and is now privately owned and admired on both sides of the Channel. Included on the (British) National Register of Historic Vessels, she has been awarded the accolade of Flagship of the Year 2010 by National Historic Ships in recognition of her wide-ranging public summer cruising programme. In this role, *Sheemaun* will be promoting the 1,200 other vessels on the National Register of Historic Vessels at events which include the Calais *Fête de la Mer*, the Swallows & Amazons Rally and the Mayor's Thames Classic Boat Festival. A prize of £1000 was also given to the vessel.

Albion
Norfolk wherry *Albion* built in 1898, valued member of the National Historic Fleet, has been named runner-up for 2010 with a prize of £250. This honour has been created for the first time, due to the high level and quality of applications received. *Albion* carried 1,400 passengers in 2009, hosting public open days on the Broads. She is said to be the only carvel-built trading wherry constructed and is listed on page 135 of *The International Register of Historic Ships.* In 1998, the Norfolk Wherry was awarded the World Ship Trust's Special Centenary Award in recognition of the Norfolk Wherry Trust's 100th anniversary. Both grants are to be spent, it is understood, supporting the vessels and promoting the NHS Flagship of the Year project. National Historic Ships, which is sponsored by the (British) Department of Culture Media and Sport, is the official voice for historic vessels in the UK. NHS offers advice on ship preservation, promotes historic vessels throughout the UK, and runs a Strategic Grants scheme for the benefit of historic vessels on the National Register.

THE ROYAL CANADIAN NAVY
This year sees the centenary of the formation of the Royal Canadian Navy. *In Peril on the Sea* is the epic story of Canada's important but forgotten role in the longest battle of the Second World War, that of the Atlantic during which the Royal Canadian Navy expanded from a tiny service of ten ships to become the third largest Allied navy. RCN's primary role was convoy escort. In 2003 the Canadian Naval Memorial

continue on page 16

and from Kent Life Magazine August 2010

THE BRAVE LITTLE BOAT

Back in 1935, little did gentleman's pleasure yacht *Sheemaun* realise what an extraordinary life she was to lead. Now, 75 years on, she has been named 2010 flagship for the UK's Historic Ships. *Kent Life* meets her proud owner

Words by Sarah Sturt pictures by Manu Palomeque

Since when I have had the privilege to become closely associated with National Historic Ships UK and have the honour to be appointed as National Historic Ships UK 'Shipshape Ambassador' to the Thames Estuary Area and to sit as one of the panel of judges who select the deserving winners for the generous Marsh Awards, given in respect of their voluntary work in restoring, promoting and sailing Historic Vessels.

2012

Sheemaun is invited To London for the Queen's Diamond Jubilee Grand Thames Pageant

Skipper - Dr Rodney Pell. Crew - Maura Pell, Tim Hunt, Dr Charles Philips, Steve Parish. Special Guests - Polly Coburn, Mike Gill Wolf Raymer. Guests – Geoff Pell, Nicola Guest, Martyn & Evelyn Heighton and Charlie Hunt

Sheemaun's inivitation from the Jubilee Pageant Committee had been received and all the complex security hurdles finally cleared. Crewed by your Skipper, Hon. Exec Officer Tim Hunt, Master Chef Dr Charles Philips and Master Shipwright Steve Parish we departed Ramsgate early on May 24th bound for the Swale where in very difficult conditions with wind over a Spring Tide we moored overnight. Casting off the following day bound for St Katharine's Dock with a deceptive but fading blue sky we passed under the QEII Dartford Bridge glad that we were not having to queue up like the vehicles above us!

Our cruise up river was unremarkable save for an exciting moment when a fast, black Police RIB[161] hove alongside and two armed officers in black all-weather gear climbed aboard to check papers and search ship. It transpired that with the co-incidence of the Queen's Jubilee Pageant and the 2102 Olympic Games in East London that security on the Thames was at Highest Alert. The Officers were fascinated to learn that armed security had been one of the tasks HMY *Sheemaun* had carried out in the last War. The Officers were amazed to see our Thames Police Division Scarab burgee and they knew of some of my old mates

---

161. Rigid Inflatable Boat

of years past in the Metropolitan Police River Division! They stayed aboard for quite a while. After some RT communications *Sheemaun* was co-opted into Operation Kraken! Operation Kraken is the UK Coastal and Maritime Security task operated jointly by the National Crime Agency and the Border Force. I was given a briefing as to what to look out for and a secure number with which to phone in to the Kraken Operations Control Centre. *Sheemaun* of course was very happy to resume such authority but as no White Ensign had been offered to go with the position, she had to put up with her prestigious Blue Ensign. Sensibly she chose to remain quiet about her past gold smuggling activities!

The forecast however was awful, we arrived to find Tower Bridge a dramatic sight set against a background of malignant gathering dark clouds! Then after milling around, while doing our best to avoid the fast ferries and general river traffic we were at last cleared to lock in by our old friends at St Katharine control.

Dark storm clouds were gathering over London as we approached Tower Bridge – Photo - RP

Duly locked into St Katharine's by Tower Bridge we made had a week in hand to prepare ship for her our part in the Grand Pageant 'Avenue of Sail'.

As Pageant Flagship representing the historic Little Ship Club, *Sheemaun* was proud that the Club had auctioned three guest places aboard for the occasion and almost £1000 had been raised for charity by generous LSC members. So, we took our place in the Avenue of Sail, set our square yard and dressed overall with fine bunting. *Sheemaun* flew several special burgees including of course that of the Royal Temple Yacht Club (Senior Flag), The Seven Seas Club, the Little Ship Club, the burgee of the Young Freemen of London, the burgee of the City Livery Club, a very senior 23rd degree Masonic burgee (provided by Dr Charles Philips) and the Hollowshore Cruising Club burgee.

In torrential rain on the Great Day our eight guests arrived by water-taxi, it was cold and grey but *Sheemaun* has good heating, generates her own 230v electricity and soon all were warmed up and dried out the better to partake in the celebrations. Somehow the eight dripping wet sets of water-proofs ended up on my cot berth Grrrhh!

Photo – Steve Parish

The rains eased slightly but it was cold! Those who wished to be on deck to view the pageant made themselves as snug as possible...

While others found tempting comforts below...

...in plenty...

... and with tasty morsels abundant...

We saluted and cheered the Grande Parade of a thousand or so passing vessels and noted, also from Royal Harbour Ramsgate, the famous '*Sundowner*' as she passed by. It had been 74 years earlier when Capt. Lightoller in *Sundowner* and Harold Bell in *Sheemaun* had moored their vessels alongside each other at Flushing!

Sundowner passes *Sheemaun* . The two little ships had first met in 1938 at the Pavillon d'Or Rally. Photo - Steve Parish

An amazing and very special day ticked its way around the clock face. Dried out and warmed, enthused, proud to be British and privileged to be involved in this historic Pageant, the intrepid seafarers on *Sheemaun* joined together in a happy comradeship and to enjoy the fireworks display.

Photo – RP

Exhausted but happy, our guests returned shoreward via (long awaited) water-taxi services and we crew tidied ship and prepared for putting to sea the following morning bound for Ramsgate.

Bidding farewell to Tower Bridge and the darkly clouded 'Shard' we headed seaward.

The voyage seaward as far as the Four Fathom Channel was un-remarkable. It became dark as expected but not as expected a heavy ENE wind and swell developed which as we ran East through the Princes Channel against a foul tide, heaped 2-meter waves against our port side and with hissing froths. It was heavy going with much pitching and rolling. Then as we were only some 100 meters North of the dangerous Margate Sands on which we could hear the seas breaking menacingly on our starboard side - we had lost steering!!!

It was pitch dark, the wind and seas were pushing us towards the sands where large waves were breaking with crashing force. Panic has no place in such a situation, it merely distracts, but serious thought was given to making a Mayday call. Tearing into the aft lazarette, heaving out six deck chairs, a vacuum cleaner, tool boxes, electric drills, spare chain, bolt cutters, emergency pumps etc, etc. I could find no problem with the stern gear there.

But still *Sheemaun's* famous wheel was mysteriously 'locked' and refused to allow the desperately needed port turns to get us away from the dreaded sands. Outside was a howling wind, heaving seas and cold, cold darkness. How trivial the lifejacket seemed in this black turmoil! Clipping on, while Charles Philips took the wheel, I heaved myself through the wheelhouse door and made my way precariously to the bridge-deck and after-wheel. There I found a large refuse bag jammed under the after-wheel! Pulling this away immediately restored full steering control and greatly relieved we powered away from those awful ship-wrecking sands, eventually making Ramsgate 2 hours later, cold and exhausted and grateful to be alive.

At the Grand Pageant there had been no facilities offered by the Authorities for the collection of 'trash' from the 100 or so vessels in the 'Avenue of Sail' and as a result we had been obliged to return to Ramsgate with seven big bags of 'trash' and bottles for re-cycling. That such 'trash' might create a life-threatening risk at sea had not been foreseen. In the event we were lucky to have survived that last part of the voyage.

So, however pretty, however historic and however media-worthy a little vessel may be. At the end of the day, if she is to safely make the 150-odd mile return voyage from Ramsgate to Tower Bridge, or any such voyage, she must be fully seaworthy, safety checked, competently skippered and crewed. If not, all the bunting in the world and all the cheering crowds and fireworks will count as nothing.

Yes, we were proud and privileged to take part in our Queen's Diamond Jubilee Pageant and proud that in so doing real grit and real seamanship was called for – Yes, we feel we are New Elizabethans

Yours Aye,

This historic letter was later received from The Most Honourable Marquess of Salisbury –

HATFIELD HOUSE
HATFIELD
HERTFORDSHIRE
AL9 5NF

Dr Rodney Pell,
National Historic Ships
United Kingdom

25th June 2012

Dear Dr Pell

I wanted to write and thank you for taking part in the Thames Diamond Jubilee Pageant – a spectacle which I imagine was the most remarkable the Thames has ever seen. I have no doubt that the Pageant will go down in history. Not only was it a remarkable spectacle, it was the central event in celebration of the Queen's Diamond Jubilee and only the second time such celebrations have taken place in this country.

In spite of the weather, the team which organised the Pageant were, I hope you will agree, an enthusiastic and highly skilled group. Even with all their experience, they had never been presented with a project of this scale and complexity. I hope you feel that they deserved all our gratitude, but I especially wanted to thank you for taking part in such a happy and constructive spirit. I so much enjoyed meeting some of the participants in the days preceding the Pageant and witnessing that spirit myself.

The Queen has already told me how much she enjoyed the day and appreciated the efforts of everyone who took part and I hope that you will remember the event with as much pleasure as all of us in the team. Who organised it.

Everyone on the Pageant Team is immensely grateful to you and your crew for joining in and being part of it all.

Yours very sincerely,

Salisbury

The Marquess of Salisbury
Chairman of the Thames Diamond Jubilee Pageant

I have copied out the letter. The signature shown is not that of the Marquess himself but was created from the best approximate font. I retain the original.

2013

Jersey in May at
St Helier Yacht Club

With roots going back to the year 1903 St Helier Yacht Club has become a proud and prestigious organisation that with a membership of more than three thousand, can reasonably claim to be one of the the largest yacht clubs in British waters! Jersey girl Florence Rowe had married Sir Jessie Boot owner and director of the Boots Company widely proclaimed as 'Chemists to the Nation'. Sir Jessie, a generous philanthropist and Patron to the St Helier Sailing Club, had in 1924 donated two rowing gigs and three sailing boats so that those who could not afford to own a boat might still be able to enjoy the pleasures and disciplines of boating and sailing. A philanthropic perspective, which as it has progressed and developed over the years, the Club has maintained and cherished.

In June 1940 Hitler's Nazi forces invading France had effectively surrounded the harbour of St. Malo trapping some twenty-one thousand British troops. In a desperate response the British Admiralty sent every available and suitable vessel to rescue and evacuate those troops but somehow those men had to be ferried out from the harbour to the awaiting rescue vessels hove to but restricted to the deeper offshore waters. On 16th June, via a message from the Admiralty the Commodore at St. Helier Yacht Club was contacted and at very short notice eighteen St. Helier Yacht Club boats set sail in two little flotillas bound for St. Malo harbour to assist with the evacuation. This brave and dangerous operation by volunteer yachtsmen would become known as the 'Little Dunkirk'. A heroic amateur action to be later marked in history by the Lords of the Admiralty, who in recognition of that historic action, in May 1952 warded the St. Helier Yacht Club the privilege of flying a defaced Red Ensign.

One drizzly day in May 2013 that bravely won, defaced Red Ensign hung damply from its yard arm overlooking St Helier Harbour. For a keen sailor it was a disappointing day. Overhead the dull grey clouds were only made the more depressing by the light drizzle they laid across the waters. Michael Dodd sitting in his silver Mitsubishi Space Star was parked on the South Pier, musing on matters maritime while he looked down at the marina where his yacht *Storm Bird* lay gently nudging at her moorings.

'Oh well… not even worth going aboard ship to tidy up…'

Leaving the parked car Mike strolled across to the St Helier Yacht Club. Like Sir Jessie before him Mike had also been captivated by the beautiful Island of Jersey and had been a Jersey Island resident since 1969 and together with his wife Dee greatly enjoyed sailing their yacht *Storm Bird*. Both are members of the St Helier Yacht Club. Upstairs, the Club Lounge Bar designed by yachtsmen for yachtsmen, provided just the right atmosphere. A spacious pitched roof with timber beams sets off grandly below it a rich blue carpet, a fitting background for various arrangements of tables and chairs, for formal meetings and social gatherings. A large oil painting of the historic St. Helier rowed lifeboat braving tumultuous seas is proudly displayed above the stone fire-place. After ordering a pot of English breakfast tea and some biscuits Mike settled himself comfortably at a window side table overlooking the harbour. Moments later the steward set a tea tray down in front of him. Gazing out across the harbour Mike reflected -

'Hmmm… now what was it that George Orwell wrote

about in his essay - A Nice Cup of Tea? It has to be Indian of course and the teapot warmed first... three heaped teaspoons and no muslin bag or strainer...'

Lifting the teapot lid however revealed a couple of tea-bags blandly pirouetting around each other on their little strings. Turning around Mike, always an avid reader, lifted a magazine from the magazine rack just behind him, poured himself a cup of tea, added a few drops of milk, and watched for a moment as two little bubbles followed each other round and round before popping. The magazine he had picked up was the 'Classic Boat' March 2011 edition. Sipping his tea and turning the pages Mike's attention was suddenly riveted. For there on pages 26 to 30 was a centre-spread article –

'NHS FLAGSHIP OF THE YEAR

Flag carrier
Sheemaun

National Historic Ships selected a 1930s gentleman's MFV yacht to represent the historic fleet this year.

Steffan Meyrick Hughes tells the story of Sheemaun and her owner Dr Rodney Pell'

Sitting as in a daze Mike Dodd sipped his tea, munched some biscuits and read and re-read the article. There could be no doubt about it. That boat *Sheemaun* was the boat his late father Stanley Dodd RNVR had served on as mechanic in the Second World War. Yes, she had been one of the 'Dad's Navy' of small armed patrol vessels. Yes, she had been armed with machine guns and yes, she had been based at Cliffe Fort in Kent where his father had been stationed and yes, she had been involved in examining incoming vessels and in destroying magnetic mines. Not only that but Mike could now recall his father talking about the *Sheemaun* which had then been his favourite boat out of the score of the Royal Naval Thames Estuary Auxiliary Patrol Service vessels in the Nore Division, and Mike could remember, from childhood all those years ago, having been taken by his father to see that very boat at its berth on the jetty at Cliffe Fort on the Isle of Grain in Kent.

'I must be the only one alive who has not only seen her as a warship but sailed on her as a warship… I'd known her name since childhood… Dad must have spoken about her a lot… I was very excited looking at the photo and seeing the strange wheelhouse arrangements as I remembered it as a child… I jumped up waving the magazine around saying 'Well blow me down it's the Old Man's boat.' I couldn't wait to contact its owner a Dr Pell and find out where the old ship had been hiding all these years… of course I wanted to 'phone Dad… but just a few years too late…'[162]

With the magazine tucked securely under his arm a very excited Mike Dodd then left the Yacht Club and drove home to show it to his wife Dee. Together they read and re-read the article and reminisced on family history. Mike's brother Barrie was contacted and both families made a search of attics and old boxes. Their searches produced some very relevant diaries and memoirs beautifully handwritten by their father the late Stanley Dodd, along with some newspaper cuttings and old pictures. An historic family treasure trove had been unearthed and the story of *Sheemaun* had been further enriched and detailed.

---

162. Email to the writer from Mike Dodd 04 April 2017

Stanley Dodd RNVR in uniform photo circa 1943 with his
H.M. PATROL VESSELS cap band. Photo courtesy his son,
Mike Dodd

The resulting search of attics, cupboards and boxes were
fruitful. Family memorabilia were unearthed and of particular
interest and excitement was the finding of Stanley's hand-written
memoirs. On those pages, in neat writing, Stanley had expressed
his experiences and feelings, including graphic details of his war
experiences. Stanley, it transpired, had been a sharp observer of
events and people and his writings reveal a savvy and humorous
mind. He was clearly artistic for his papers also included some
line sketches in which with a few strokes he had cleverly captured
some of the Thames river scenes. Mike duly set about contacting
National Historic Ships UK.

Out of the Blue - I received a call from Debbie Williams at National Historic Ships UK informing me that a Mr Michael Dodd in Jersey wished to make contact. I duly 'phoned Mike and was amazed to learn that his late father Stanley had served as mechanic to the Thames Nore Division Auxiliary Patrol Boats in World War II, and that of all the Thames Auxiliary Patrol Boats *Sheemaun* had been his favourite. Stanley Dodd had later written comprehensive memoirs.

Stanley Dodd RNVR and his sons Michael and Barrie were now destined to be enrolled along with many others in bringing together the amazing and fascinating history of a brave little boat.

Barrie Dodd, his son Alex and Mike Dodd in *Sheemaun*'s saloon 2013. Photo - RP

2013

Sheemaun attended at the Mayors Thames Festival and St Katharine Docks Classic Boat Festival

Where *Sheemaun* was proud to receive the 1st Prize in the form of an historic St Katharine Docks cast-iron mooring bollard. It was so heavy that two men had to deliver it to the boat and then it had to be stowed low down and very securely for the seventy-five-mile seaward voyage home!

It was a pleasure to welcome aboard Old Pangbournian Mr Tudor Rose who had first been to sea when a naval cadet on *Sheemaun* some thirty years previously. Tudor was delighted to see around his old ship and to once more put his hand to her wheel!

Mr Tudor Rose – former *Sheemaun* Naval Cadet with his hand once again on that historic wheel. Photo-RP

The Royal Temple Yacht Club Committee honoured *Sheemaun* by awarding her a Silver Tray which her owner was pleased to accept on her behalf - Photo RTYC

2014

The Dunkirk and the Oostende voor Anker Festivals
Cruise Journal of *Sheemaun*

Skipper Dr Rodney Pell

CREW

Mike Emmett   Capt. David Lee   Rodney Pell Jr

First Mate
Maura Pell

Maura's son
James West

By invitation from the FRCPM (Federation Regionale pour le Culture et Patrimonie Maritime) and from Hon. Admiral Hubert Rubbens organiser of the of Oostende voor Anker Festival, *Sheemaun* set off from Ramsgate at HW -2 on May 15th at low water

Sheemaun departing Ramsgate May 15th Photo – Dr Andrew Morgan

Rodney Pell Jr took the aft wheel for part of the Channel crossing. Photo - RP

With sails hoisted - Photo RP

We arrived some five hours later at East Dunkerque and were shepherded through les Grandes Ecluses to our berth in the Basin du Commerce. As ever generous French hospitality was to the fore. Berthing, electricity and partying etc. were complementary. We berthed opposite the magnificent square rigger the *'Duchesse Anne'*. Festival Skippers and Crews were duly invited aboard the *'Duchesse Anne'* and introduced generously by the Festival Organisers and the Dunkerque Chambre du Commerce to la belle vie with an abundance of good company, good food and good wine and music.

The *Duchesse Anne* picture taken from *Sheemaun* at night - RP.

The Basin du Commerce, convenient to the Centre-Ville. RP.

While walking in the Centre-Ville we paid our respects at the statue of The famous French Admiral and sometime privateer, Jean Bart. - RP

Sheemaun was berthed behind the *Christ Roi* an historic French Prawner from Gravelines. Meeting up with the Skipper refreshed some poignant and sobering memories - In 2009

Sheemaun while en route to the Boulogne Festival, had witnessed the brave Skipper of the *Christ Roi* rescue the crew from an historic Gravelines Lobster Boat foundering in the heavy seas. We were one among a number of historic vessels all heading for the Boulogne Fete de la Mer but the seas were formidable and entering the Boulogne outer harbour we had to call on every sinew and skill. The photograph here-under was taken just after we had entered the shelter of the Outer Basin at Boulogne in 2009 and shows the fury of the seas through which we had sailed!

We had just come through these heavy seas seen pounding the Boulogne Outer Harbour Wall! - Photo Dr Charles Philips.

There were many demonstrations, included the amazing feats put on by the Dunkerque Cotes d'Opal Society for Training of Sea Rescue Dogs – performed here with volunteer 'victims'. Hereunder is a photo of a 'victim' holding onto the harness of the Newfoundland Rescue Dog, while being powerfully towed back to dry land and safety.

Photo - RP

The crowds turned out in their hundreds to view
the historic vessels Photo - RP.

After doing 'our bit' in the Grand Parade of Sail and greeting
many sightseers and visitors it was time to depart for Oostende
and after traversing the vast Canal du Bourbourg we locked out
from the huge Ecluse Trystram.

The lonely but welcome Zuidecoote Buoy was passed this time in a limpid sea – but don't ever underestimate this awkward 'dog-leg' through hazardous and narrow shifting sands shallows which in anything of a nasty sea and adverse wind can quickly become extremely dangerous. We put into Nieuwpoort for a couple of days and much enjoyed the excellent poisonniers. If only wet-fish shops in the UK could be like that. Mouth-watering counter displays of the freshest fish and crustacea all spotlessly clean. A huge choice was on offer, no fishy smells, no flies. Juicy lemons were given away with purchases and tempting bottles of chilled Chardonnay and Chablis available at very reasonable prices.

We then took the flood tide to bring us swiftly to Oostende in time for an easy lock-in.

The Skipper and Crew managed to squeeze *Sheemaun* into her berth amongst some other two hundred or so splendid Classic and Historic vessels. We then set about 'dressing ship'. Proudly flying the UK Historic Flagship pennant, our Royal

Temple Yacht Cub Burgee, our Little Ship Club Burgee, our Hollowshore Cruising Club Burgee and our St Katharine Docks Pennant all atop the usual hoists of colourful bunting and the Oostende voor Anker pennant! *Sheemaun* looked every bit the splendid historic vessel that she is.

Just one perspective – but it gives a real feeling of the Festival atmosphere. RP.

Seagulls find sufficient food in the sea
(their natural habitat).

There is no need for additional feeding.
Moreover, feeding seagulls is harmful to their health and it makes them very aggressive. Feeding also causes the seagulls to settle in the city centre, which results in extra pollution. Therefore, feeding seagulls is prohibited.
Tourists and residents who feed seagulls may face fines of up to 250 euro.

The Skipper and Crew very much approved of a local Bye-Law which forbids the feeding and encouraging of seagulls and encouraged by a significant penalty. The Port of Oostende is much bigger that Ramsgate and with many restaurants spilling over onto the pavements and squares. Seagulls are not encouraged and in consequence are they nothing like such a nuisance as they are over here in the U.K.

Historic Vessels literally were being crammed in. RP

...while yet more were arriving...

Capt. David Lee watching the arrival of the tall ship *Etoile Roi* aboard which by courtesy of the Festival Authorities, the participating crews were duly welcomed each evening to enjoy true Belgian Royal hospitality!

Some 300,000-welcoming sight-seers ensured that the Oostende voor Anker Festival 2014 was another great success. The floating pontoons were opened to the public 10.00 – 16.00 each day and thousands filed past the historic vessels with many being welcomed aboard as was manageable by the skippers and crews.

The Oostende City Band led a Grand Parade of the Captains and Skippers of the participating historic vessels through the

Oostende streets to the Town Hall where were addressed by the Lady Mayor and Viscount David Montgomery, son of the late Viscount General Bernard Montgomery of El Alamein and who with his valiant troops had 70 years earlier freed Oostende from the occupation and oppression of Hitler's Nazi invaders during the Second World War.

Reluctantly on 3rd June we locked out from Oostende on the early ebb tide and set course for the Royal Harbour Ramsgate having taken part in a poignant and historic event and proud of our historic vessel. *Sheemaun* had after all born arms and had served in WW2 as one of the Thames Estuary Patrol Boats of Nore under command of Admiral Sir Reginald Emlie Plunkett-Drax KCB,DSO.

Mid Channel while making good speed with our Beta Marine Diesels purring, we overhauled the historic WW2 steam Puffer VIC 96 and were later to rapidly close on a splendid sight - The Little Ships of Dunkirk - who had preceded our departure from Oostende by some 2 hours. We entered Ramsgate and as the lock gates were still open had the good luck to motor straight into the inner marina to tie up at our berth ahead of the 'Dunkirk Little Ships'. We were proud to have been asked to take *Sheemaun* across the Channel to take part in such a splendid commemoration of maritime history.

Your Skipper

2015

MY *Sheemaun* and MV *Havengore*
share some History

Commissioned by the Port of London Authority the MV[163] *Havengore* was launched in 1956 from the Tough Brother's internationally acclaimed Boat Yard at Teddington-on-Thames. Built to highest standards at the time with double diagonal Teak planking set on Oak frames, the MV Havengore at 84.7 feet long (25.81 metres) and weighing 89 tons was a substantial vessel. She was fitted with what at the time was state-of-art survey equipment – output on punched tape! And she had been designed to pass under all the bridges that span the River Thames. I used to watch her from my Docklands Thames-side balcony as she criss-crossed the river taking soundings. Later MV *Havengore* became the Flagship of the Port of London Authority Fleet and would take part in ceremonial occasions on the London Thames, her Motto –

'Walk always in the Ranks of Honour'

Havengore came to the Nation's attention, when in 1966 the Port of London Authority assigned to her the solemn role of bearing the coffin of the late Sir Winston Churchill. Sir Winston Churchill had suffered a series of debilitating strokes, but on Sunday 24th January 1966, Britain's National Wartime Hero and former Prime Minister, suffered a severe and final and stroke. He was 90 years of age and his political career had been one of the longest and most prestigious among British Statesmen. He had skilfully steered Great Britain and her Allies through the

---

163. Motor Vessel

terrible and treacherous 1939 – 1945 war imposed by Fuehrer Adolph Hitler on Europe and the World.

At the request of Her Majesty Queen Elizabeth, Sir Winston's body was laid to Rest-in-State at Westminster Hall for three days, then following a state funeral service at St Paul's Cathedral on 30th of January, Sir Winston's coffin was placed on a gun carriage and taken to Tower Pier on the Thames where it was transferred aboard the Port of London's Flagship the MV *Havengore*. The coffin was laid on the after-deck, attended by a ceremonial guard and with the mourning Churchill family aboard in the saloon. Then, MV *Havengore* with an escorting fleet of vessels, made a dignified procession solemnly westwards up the Thames to the Festival Pier. As the solemn funeral entourage processed, the jibs of the waterside cranes were lowered and raised again one after the other in a never-before-seen undulating salute. It was as if London's docks, wharves and the crane jibs as they bowed to the great man, were thanking Sir Winston for having delivered them from Hitler's savage and terrible Blitzkrieg two and a half decades previously. Televised and reported World-Wide, the scene was described as one of the most poignant of sights. It was a scene that moved playwright Noel Coward to weep.[164]

The *Havengore* was decommissioned and sold out of service in 1995, by which time she needed substantial repairs and re-fitting. Christopher Ryland, her current owner and custodian, commissioned Fox's Boat Yard at Ipswich to undertake a comprehensive refit to both the hull and machinery at Fox's Boat Yard in Ipswich. Now restored, *Havengore* is currently based at London's Historic St Katharine's Docks by Tower Bridge, from where she undertakes ceremonial cruises and various commissions skippered by her captain, Ian Ruffles. *Havengore* conveyed members of the Royal Family on the occasion of the Queen's Diamond

---

164. B. Riley-Smith writing in the Telegraph 23rd January 2015

Jubilee Thames Pageant in June 2012, at which *Sheemaun* was also invited to be present.

Captain Ian Ruffles is an old friend of *Sheemaun*, he too has put his capable hands to her wheel. Ian's knowledge of the Thames, its Estuary, its barges and the river Medway is almost encyclopaedic and the stories he tells are fascinating. Ian also enjoys a practical joke, but he was very nearly keel-hauled by me after it transpired that he had hoisted a rather novel piece of bunting to *Sheemaun*'s topmast at a St Katharine Dock's Classic Boat Festival. 1st Mate Maura had been puzzled as to how she came to be missing a bra. However, the cheering dockside crowds of sightseers with their cameras and hands pointing upwards helped her to locate it!

Sheemaun (on the left) berthed together with the Royal Rowing Barge *Gloriana* and MV *Havengore* at St Katharine Docks by Tower Bridge on the occasion of the Mayor's Thames Festival in September 2015. Photo reproduced by kind permission of Jeff Berger at www. jaybee, Closter USA.

Honorary Master-of-Oar to the Royal Row Barge *Gloriana*,
Andrew Adams found his sea-legs when he was a Pangbourne
Nautical College Cadet on *Sheemaun* - Photo RP

Sheemaun
Is a Grand Old Lady
deserving respect
She changes the lives of those who sail in her

One has only to glance at *Sheemaun* to see at once how different she is from her modern peers. While oozing history and classic character, she is also clearly a strong and very sea-worthy vessel. With her two diesel engines and traditional gaff rig she is well capable of serious off-shore cruising and over many decades has proved herself time and time again. Built of sound timbers using techniques and principles that have stood the test of time over the centuries, *Sheemaun* has taught me to understand and value wooden boats and she has gently persuaded me to completely re-invent myself.

Like any aristocratic elderly lady, *Sheemaun* likes nothing better than to be admired, talked about and photographed; and where better for this than at maritime festivals! She has taken me and my 1st Mate Maura to some wonderful places, varying from muddy creeks to grand harbours. She has introduced us to interesting fellow boat-owners and sailors and to actors, historians, members of Parliament, captains, admirals and Royalty. It was through *Sheemaun* that I was admitted an Associate of the Royal Institution of Naval Architecture, it was through *Sheemaun* that I came to be closely associated with National Historic Ships UK and it was through *Sheemaun* that I and 1st Mate Maura, received the Freedom of the City of London. *Sheemaun* has a presence, an energy and personality of her own and she makes things happen and she changes people.

Actress Brenda Blethyn, Rodney and Maura Pell on *Sheemaun*
Photo Lindy Tweedell

2012 RP with Admiral the Right Honourable Baron West of Spithead GCB. DSC. PC. ADC former UK Sea Lord, at a National Historic Ships awards ceremony - Photo Matt Spour

2012 RP with Her Royal Highness the Princess Royal at a National Historic Ships awards ceremony - Photo Matt Spour

Maura Pell and Rodney Pell receive the Freedom of the City of
London – Photo Dr Charles Philips

Even as this is being written, *Sheemaun* is receiving invitations
to attend at Maritime Festivals and events. She is registered for
the prestigious Oostende voor Anker Festival in due in May
2018 due to be attended by His Majesty King Phillippe of
Belgium. Over a hundred and fifty historic, spectacular and
famous ships will be gathered together and more than a quarter
of a million spectators will be catered for. But, now it is time for
me to end this phase of the story which relates the events and
adventures over the past eighty-three years in which *Sheemaun*
has been engaged, and the amazing stories of those who over the
past eight decades have put their hands to her historic wheel.

A wheel that will in future years be held by new hands and
no doubt with many more adventures to experience and stories
to be regaled. There is every reason to anticipate that *Sheemaun*
will be present and seaworthy in the year two-thousand and
thirty-nine to commemorate the Centenary of the creation of
the Royal Navy Thames Auxiliary Patrol Service.

POST-SCRIPT

Sheemaun crossed the Channel to attend at the 2018 May Oostende voor Anker Festival, which as ever was a colourful, lively and musical event with hundreds of craft stalls, side-shows, parades and ceremonies all master-minded by Hon. Admiral Hubert Rubbens. Some two and a half thousand visitors attended over the four days. A significant highlight of the festival was 'Open Ships' when the two hundred beautiful and historic craft were opened to the public.

Among the many who came aboard *Sheemaun*, was a family who were keen to photograph their small sons with their hands on her wheel. On being asked if any famous people had put their hands to the wheel, I replied, and that amongst them in 1938 a certain Captain Lightoller, 2nd Captain of the RMS *Titanic*, had put his hands to *Sheemaun*'s wheel. An hour later a Belgian TV News crew arrived to film the wheel and relate the story. Soon afterwards people were arriving in their hundreds to put their hands to her famous wheel and have their photographs taken!

Sheemaun is a Grand Old Lady deserving of respect, she has changed the lives of many of those who have put their hands to her wheel over past decades and continues to stalwartly serve those who sail in her. We salute her.

2018

PEACE. 5·5·45 §

S.S. "VENUS". NEWCASTLE — BERGEN. § 10·8·44.

and one for luck. Shaw.
10 th Aug 44

TOWER BRIDGE

DUTCH COASTER. 318 TONS. 6·5·43.

Drawings by Stanley Dodd Royal Navy Volunteer Reservist
(RNVR) Mechanic on the armed HMY *Sheemaun*.